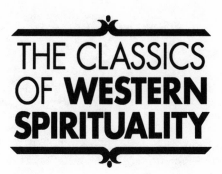

THE CLASSICS
OF **WESTERN**
SPIRITUALITY

Elisabeth of Schönau
THE COMPLETE WORKS

TRANSLATED AND INTRODUCED BY
ANNE L. CLARK

PREFACE BY
BARBARA NEWMAN

PAULIST PRESS
NEW YORK • MAHWAH NJ

Cover art: Mother Placid Dempsey, a Benedictine nun of the Abbey of Regina Laudis in Bethlehem, Connecticut, is a painter and sculptor who employed both these mediums to create the cover image for *Elisabeth of Schönau.* Regarding her work she says: "The cover of *Elisabeth of Schönau* depicts the vision of the Virgin clothed with the sun as Elisabeth has recounted it. The Virgin clothed with the sun is a well-known image, which occurs first in the New Testament and recurs over and over again in Christian art and iconography. It is usually understood to represent the church and/or the Virgin Mary. However, in Elisabeth's vision, and perhaps uniquely there, the Virgin represents Christ himself. As I thought about it, I realized what I already knew—that Christ is the Source and Exemplar of every grace that comes to humanity. All graces and blessings flow from his passion, death and resurrection. This Christocentric reality glimpsed by Elisabeth in an unusual way underlies and assumes every Marian and ecclesial expression of the same image. It is perhaps the most important of her visions and, within our own times, pertinent to ecumenical dialogue. Certainly it is enlightening and consoling for everyone, for it is a vision of Christ unvanquished by death and radiantly alive, transfiguring the world in the grace of his resurrection, in which we are all called to share."

Library of Congress Cataloging-in-Publication Data

Elisabeth, of Schönau, Saint, 1129–1164.
    [Works. English. 2000]
    The complete works / Elisabeth of Schönau ; translated and introduced by Anne L. Clark.
      p.   cm.—(The classics of Western spirituality)
    Includes bibliographical references (p.) and index.
    ISBN 0-8091-3959-6 (alk. paper)—ISBN 0-8091-0521-7 (cloth : alk. paper)
    1. Spiritual life—Catholic Church. 2. Mysticism—Catholic Church. 3. Visions.
    I. Clark, Anne L. II. Title. III. Series.
BX2350.2.E4513 2000
248.2′9—dc21

00-020982

Published by Paulist Press
997 Macarthur Boulevard
Mahwah, New Jersey 07430

www.paulistpress.com

Printed and bound in the United States of America

Contents

Translator of This Volume

ANNE L. CLARK is an Associate Professor of Religion at the University of Vermont, where she teaches courses on medieval Christian traditions, especially the religious life of medieval women. She received the Ph.D. from Columbia University in 1989. It was in the course of graduate study that she first encountered the works of Elisabeth of Schönau. She has published *Elisabeth of Schönau: A Twelfth-Century Visionary* (University of Pennsylvania Press, 1992), as well as several articles on Elisabeth. Her current work includes research on Gertrude of Helfta and on the veneration of the Virgin Mary in the later Middle Ages.

Author of the Preface

BARBARA NEWMAN is professor of English and religion at Northwestern University. She earned her doctorate in medieval studies from Yale University in 1981 and has published widely on medieval religious women. Among her books are *Sister of Wisdom: St. Hildegard's Theology of the Feminine* (1987), an edition and translation of Hildegard's *Symphonia* (1988); *From Virile Woman to WomanChrist: Studies in Medieval Religion and Literature* (1995); and *Voice of the Living Light: Hildegard of Bingen and Her World* (1998).

For my husband
Kevin Trainor

Acknowledgments

I would like to thank the many people who have helped me in my work on this volume. Most significant among them are Priscilla Throop, who carefully reviewed all my translations and made thoughtful suggestions about interpreting the Latin texts; Karen Green, who very generously aided me with her skill in electronic database searching for identifying sources, especially elusive liturgical references; and Laurel Broughton, who came to my rescue with numerous other references. The University of Vermont College of Arts and Sciences Dean's Fund and the University Committee on Research and Scholarship financially supported this project. I also wish to extend my deepest thanks to my husband, Kevin Trainor, who continuously supported me throughout the many years of work on this book.

Preface

Elisabeth of Schönau (1129–65) was among the most widely read of all medieval visionaries. Her works were studied not only in her native Germany, but also in France and England; individual writings were translated into French, Anglo-Norman, and Icelandic; and the Latin texts survive in at least 145 manuscripts—more than we have for the works of Hildegard of Bingen, Hadewijch of Brabant, Mechthild of Magdeburg, and Julian of Norwich combined. Yet in the modern rediscovery of medieval women writers, Elisabeth has been among the most neglected, even though a reasonably good edition has been available since 1884. What accounts for this striking discrepancy between her medieval and modern reception?

The answer to this question can tell us a great deal about the distance between medieval spirituality and contemporary reasons for our interest in it. We tend to value mysticism insofar as it represents the uniquely personal, anomalous, and subversive elements in religion; we prize the heroic achievements of individuals, and especially their resistance to oppressive authorities. But Elisabeth does not offer us the daunting intellectual gifts of Hildegard, the dazzling lyrical talent of Mechthild, or the theological depth of Hadewijch and Julian. Much less can we hold her up as a defiant heroine of the Resistance, like Marguerite Porete or Joan of Arc. Rather, she confronts us as a mystic of supreme objectivity, one who spoke in and for her community, and through whom her community spoke. Few seers have ever been so profoundly ecclesial as Elisabeth. She was a window through which the community of nuns and monks at Schönau, and later the church at large, could gaze on the mysteries it proclaimed and adored. She was a mirror to reflect its own deepest convictions back to it, heightened by the radiance of objective truth. What she offered her contemporaries, or rather what God offered through her, was, in her own words, "confirmation of the faith and consolation of those who are troubled."

Elisabeth became a Benedictine at twelve, the earliest age at which a girl was considered competent to take adult vows of either marriage or virginity. In 1152, when her visitations began—just a year after her mentor, Hildegard of Bingen, had published her book *Scivias*—Elisabeth was twenty-three and already a seasoned nun. But her visionary career began with a devastating inner crisis. Hers is a classic account of *acedia* or the "sin of sadness," dreaded bane of the contemplative life. Suicidally depressed, tormented by demonic apparitions, Elisabeth was rescued at last by the prayers of her sisters and brothers, but also by consoling visions of the Virgin. Already at the outset, we see what would become the overarching theme of her visions: the saints of earth and heaven form but one company, separated by the thinnest of veils, which divine grace allowed her to pierce almost at will. For the next year, Elisabeth's visions would conform to the church calendar, confirming the rightness and validity of the community's worship down to the last detail. Saints appear to her on their feast days, crowned with celestial glory; Mary falls prostrate in prayer before the divine majesty at the precise moment when the community beseeches her intercession; the holy cross shines forth on the feast of its exaltation. When the visionary figures speak or Elisabeth responds, it is almost always in liturgical and scriptural verses. What we observe here is an extreme liturgical realism: Each prayer, each hymn, each lesson corresponds to some reality in the world above, and these realities become visible and audible to Elisabeth in her trance state. There is nothing "subjective" or idiosyncratic about the content of her visions; they are living iconography. Elisabeth is represented in her *First Book of Visions* as the ideal Benedictine—a nun so perfectly attentive to the communal worship that both she and it become transparent to celestial worship.

The bridge that enables Elisabeth to cross from earth to heaven is her bodily suffering. In recurrent, formulaic phrases she reports that only after experiencing torment, anguish, or violent struggle could she "relax into ecstasy" and enter the region of light, where her celestial interlocutors awaited her. These agonies suggest neither ordinary sickness nor self-inflicted penance: They seem necessary to mark the passage, otherwise so tenuous, between here and hereafter. Once she has achieved the trance state, Elisabeth not only sees but also speaks. Some of her locutions and prophecies seem to have been transcribed directly from ecstatic utterances, while others were reported to her brother Ekbert or her sisters after the ecstasy ceased. Trance speaking is a phenomenon that has been widely attested cross-culturally, especially among women; it is often, though not always, connected with mediumship or spirit possession. At the Spiritualist assemblies of mid-nineteenth-century America, female trance speakers held large audiences spellbound with their eloquence and wisdom. The practice of trance speaking is acceptable because it reinforces stereotypes of female passivity, which the subject herself usually shares, but at the same time it enables women to speak with a degree of clarity and confidence they could never summon in their conscious state. Elisabeth comments perceptively on the relationship between her trance revelations and her native intelligence in a vision that concerns, appropriately enough, the raptures of Saint Paul. One December night at Matins:

> By chance it occurred to me to think about the words of the Apostle [2 Cor 12:2] about which I had questioned the angel. I began to pray to the Lord in my heart saying, "Lord, if any benefit could come from this, I ask you to deign to make manifest to me that divine understanding which I have begun to seek." While I was turning this over in my heart, I suddenly conceived in my mind the whole understanding of the thing I had been seeking and I pondered within myself many words which I had previously not known. While I was greatly marveling at this to myself, I went into a trance and collapsed. And behold the angel of the Lord stood in my sight and said to me, "What you were seeking, I spoke to your heart." (*Third Book of Visions*, ch. 8)

Elisabeth thinks about a theological problem, prays, and receives illumination in her conscious state, but then immediately goes into trance. It is as if she required the confirmation of ecstasy to validate her own thoughts. But she is not alone in this: Her abbot Hildelin, her brother Ekbert, and other authorities also accepted her revelations as objective truth. Without that belief, the learned Ekbert would have seen no reason to pose tough theological questions to his sister—or rather to her angel, whose explanations she faithfully mediated. Such questions were a common currency of intellectual and spiritual exchange among twelfth-century monastics. Heloise sent a long list of them to Abelard, trusting in his philosophical wisdom; the monks of Villers sent thirty-eight conundrums to Hildegard, trusting in her access to divine mysteries. Ekbert and his friends wanted to know a variety of celestial secrets. For example, was the Virgin assumed bodily into heaven? How fully did the angels foreknow the details of Christ's passion? Was it a whole order of angels that fell with Lucifer, or did some of the fallen spirits come from each of the nine ranks? Unlike Elisabeth's medieval audience, modern readers cannot blithely trust her angelic guide and avoid the question of where the answers actually came from. Only a naive cynic would imagine that Ekbert himself created them; he would not have abandoned his promising ecclesiastical career and become a monk merely to engage in intellectual fraud. We might rather suppose that Elisabeth, entranced, knew and understood much more than she consciously knew she knew. But it was certainly not her unconscious, in a psychoanalytic sense, that supplied the answers. It might be truer to say that the mind of the church supplied them, speaking through one who was totally immersed in the church yet keenly aware of its shortcomings.

Elisabeth's initiation into prophecy came after her visionary charism was well established. It is here that Hildegard's influence on her seems most pronounced. The ten sermons in Elisabeth's *Book of the Ways of God* bear a strong resemblance to the older visionary's prophetic writings, and it is no coincidence that contemporaries linked the two women's prophecies as manifestations of the same grace. Elisabeth's sermons are less obscure, thanks to Ekbert's editorial work, but no less forceful. Her critique of ecclesiastical abuses is very much that of an insider, and the sins she denounces—avarice, pride, simony, pastoral negligence, sexual pollution—are the same ones that male reformers and moralists vehemently denounced. In conjunction with Ekbert and Hildegard, Elisabeth also took part in a well-orchestrated campaign against the Cathar heresy. But she did not presume to preach her own inspired sermons, as Hildegard did. Rather, she sent them to the archbishops of Trier, Mainz, and Cologne to be proclaimed "to the Roman Church and to all the people and all the Church of God." In her envoy we see audacity and deference conjoined: She did not want the bishops to dismiss her words as mere "figments of women," but she also flattered them as God's chosen instruments because they were "renowned for piety"—an assessment not all observers would have shared. At the time (1157), Arnold II held the archdiocese of Cologne and Hillin the see of Trier. Both were correspondents and admirers of Hildegard. But the incumbent of Mainz, also named Arnold, was an imperial appointee who shamelessly taxed the city to pay for Barbarossa's wars, imposed an interdict when the citizens revolted, and was murdered by a lynch mob in 1160. It seems unlikely that he ever obeyed Elisabeth's command to proclaim her message as the word of God. Nor did Hillin of Trier, as we learn from Elisabeth's later epistle (Letter 4) chastising him for the oversight.

Of all the seer's writings, the most widely read throughout the Middle Ages was her book of revelations on the virgin martyrs of Cologne—a work that, tellingly, is the most alien and even repugnant to modern taste. The martyrs in question were Saint Ursula and her band of virgins, whose numbers had been multiplied by a tenth-century scribal error from eleven to eleven thousand. Elisabeth's narrative presupposes the received history of their martyrdom, which entails two other extraordinary transpositions. First, by the alchemy of faith, medieval piety had transmuted the imagined massacre of eleven thousand women into a glorious victory, not unlike the "victory" of a crusading army which, win or lose, could not be defeated in the eyes of God. Subsequently, as the walls of Cologne were being enlarged in the twelfth century, piety and hucksterism alike transformed an ancient Roman necropolis excavated by the workmen into a treasury of miracle-working bones. Among these bones were found numerous inscriptions, some perhaps authentic, but many more fabricated by individuals who wished to profit from the trade in relics. A skeptical abbot, Gerlach of Deutz, appealed to Elisabeth in the hope that she could identify and authenticate (or possibly debunk) these hitherto unknown saints. Greatly complicating the affair was the fact that many male skeletons had been unearthed among the supposedly all-female martyrs, including that of a "Saint Cyriacus, Roman pope," whose name was awkwardly missing from the official list of pontiffs.

Faced with this request, Elisabeth had what can only be described as a series of visions-to-order in which Saint Verena, a virgin whose relics had just been translated to Schönau, patiently expounded the histories and family ties of the troupe. More than one historian has dismissed the text Elisabeth produced as a superstitious fiction and, moreover, one in which she allowed her gift to be manipulated for blatant commercial ends. But this unsympathetic assessment does not account for the sense of joyful discovery (along with some nervousness about being an author of novelties) that pervades the nun's hagiographic romance. We will come closer to understanding its place in her spiritual life, and its resonance for the medieval public, if we read Elisabeth's *Book of Revelations* as an idealized representation of the religious life. In the service of her own piety, as well as Abbot Gerlach's, she was not merely explaining away discrepancies between the received legend and new archaeological finds, but constructing a self-consciously revisionist history.

In spite of the great bloodbath that she ostensibly celebrates, Elisabeth downplays the violence and voyeurism typical of virgin martyr legends and wastes little space on identifying or vilifying the persecutors. More strikingly, she transforms a legend about a vast amazonian army—for the martyrs were supposed to be virgins who had all renounced family, fled marriage, and eschewed the company of men—into a vision of harmonious friendship and collaboration between the sexes. Ursula's father, far from resisting his daughter's plans, tenderly provides her retinue with a male escort, and in the end her pagan fiancé Etherius—together with his mother, sister, and first cousin—all accept baptism and go joyfully to meet the virgins in response to a divine command. Pope Cyriacus becomes a sympathizer, his name expunged from the record books by malicious clerics who mocked his decision to resign the papacy and "follow the foolishness of little women" on their stately procession toward martyrdom. Numerous supportive bishops swell the throng. As Saint Verena's revelations unfold, the company of martyrs takes the shape of a tangled, all-encompassing genealogy: each saint enjoys the company of at least one brother or sister, aunt or uncle or cousin. Reconstituted as a Holy Kindred, like the thriving extended family that surrounded Mary and Jesus in late medieval paintings, the "sacred company" becomes a microcosm of the heavenly church and an idealized mirror of the earthly church.

More specifically, it would not be amiss to see in this throng of pilgrims—men, women, and children en route to a glorious destiny—an image of Elisabeth's own religious family. Her great-uncle Ekbert, after all, had been bishop of Münster; her brother Ekbert would in time become abbot of Schönau, where she herself was mistress; another sibling, Ruotger, was prior of the Premonstratensians at Pöhlde; three of her cousins or nieces were nuns at the house of Andernach; and she counted yet another kinswoman among her sisters at Schönau. Living as she did in a double monastery, Elisabeth enjoyed close relationships with monks and nuns alike, and both her brother and her abbot encouraged her in her prophetic vocation. So if, in one sense, her visions corroborated the findings at Cologne, in another it was the newly discovered inscriptions that confirmed her own vision of religious life as a glorious, equal-opportunity venture in which women and men could provide mutual aid and comfort. Fittingly, however, it is a woman who leads the whole enterprise; male authorities, including the pope and half the episcopate, leap cheerfully onto her bandwagon. Martyrdom is no longer the focal point of their story, but the rite of passage that transports this devout and loving clan from earth to heaven. For Elisabeth, the virgin martyrs' torment might have seemed like an analogue, writ large, of the bodily struggles she herself endured each time she made that crossing.

It is oddly fitting that neither Ekbert nor anyone else ever wrote Elisabeth's life: She would not have wished to stand out so far from her sisters. Instead, he wrote an account of her death, which in its utter fidelity to liturgical and hagiographic conventions is perhaps the truest index of her character. Elisabeth, we are told, remained lucid until the end, constantly praying, exhorting, consoling, forgiving; in one of her final ecstasies, she received the comfort of the Virgin together with Saints Ursula and Verena; dying, she told each attending priest exactly which psalm to recite for the good of her soul. Neither a maverick nor a pioneer, she bore witness to the last by making her body and her whole life transparent to the faith of the Apostles' Creed: "I believe in the Holy Spirit, the holy catholic Church, the communion of saints, the forgiveness of sins, the resurrection of the body, and the life everlasting."

Introduction

The Life of Elisabeth of Schönau

Elisabeth of Schönau was raised in a Benedictine monastery from the age of twelve. At the age of twenty-three, in the year 1152, she began to see visions from heaven. So her secretary tells us. Neither Elisabeth herself nor her secretary tells us much more about her early life, other than that from her entry into the monastery, the hand of the Lord was heavy upon her. These terse but evocative characterizations can be filled out by external evidence and scattered references within Elisabeth's works, although it is striking that neither Elisabeth nor her dedicated secretary chose to create a fuller biographical sketch of this visionary who became one of the most famous women of her day.

Elisabeth seems to have come from a well-established family in the Rhineland. In a previous generation, her family was distinguished by the accomplishments of Ekbert, bishop of Münster from 1127 till 1132, who played a visible role in papal and royal politics. Bishop Ekbert's niece was the mother of Elisabeth, her brother Ekbert who was named after this famous uncle, and at least one other sister and brother. Of these four known siblings, three are identifiable as heads of monastic communities.[1] Other kin are also known as monastics both at Schönau and other institutions. Family connections with local minor nobility are also attested, particularly with the patrons of Schönau. Elisabeth's removal from her family at the age of twelve should not obscure a very significant feature of monastic life in this period, which is the continuation of family networks through monastic institutions. This can be no better illustrated than Elisabeth's relationship with her brother Ekbert, which will be discussed below.

The community at Schönau, Elisabeth's home from the age of twelve until her death, was a relatively new foundation. It had been established in 1114 as a Benedictine priory for men, dependent on the abbey of Schaffhausen in Swabia. In 1125 or 1126, it was converted to an independent monastery and soon thereafter the nuns' cloister was added.[2] It had been founded as part of the Hirsau movement, a major movement of monastic reform among German Benedictine communities. Many communities within this network were committed to providing possibilities for women's religious life, often by the creation of nuns' cloisters in conjunction with those for monks. The monasteries associated with the Hirsau movement also tended to maintain ties to their local bishops and lay nobles.[3] Thus Elisabeth lived in a community founded as part of a movement for spiritual renewal, a renewal that encompassed a commitment to women's monastic life. The characteristic ties to local bishops and lay nobility can also be seen throughout Elisabeth's works. Several visions relate to the activities of Count Rupert of Laurenburg, the patron of Schönau, and his widow, Beatrice, was at Elisabeth's side in the final days of her life. Likewise Elisabeth's connection to Archbishop Hillin of Trier, to whom she directed letters of admonition and advice and whom she even came to see as a mouthpiece for her own revelations, may also have been encouraged by the particularities of this style of monastic life.

Yet the supportive environment of Schönau could not guarantee security; in fact, Elisabeth's visionary experience began in a time of religious turmoil. She describes herself as tormented by doubt about her faith and enervated by her religious practice. In this almost suicidal state, she began to have visions of both demonic and celestial apparitions. The devil appeared to her in various guises, but she was fortified by her contact with the Virgin Mary and various saints. Eventually the demonic visions subsided, and Elisabeth then narrates a fairly regular course of contact with the Virgin and other saints, transports to the otherworld, and visions of events described in the gospels.

Intimately connected with this visionary experience was her ongoing experience of physical suffering. Elisabeth was often afflicted with sickness that weakened and pained her. In addition, her ecstatic trances were usually preceded by an intensification of pain. Her attitude toward this suffering is interesting in its complexity. Elisabeth understood her physical affliction as part of God's working in her and thus eschewed medical treatment. Yet, she did not feel the need to portray herself as a silent sufferer. At various times she complained about the extent of her agony and beseeched her celestial patrons for relief from her suffering. On the other hand, she also engaged in mortifying her body with physical duress and understood ascetic practices as voluntarily adding to what the Lord would inflict upon her. By the time of her death, she also worried that her physical torment might be interpreted by others as a divine punishment that undermined the veracity of her visions.

A significant new development in Elisabeth's experience is introduced in a vision dated March 27, 1154, almost two years after the onset of her visions. In language evoking the memories of Saint Paul's experience on the road to Damascus as well as the commissioning of Old Testament prophets, Elisabeth describes a ray of light from heaven pouring over her and warming her. She fell to the ground with a violent force and couldn't be moved by the sisters who tried to help her. She continues:

> After a little while, the angel of the Lord came, and quickly raised me up and stood me on my feet saying: "O person, rise and stand on your feet and I will speak with you, and do not be afraid, because I am with you all the days of your life. Act manfully and let your heart be strengthened and wait for the Lord. Say to the apostates of the earth, 'Just as once the people crucified me, so I am daily crucified among those who have sinned against me in their hearts.' Indeed, they turn their faces from me and their heart is far from me lest they see, lest they acknowledge how I have suffered and how I have freed them by my blood." (*First Book of Visions*, chap. 67)

From this point on, Elisabeth continued to understand herself as divinely commissioned to announce to the world the content of her revelations, revelations that increasingly included explicit condemnation of wayward Christians as well as instruction for their moral regeneration.

Elisabeth accepted the charge to "act manfully" with some trepidation. This phrase itself suggests some of the tension she felt in taking on the prophetic role of shouting God's word to a sinful people, a task incompatible with the Pauline injunction for women's silence. The first public announcement of her visions came through the preaching of Hildelin, the abbot of Schönau. Her visions garnered a mixed reception: Many faithful were moved to sincere penitence but some, including ecclesiastical authorities, were unimpressed and even suggested that she might be deluded by the devil. These events, described in the *First Book of Visions* and her first letter to Hildegard of Bingen, unequivocally taught Elisabeth the vulnerability of her position. She learned about the difficulty of controlling the public dissemination of her works, the likelihood of being dismissed by some as an author of "womanish fictions," and that even the appropriate response to her visions—genuine repentance for sin—could have its cost for the public understanding of her message.

Throughout this period, Elisabeth was often visited by her brother Ekbert (not to be confused with their great-uncle, Bishop Ekbert of Münster). Ekbert, a deacon at Saint Cassius in Bonn, was very interested in his sister's visionary experience, and he shared with other nuns at Schönau the task of recording Elisabeth's descriptions of those visions. According to his biographer, Elisabeth strongly encouraged Ekbert to be ordained to the priesthood and to enter the monastic life, both of which he did.[4] In 1155, Ekbert joined the community at Schönau, "drawn," as he put it, "by the marvelous workings of God." Abbot Hildelin enjoined Elisabeth to tell Ekbert all her visions for him to record, thus formalizing the literary collaboration they had initiated. Elisabeth describes herself as relieved at this arrangement, perhaps being more confident of Ekbert's judgment than that of Hildelin, whose preaching of her visions left her exposed to disbelief and suspicion.

Ekbert's permanent move to Schönau and Hildelin's order for the systematic recording of Elisabeth's visions led to some significant changes in her life. Initially, Elisabeth and Ekbert had agreed that none of her visions should be published during her lifetime, but with Hildelin's intervention, that plan was superseded. And although Ekbert's role as secretary did not completely displace the other Schönau nuns from their activity in recording Elisabeth's visions, all the visionary records were now gathered, organized, and edited by him. Furthermore, Ekbert did not confine himself to the role of a passive amanuensis. Relying on his intimate bond with Elisabeth and the obedience she owed to their abbot's command, he sometimes coaxed from her more than she originally chose to say. And what she did say he "investigated," recording only what he thought would be useful for the faithful. Most significantly, Ekbert sometimes introduced certain questions into Elisabeth's visionary experience, seeking to use her extraordinary gifts to resolve issues of current controversy.[5]

Although the recording of Elisabeth's experiences continued and probably increased in this period after Ekbert's move to Schönau, we still know little of her day-to-day life. She became mistress of nuns sometime before 1156, but the only information we have about her activity in this capacity comes from Ekbert's lament about her death. Here he gives us a touching picture of her intimate relationship with her fellow nuns, a relationship incorporating but not limited to Elisabeth's extraordinary position as visionary. It is primarily as visionary that we know much else about her life, and in this capacity her reputation began to spread widely during this period. And the spread of her reputation led to the creation of yet new works. For example, a monk who heard about Elisabeth's visions came to visit her. After having satisfied himself that her visions were truly from God, he requested two letters from her in which she would pour forth insight from that same divine source. Elisabeth responded to his request, and this inaugurated her composition of other letters as well.

Perhaps the most famous example of how her reputation led to further composition of visionary texts is the series of events surrounding the discovery of the relics of Saint Ursula and the eleven thousand virgins of Cologne. A cemetery outside the city walls of Cologne was being excavated in the belief that it was the site of the famous martyrdom. When the monastery at Schönau acquired several relics from that collection, Elisabeth had visions in which she conversed with those martyrs. Elisabeth's reputation as one who could have contact with the inhabitants of the celestial realm spurred Abbot Gerlach of Deutz, who was orchestrating many of the exhumations, to seek her help. She had the power to confirm or disprove the rather troubling inscriptions that were said to have been found among the corpses. Elisabeth well understood that this was a controversial undertaking. The bodies being exhumed from the cemetery did not correspond to the accepted history of the martyrdom. But it is this most controversial subject that led to her most imaginative creation, a text that would also prove to be the most widely transmitted of all her works.

The Cologne excavations and inquiries were not the only activities beyond the walls of Schönau that attracted Elisabeth's attention. She addressed what she perceived as the general need for pastoral guidance in the church with her work *The Book of the Ways of God*. More specifically, she addressed what she saw as a major crisis in the church, the flourishing of a heretical group, the Cathars. Cathars had been active in the Rhineland since the 1140s.[6] They were known primarily as dualists who denied the incarnational aspects of Christian belief. Not surprisingly, such a perspective stood in stark contrast to Elisabeth's faith, nurtured as it was by a strong eucharistic piety, a recurring vision of the bloody Christ reminding the world of his physical sufferings, and a devotion to saints whose bones she honored. The full force of Elisabeth's apocalyptic foreboding comes into play in her tract about the Cathars. And yet, it is so characteristic of her thought in that the fundamental problem at issue is not simply Cathar belief but the failure of pastoral care. The shepherds of the church—those with the authority and learning to lead the church along the right path—are sleeping or else too busy feathering their own nests to exert the necessary vigilance over their flocks.

These sentiments about the Cathars were written in a letter to Hildegard of Bingen, a Benedictine nun at the nearby monastery she had founded at Rupertsberg. Elisabeth wrote in response to Hildegard's own text about the Cathars.[7] This letter is only one of several testimonies to Elisabeth's relationship with Hildegard. Like many other women and men of her day, Elisabeth sought the advice of Hildegard in letters. But Elisabeth stands apart from most of Hildegard's correspondents in sharing Hildegard's prophetic vocation of announcing visionary revelations. Elisabeth acknowledges Hildegard's influence in her *Book of the Ways of God*, when she declares that she learned from the angel that she would receive the revelations of that book after she had visited Hildegard. Thus their relationship was forged through personal visits, the exchange of letters, and some familiarity with each other's work.[8] But although Elisabeth greatly respected Hildegard and appreciated her as a model of visionary proclamation, Hildegard's influence did not generally extend to the content of her visionary texts. Elisabeth's later works show an occasional allegorical turn that suggests her familiarity with Hildegard's *Scivias*, but the greatest similarity can be seen in their respective works on the Cathars, where they clearly shared an apocalyptic idiom of condemnation.

The flurry of writing that followed Ekbert's permanent move to Schönau seems to have subsided after several years, although there are significant portions of the *Third Book of Visions* and many letters that cannot be dated and may derive from the later years of Elisabeth's life. Her final illness overtook her at age thirty-six, probably in 1165.[9] Ekbert leaves us with a picture of these last days in which Elisabeth was marvelously sustained, perfectly balanced in mind despite the ravages of her body. In this text we still see traces of the Elisabeth visible in her own works: a Benedictine nun eager to fulfill the duties of her rule, a visionary who knows the message she delivers is vital but may be dismissed on the basis of her sex, a Christian who yearns with both fear and joy to be delivered to her Creator.

Elisabeth's Works

The works of Elisabeth are collections of her pronouncements about what she saw and heard in ecstatic trances. Several of the texts have brief introductions by Ekbert, but other than these introductions, the narrative is in the first person. And that first person perspective remains an identifiable, autobiographical voice in these texts. In this way, Elisabeth's works differ from, for example, the *Scivias* of Hildegard of Bingen. Except for the opening declaration and the introductions to the first vision in each of the three sections, the seer-narrator is not a major presence in the visions. Hildegard's role as visionary is contained in the phrases "I saw" or "Then I heard," but everything that follows—even the sophisticated theological meditation on the meaning of the visions—is presented as somehow apart from her experience or her agency. In contrast, Elisabeth describes her state—physical and mental—when her visions occur. Her experiences are often interactive; she reacts to what she sees or hears; she questions the meaning of her visions and learns more in so doing; she describes herself meditating on previous visions and she breaks forth in unguarded response to what she sees. But the texts themselves are not verbatim transcripts of Elisabeth's ecstatic utterance while in trance; rather, they are records of her attempt to articulate in retrospect the totality of her experience.

These works, all preserved in Latin, were produced as the result of a complex collaboration between Elisabeth and her brother Ekbert, who served as her secretary. In his earliest comments about the texts, Ekbert emphasized the miraculous nature of Elisabeth's Latin expression, referring to her minimal knowledge of Latin. Yet, throughout the texts there are numerous casual references to Elisabeth reading, ostensibly in Latin. More to the point, Ekbert's references to the miracle of her Latin expression serve an apologetic purpose: His denigration of her Latin skills is a means of asserting the divine origin of her visions. By declaring her inability to express herself in Latin, he tries to forestall any accusation that her visionary works may be just a woman's fabrications.

In his final comment on the subject, the preface to the visionary collection, he says something rather different about the language of Elisabeth's visionary experience. Here he refers to his own role in translating some of the visionary pronouncements because some were originally uttered in German. Like his previous comments, this one is also made in an apologetic context; this time he is defending himself from any suspicion of having fabricated the texts. Elisabeth herself twice refers to a particular visionary utterance in German, seemingly distinguishing them from the rest of her experience.[10] Given the obviously apologetic motives in Ekbert's comments, and given the various references within the text that suggest Elisabeth's

Latin skills and the unusualness of German speech, we should be wary of accepting Ekbert's words at face value. Elisabeth had the benefit of monastic training from a young age, and her expression deeply reflects that culture. She probably described some of her visions in German, and these would have been translated by Ekbert, as he declared in his preface, but we should not jump to the stereotype of equating women solely with vernacular expression.

Elisabeth's visionary texts, like many other medieval texts, were produced within the context of a scribal culture in which composition was sometimes separate from the physical activity of writing. But Ekbert's role as secretary goes even beyond this process of dictation by an author and transcription by a secretary. Ekbert understood himself as charged with investigating Elisabeth's announcements and creating texts that would serve to edify the people of God.[11] Obviously, this involved the use of his judgment, something that Elisabeth describes herself as welcoming, given her own uncertainty about which visions should be made public. It also suggests that there could have been visions that Ekbert chose not to include in the texts.[12] In a letter to Abbot Reinhard of Reinhausen, he admitted to not recording everything that happened to Elisabeth. His other responsibilities, the scarcity of parchment, and the tedium he experienced due to the "malice of detractors" led him to pass over some things. Thus the works of Elisabeth exist as they have been assembled and edited by Ekbert. Over the course of her career and even after her death, Ekbert continued to hone the collection of her visions. He added new texts (both of Elisabeth's visions and his own writings[13]), polished those already published, and occasionally suppressed pieces he found questionable.

Although Elisabeth was very interested in the correct transmission of her visions,[14] there is no evidence that she scrutinized the literary texts that recorded them. Yet, her confidence in Ekbert's management of the publication of her visions had its limits. Despite the abbot's order, her professed love for her brother, and his authority as a learned investigator, there were some things that she refrained from telling him, thus retaining some control over public access to her interior experience.[15]

The most fascinating part of the collaboration between Elisabeth and Ekbert was the interaction that resulted from Ekbert's "investigation." What Elisabeth declared to have learned in her visions was subject to Ekbert's questions. For example, Elisabeth concluded a letter to the abbess of Dietkirchen with a picture of the final reward for faithful virgins. She described the rejoicing of the angels, the feasting with the Lord, freedom from all tribulation, as well as "cinnamon and balsam and the sweetest aroma." When Ekbert saw this letter (presumably transcribed by one of the other nuns of Schönau), he questioned the meaning of cinnamon and balsam, perhaps struck by this sensory, unallegorized image in this context of otherworldly bliss. Elisabeth responded to this query with another vision in which she learned that the Lord shares the qualities of sweetness and piquancy found in cinnamon; the initial sweetness of contact turns into a penetrating spiciness that enflames one with greater love, an altogether appetizing process.[16]

Sometimes, the "investigation" took a very different turn, when instead of Elisabeth's visions being investigated, her visions became the means of investigating difficult or even otherwise unanswerable questions. Particularly after Ekbert's permanent move to Schönau, this kind of questioning—and not by Ekbert alone—became more frequent as Elisabeth was increasingly recognized for the extraordinary possibilities afforded by her visionary experiences. The questions ranged from information about the otherworldly fate of the deceased (including that of the great theologian Origen, known for his work of deep devotion yet heretical expression), to clarification of mysterious parts of scriptural and patristic writings. Most of these questions had to do with "celestial" matters, such as angelology, the bodily assumption of the Virgin Mary, and Paul's references to his mystical experience, but occasionally the questions veered dramatically toward earthly affairs. The "heretical" belief of the Greeks who denied the procession of the Holy Spirit from the Son, or the validity of sacraments celebrated by simoniacal bishops were questions of current ecclesiastical and theological interest in Elisabeth's day, and Elisabeth's associates hoped for divine insight on these issues. Straddling celestial and earthly matters were the questions about the bones and their inscriptions being unearthed at

Cologne: Did they belong to those great martyred virgins now enjoying their well-earned reward, or were they the work of crafty profit-seekers?

Elisabeth must have dreaded some of these questions. Sometimes she refers to her trepidation in exploring these issues, and sometimes she is hesitant to publish the resulting visions. She was aware of the controversial nature of some of the questions and sometimes declares that the sought-after answers would not be forthcoming. Occasionally these rejoinders are subtle reflections on the questioners themselves: She suggests that Origen got himself into trouble by excessive scrutiny of divine mysteries, and that the Lord would reveal more about issues like simoniacal bishops if people weren't more corrupted than corrected by the revelations.

Despite her reservations, Elisabeth usually took the questions very seriously and devoted her interior life to reflection upon them. The texts that seem to reflect the latest stages of composition, especially the *Third Book of Visions*, contain more of this type of discussion, and Ekbert's influence is most visible here in suggesting subjects to which she should devote her attention. But even here, this influence should not be overestimated. In asking questions (as well as in his own desire for visionary experience),[17] Ekbert revealed his belief in the objective reality of Elisabeth's visionary experience. A modern perspective may emphasize the subjectivity of Elisabeth's experience and its openness to social and cultural forces, its vulnerability to the powerful sway of authoritative opinion and pressure from others. Yet, for Ekbert and Elisabeth, the questions posed certainly did not determine the answers received. If so, it is highly unlikely that Ekbert, who was very concerned to emphasize the divine origin of these visions, would have left such evidence to the contrary in these texts. His belief in the power of Elisabeth's experience also shaped their relationship in such a way that asking her a question involved his openness to receiving unexpected answers.

These dynamics of investigation and influence, visible in many places throughout Elisabeth's work, are crystallized in one of her most famous visions. One Christmas Eve, Elisabeth had a vision in which she saw the sun, and in the middle of the sun sat a virgin, "with her hair spread over her shoulders, a crown of the most resplendent gold on her head, and a golden cup in her right hand." Soon she learns that the virgin is a symbol of the humanity of Christ, the sun a symbol of his divinity. The vision is further interpreted to offer a condensed picture of the sin and salvation of humankind focusing on the humanity of Christ, a subject intimately linked to the liturgical celebration of the day. However, Elisabeth was advised to question this interpretation since it involved the very unexpected use of a feminine symbol to represent the humanity of Christ. She then learned that the humanity of Christ was represented in this way so that this female symbol could also represent the Virgin Mary. The various aspects of the vision are then interpreted to show Mary's salvific activity.[18]

Elisabeth's unconventional vision is thus "investigated." She seems to offer no resistance to this questioning and responds with what may be considered a more conventional interpretation of the vision. Yet several other aspects of this incident are also noteworthy. First, Ekbert did not delete from the collection of visions the troubling material. Second, Elisabeth did not withdraw her original statement. The more conventional association of the Virgin Mary does not supplant the first association of the humanity of Christ with a feminine symbol; rather, the two interpretations of the vision are seen as complementary. Third, the investigation became Elisabeth's opportunity for further reflection on this vision. The powerful set of associations between the saving humanity of Christ and the saving work of the Virgin, even the shared identity between the humanness of Christ and the person of the Virgin, a complex of ideas supported by the liturgy celebrating the incarnation, was sparked by the question. The issue of Ekbert's influence in this investigation is undeniable. But perhaps the whole subject is better understood in terms of the dialogical or relational nature of Elisabeth's visionary life.

The relationships in which Elisabeth participated and that shaped her piety and the texts recording her visions were indeed relationships of inequality. Her abbot ordered her exposition of her visions and her brother, as "the more learned one," decided what to investigate and what to publish. Yet, despite her subordination in status to both of these men, Elisabeth's understanding of the grace she received and their belief in it as well undermined the possibility of their absolute control over her expression of her visionary experience. Ekbert submitted questions to Elisabeth, and in so doing, participated in a relationship in which he acknowledged that the answers were out of his control. Elisabeth accepted his questions, and in so doing allowed herself further scope for reflecting on what was most important to her, the revelations she understood to be God's will working through her. It was through the dynamics of this relationship that Elisabeth's experiences became textualized as the visionary books we now associate with her.

These books can be divided into two main categories: the diary-like, chronologically organized collections of visions and the thematic collections. There are three texts of the first type, known simply as *First, Second,* and *Third Book of Visions.* The thematic collections are comprised of a short text about the assumption of the Virgin Mary, the visions about the martyrdom of Ursula and her companions, and *The Book of the Ways of God,* all of which postdate Ekbert's move to Schönau. There is also a book comprised of Elisabeth's letters that were not integrated into other texts.

The *First Book of Visions* chronicles the onset of Elisabeth's visionary life. In its original form, it is a small text of twenty-five chapters, describing events from around May 18 until August 29, 1152. After a very brief introduction by Ekbert, the narrative begins with Elisabeth's declaration of her relief at his willingness to take up the task of recording and publishing her visions. Following this is her description of her state of religious malaise and the beginning of her celestial visions. Usually the events described are fixed in time according to the liturgical calendar and office of the day, followed by Elisabeth's description of her physical as well as interior experience. The incidents described in this text are the most purely "visual" of Elisabeth's experiences. Later texts describe more auditory sensations and a great deal of verbal communication between Elisabeth and the celestial figures she sees.

Although these are the earliest records and often show the least evidence of theological reflection upon the nature of her experience, even here Elisabeth reveals aspects of her perspective that become more explicit in the later records. For example, having had several visions of a dove that she assumed represented the Holy Spirit, Elisabeth then began to wonder if perhaps she was being deceived by Satan, who was known to be able to transform himself into seemingly celestial forms. She sought guidance from Abbot Hildelin, and he reassured her that he had never heard of such a thing. Yet, she declared, "I remained dubious." It was not until she had a vision that she could interpret as an answer to her question that she was reassured.[19] It is her continued visionary life that was authoritative here. This is particularly noteworthy given the modern tendency to picture Elisabeth as insecure and always seeking the approval or confirmation of others. In this regard, she suffers by comparison to her sometimes imperious contemporary, Hildegard of Bingen, as almost anyone would. But even this early and rather simple visionary account suggests a certain streak of independence in Elisabeth's way of working out the implications of her experience.

This brief, original form of the *First Book of Visions* ends with two incidents that foreshadow Elisabeth's later development of prophetic identity. Chapter 24 recounts her first experience of what can be called pastoral preaching. She opens her mouth and a sermon calling the sinful to repent pours out. Following chapter 25 is a vision full of apocalyptic foreboding, which Abbot Hildelin seems to have later incorporated into his controversial preaching. Perhaps because of the way Hildelin represented this prophecy, or because of the way it was misinterpreted by others as a prediction of the Last Judgment, Ekbert later suppressed this vision when he expanded the text.

In the expanded version of the *First Book of Visions*, Ekbert elaborated his introduction, made minor revisions in the original chapters, and added the records of Elisabeth's visions up to August 15, 1154. This addition of over fifty chapters made the *First Book of Visions* the longest of all Elisabeth's works. In these chapters, Elisabeth describes much more complex experiences than are found in the earlier chapters. Her visions now have very significant verbal components; they are often described as experiences of rapture in which she is carried away to the otherworld; and most of them now include the presence of an angel who serves as her guide and interpreter of what she sees. This later version of the text also encompasses the records in which Elisabeth describes her sense of prophetic commissioning. Yet, curiously, these events are almost immediately followed by two visions in which Elisabeth sees herself at her final judgment, and the book concludes with explicit reference to her death.

The *Second Book of Visions* also begins with an introduction by Ekbert and exists in two forms. The original one is comprised of eighteen chapters spanning Elisabeth's experiences from May 14 till August 10, 1155. The gap in time from the events described at the end of the *First Book of Visions* to the beginning of the *Second Book* is filled by the events surrounding Abbot Hildelin's preaching of Elisabeth's visions, as described in Elisabeth's first letter to Hildegard. Thus it is not surprising that one of the main differences between Elisabeth's narratives in these two books is the much greater presence of Hildelin in the *Second Book*. With Elisabeth's prophetic commissioning—which involved her disclosure to him about the full range of her experience—and his decision to publish her visions through his own preaching, he took a much more active role in her life. His presence, primarily as priestly officiant at Mass and her confessor, is repeatedly highlighted in these records.

Eleven more chapters were later added to the *Second Book of Visions*, ostensibly continuing in chronological order, but there is no longer sufficient internal evidence to date them. This is also a characteristic of the *Third Book of Visions*. These later chapters in the *Second Book* and the entire *Third Book of Visions* are also distinguished from the earlier material in their decreased attention to some autobiographical elements, such as Elisabeth's physical condition, and in their witness to Ekbert's greater presence in Elisabeth's life and his occasional direction of her attention to subjects he was interested in. The later addition of these chapters and their evidence about Ekbert's influence suggest that these chapters record Elisabeth's experience after Ekbert had made his permanent move to Schönau. It may seem ironic that the records of Elisabeth's experience occurring after Ekbert began his systematic effort to preserve her words were vaguer than the material recorded earlier. But there are several factors that help explain this. First, it may be that the other Schönau nuns who recorded Elisabeth's words were more interested in preserving all the details. Second, it is also possible that Ekbert's own earlier efforts were more diligent in recording Elisabeth's words. Third, and most significant, this period after Ekbert's move to Schönau also saw the development of a new type of visionary text, thus perhaps contributing to a decreased attention to the kinds of visions recorded in the earlier texts.

Elisabeth began a very fertile period of visionary experience in 1156. The three thematic collections of her visions all stem from this period. In June, she began to have a series of visions that would last till August of the following year. These visions are the basis for *The Book of the Ways of God*. In this text, Elisabeth describes seeing a mountain with ten paths leading to the summit. A mountain with paths is an image found in her earlier visions, but it is most fully elaborated in this text. The paths represent ten groups within the church: contemplatives, actives, martyrs, marrieds, chaste, leaders, widows, hermits, adolescents, and young children. After describing the various paths with their respective degrees of difficulty, she announces a sermon for each to guide the faithful in their ascent to God. This is the most systematically organized and executed of all Elisabeth's works. But even here, the basis in her visionary life is still very apparent. The ten paths came to her in three separate visions, or rather in a series of three visions in which she saw the same thing with increasing detail. There is a kind of "logic of inclusion" in these visions; that is, more and more paths seem to be added without necessarily an attempt to rationalize their relationship to each other. After having had the initial visions revealing the ten paths, she begins to wonder about the potential confusion among them: She recognizes that the proliferation of paths does not actually correspond to a tenfold division among the people of God. But the overlaps and redundancies enable a broad scope for pastoral guidance, and each path is addressed in turn. Nor are the sermons homogenized; they vary in length and in fervor, and it is clear that Elisabeth's reflection turned more easily to some paths than others. Although she explicitly affirms that all paths lead to celestial beatitude, she does assert the primacy of one in particular. The path of contemplation is the path that Christ himself walked and the only permanent path, since contemplation is what the elect will do for all eternity. Elisabeth's commitment to the importance of this work can be seen in a letter that she wrote to the bishops of Trier, Mainz, and Cologne commanding them to preach the message of this book to the entire church.

Shortly after the onset of the visions revealing *The Book of the Ways of God*, Elisabeth also had a series of visions about the assumption of the Virgin Mary. The visions stretched out over the course of three years, but were confined to the times around the feast of the Assumption. They were elicited by a question posed to Elisabeth by an unnamed authority ("one of our elders"). Elisabeth, expecting to see the Virgin around the time of the feast of the Assumption, was advised to ask her about whether her assumption into heaven was physical as well as spiritual. The question was so pressing because "what is written about this in the books of the Fathers is found to be ambiguous."

The nature of Mary's assumption was in fact a point of doctrinal controversy in Elisabeth's day. Scripture was silent on this point, as on so many aspects of Mary's life that later captured the loving attention of those devoted to her. Despite enthusiastic elaboration of the events in Mary's life in apocryphal texts, *assumptio* was commonly understood to refer to the ascent of Mary's soul after her death. In the early twelfth century, an anonymous treatise ascribed to Augustine offered rational arguments for the bodily resurrection of Mary, but this text hardly produced a theological consensus. If scripture, patristic authority, and even rational argument couldn't resolve the problem—which after all, was fueled by loving devotion to Mary and not recourse to these more restrained sources—Elisabeth must have seemed like a promising new source of authority. Thus when her first inquiry yielded no information, her assiduous questioner only urged Elisabeth to more prayer to elicit the desired visions. Ultimately Elisabeth announced a series of visions interpreted to support the belief in Mary's bodily assumption. The visions went even further: Elisabeth announced a new date for celebrating the assumption of Mary. August 15, the traditional date, was established by the church fathers in ignorance of the reality of Mary's bodily assumption, which Elisabeth declared to have transpired on September 23.

The short text recording these visions, *The Resurrection of the Blessed Virgin*, is unusual among her works in that Elisabeth seems to have remained unconvinced of its universal value. Despite general concerns about publishing her visions, her other works reveal her widened sense of their pastoral importance for the edification and consolation of the faithful. But *The Resurrection of the Blessed Virgin*, perhaps because it affirms a specific divergence from the current liturgical calendar, is understood by Elisabeth as a work that could at most be shared with those like herself, that is, those who especially love the Virgin, those who are her most intimate servants.

The third thematic text originating in this period of rich visionary activity is *The Book of Revelations About the Sacred Company of the Virgins of Cologne*. By Elisabeth's day, the legend about the martyrdom of Ursula and her companions was known through liturgical texts and Latin stories of their passion. The best-known account was *Regnante domino*, written around 1100 for the convent of Saint Ursula in Cologne.[20] Elisabeth knew *Regnante domino* and made reference to this "history" at several points in her own account of the martyrdom. According to this legend, Ursula, the young, beautiful, and saintly daughter of a Christian king of Britain, sought to escape a marriage offer from a neighboring barbarian king and received a revelation of her impending martyrdom as a divinely ordained solution to the undesired proposal. She announced as her conditions for accepting the proposal that she be provided with eleven thousand virgins to accompany her for a respite of three years, as well as eleven ships to accommodate this company of young women. When the three-year respite ended, God sent a strong wind that blew their ships far from Britain. Finding themselves sailing down the Rhine, the maidens disembarked at Basel. They continued on to a quick pilgrimage to Rome, paying their respects to the tombs of the saints and spiritually preparing themselves for their ensuing ordeal. On their return, while they were approaching Cologne, they were attacked by Huns, who had been besieging the city, and they were slain when they resisted the barbarians' advances.

Abbot Gerlach of Deutz sent Elisabeth more and more inscriptions from the Cologne cemetery that was thought to be the site of this great martyrdom. For each inscription received, Elisabeth announced descriptions of visionary conversations with those martyred virgins. Most troubling among the inscriptions were those associated with the bodies of men and children, since the eleven thousands virgins were known to have been women. And most troubling among the inscriptions of male bodies was that of Pope Cyriacus, whose existence should have been verifiable in authoritative texts such as lists of pontiffs. In *The Revelations About the Virgins of Cologne*, as in *The Resurrection of the Blessed Virgin*, Elisabeth confronts the divergence between the received tradition of the church and what she learns in her visions. As in the text about Mary, here too the juxtaposition of tradition and revelation is the result of an inquiry initiated by someone other than Elisabeth herself. Yet here Elisabeth's confidence in her revelations seems greater, and she creates an elaborate scenario to encompass the troubling discoveries at Cologne.

In addition to the three chronological collections of visions and the three thematic texts, Elisabeth's visions were also recorded in letters addressed to specific individuals. There are twenty-two known letters, most of which are directed to other monastics about their life of contemplation and praise of God. Only the letters to Hildegard of Bingen are part of an extant, mutual correspondence; several letters from Elisabeth suggest that they were responses to letters sent to her, and others seem to originate in Elisabeth's motivation to communicate with her addressees. The letters were for the most part collected into a book, which was introduced by Ekbert's account of a monk from Busendorf who visited Elisabeth and requested letters from her. Several others, however, were incorporated into other visionary texts.[21] Many of the themes of pastoral exhortation found in *The Book of the Ways of God* can also be seen in these letters.

After Elisabeth died, Ekbert wrote a letter to their kinswomen at the convent of Saint Thomas in Andernach, describing his sister's final days. He added this letter as a conclusion to the collection of Elisabeth's works, as if to provide the account of the holy death of the person whose life was described in the visionary works. *The Death of Elisabeth* begins with the closest thing to a eulogy that Ekbert wrote. In contrast to the restrained tone of his introductions to her visionary works, here his grief unleashes a flood of praise and wonder. Following this lament is his account of Elisabeth's final illness, her preparation for her death, and the words of guidance she spoke to those who came to see her. Like the *First* and *Second Book of Visions*, Ekbert worked on this text even after its initial circulation, and thus it exists in two versions.

These eight works—the three chronological books, the three thematic books, the letter collection, and Ekbert's letter about Elisabeth's death—compose the collection of visionary works associated with Elisabeth. Smaller collections of these works circulated outside Schönau during Elisabeth's lifetime. The earliest collections of her works included the books about the Cologne martyrdom and the bodily resurrection of the Virgin Mary, usually *The Book of the Ways of God*, and sometimes the original version of the *First Book of Visions*. To this core collection, the later chronological books were added, as well as the collection of letters and Ekbert's lament about Elisabeth's death. The texts about the Cologne martyrdom and the assumption of the Virgin Mary also circulated independently from the collections of Elisabeth's visions.

Elisabeth's Visionary Piety

We have already noted certain ways in which the community at Schönau afforded Elisabeth a culture conducive to the development of her visionary piety. Other aspects of the life at Schönau are also visible in reading Elisabeth's works: the role of Abbot Hildelin and the mistress or head of the nuns' community; evidence about the separation of the nuns' and monks' communities; references to relationships with other monasteries; and practices followed in accordance with the Rule of Saint Benedict or the customary of the community. But the aspect of monastic culture that had the greatest impact on Elisabeth and her visionary piety was undoubtedly the liturgical life. Even a cursory glance at her works reveals how her visionary experience was deeply embedded in the regular cycle of communal praise of God. It was often during the services of the divine office, or, as Ekbert put it, "around the hours in which the devotion of the faithful was especially inflamed," that Elisabeth went into ecstatic trance and had her visions.

This intimate connection between liturgy and vision is made explicit in the texts, for accounts of her experience are usually introduced by noting the day of the liturgical calendar and the office of the divine liturgy. But the liturgy is not simply a ritual setting that enabled extraordinary experience. The content of the specific liturgy—its antiphons, its scriptural readings, its dedication to particular feasts or saints—saturated the visions Elisabeth saw. Then, when she conceptualized and articulated her experience, she did so in an idiom profoundly shaped by certain texts of the Bible—the Psalter in particular—and the words of the divine office that temporally structured her days and years. Thus her pronouncements were often evocations of biblical or liturgical passages, the former often mediated by the liturgy itself.

Elisabeth's visionary works thus give great insight into one way in which the monastic liturgy could come to shape the interior life of its practitioners. As the liturgy itself offers a structure of connection to the otherworld, Elisabeth's experience offered a consolidation—a making solid of—that connection. Understanding the monastic liturgical life to mirror the continuous celestial liturgy, Elisabeth saw angels descend from heaven to participate in and protect the prayer of her community. Thus it is also not surprising to find her concerned about proper liturgical observance. When she heard a collect for Saint John the Evangelist read on the feast of the martyrs John and Paul, she had a vision in which John the Evangelist confirmed the correct date of his death, and on this basis, she suggested a reason for the current liturgical observance of his feast on a different date. And despite her misgivings about appearing to be an author of novelties, Elisabeth announced an emendation of the liturgical calendar in order to enable the proper observance of the feast of the Assumption.

The connection between the liturgy and Elisabeth's visions also suggests another important characteristic of her piety. This is the fact that Elisabeth understood her own life of prayer to be the context for her visionary experience. Visionary experience could be prayed for and nurtured by prayer. Although it was extraordinary—that is, unusual—nonetheless, it was not something that made for a radical departure from what preceded or followed it. It

21

was a heightening of rather than a divergence from the usual experience of prayer.

Related to the liturgical character of Elisabeth's visionary experience is another quality we might link with her monastic life. This is the way in which Elisabeth's visionary life reflects and is shaped by her participation in a community. For example, in one of the earliest accounts of her experience, Elisabeth describes her spiritual turmoil and physical debilitation due to the harassment of the devil. But this is not cast in a heroic mode of the rugged individual battling the forces of evil. Instead, she declares:

> Seeing my difficulties, the sisters and brothers came together and decided to pour out communal prayers for seven continuous days, to mortify themselves in the presence of the Lord for my sake, and to celebrate a Mass each day for my distresses. One of these seven Masses, the Mass of the Holy Spirit, was to be sung on Thursday, so I awaited that day with great desire, hoping that I might then receive some consolation. The longed for day arrived, and while the brothers were celebrating the divine rite, I was lying prostrate in prayer with the sisters. And my heart was enlarged and I saw a great light in the heavens, and behold, a dove of great beauty, such as I had seen earlier coming from the light, flew to me. With wings outspread it circled around my head three times, and then flew to the heavens. (*First Book of Visions*, chap. 9)

The whole community responds to her distress, and it is when lying prostrate in prayer among the sisters while the brothers celebrated the Mass that Elisabeth has a vision that consoles her. She anticipated this moment, and with her sisters and brothers focused in prayer, she sees.

The course of Elisabeth's communal life can even adversely affect her visions. She describes a prolonged experience of disapproval from the Virgin Mary. Again, the response suggests the degree to which Elisabeth's visions were embedded in the life of her community: "Fearing that we had offended our Lady's benevolence with our communal negligence (*communi negligentia nostra*), we began to request with our communal prayer (*communi oratione*)" the indulgence of the Virgin. Elisabeth is also aware of how much the stresses of her visionary life have negatively affected her sisters ("My long and varied illnesses have troubled not only me, but also all the sisters who are around me"). And the fruits of Elisabeth's visionary experience are not simply for her personal benefit: In her vision she learns how to comfort one of the priests of Schönau (probably Ekbert) for his accidental profanation of the Eucharist; she learns that the abbot's prayers have been especially pleasing to the Virgin Mary; when she learns of the purgatorial distress of three deceased nuns, the nuns of Schönau immediately undertake prayer and bodily mortification on their behalf, and when the deceased nuns are liberated, Elisabeth reminds them of their debt to her sisters; she learns that a dying sister will have a respite to amend her life.

The communal dimension of Elisabeth's piety is thus not simply the dynamics of monastic hierarchy that led to the recording of her visions when Abbot Hildelin ordered Elisabeth to narrate her experiences to Ekbert, although this is certainly a significant part of it. Elisabeth's works reveal a religious sensibility in which being attuned to divine grace is not something that happens in isolation from others. Elisabeth was shaped by a monastic culture in which the individual identity was being constantly refashioned in such a way as to minimize ego. The Rule of Saint Benedict structured an environment in which the individual self was cultivated as a member or limb of a body whose primary activity was communal praise of God and battle against the devil. Thus in *The Death of Elisabeth*, when Elisabeth is described as reminding her brothers and sisters of the value of what God has done *for their community*, this is not merely referring to the prestige Schönau has garnered from Elisabeth's reputation as a visionary.

We may tend to understand Elisabeth's experience as fundamentally personal or intimate. And the visions in the early stage of Elisabeth's career may strike the reader as the most personal; no theological mysteries seem to be limned and the experiences seem to transpire within the framework of Elisabeth's private religious needs. But to see these experiences as only private would be to miss a vital part of Elisabeth's piety. Elisabeth describes her own sense of these visions as something much more significant. Through conversation with others, she came to understand these visions as not being granted for her sake alone. Rather, she believed that the Lord acted through her to provide "confirmation of the faith and consolation of those who are troubled in heart." The present-day reader must take seriously this affirmation, which itself is attested to in the popularity of Elisabeth's works, an unlikely phenomenon if her visions were perceived to be relevant only to her own life. The claim of personal experience is indeed crucial; it is the central fact of these texts. Yet personal experience here is not understood to be idiosyncratic or private. Elisabeth's testimony of direct experience of seeing heaven or hell, of seeing the Virgin cradle the infant Jesus in her arms, of being fortified by the Virgin against the powers of the devil is offered to the world as consolation, as witness to the power of divine intervention in the course of troubling human history.

For Elisabeth, this consolation is absolutely inseparable from moral regeneration, and here the universalist dimension of her visions becomes most explicit. This concern with righteousness permeated her thought. She returned repeatedly to certain themes such as the duty of religious leaders to extend their pastoral staves and "strike strongly but gently" and be accountable for the awesome responsibility of souls entrusted to their care. This sentiment could be directed to friends who specifically sought her advice or incorporated into *The Book of the Ways of God*, and its recurrence suggests Elisabeth's view of the centrality of pastoral care for a faithful Christian people.

Although much of her moral teaching is tied to the image of path—that faithfulness is embodied by unswerving progress along the path one finds oneself on—Elisabeth was also concerned with more subtle dynamics of moral consciousness. In a striking passage in *The Book of the Ways of God*, she describes her reflection on desire, will, and intention. Any discussion of these issues has the potential for obscurity and difficulty, and Elisabeth engaged in this reflection in the very sensitive area of sexual purity. Because the question was framed in terms of sexuality, it is not surprising that the visionary response was framed in terms of filth and pollution. Questioning her angel guide about the guilt of lust that isn't acted upon, Elisabeth must immerse her hand in a pile of filth to learn the difference between desire and action. But still she wonders, knowing well the gospel equation between looking with lust and committing adultery. The category of will is introduced to illustrate the difference between unwillingly suffering temptation and willingly nurturing desire, even if neither of those interior states eventuate in an act. Throughout this passage, it is clear that Elisabeth's concern is not about abstract moral theorizing. Penance is repeatedly stressed as the proper technique for dealing with these problems, and thus the practical, pastoral dimension of the reflection is foregrounded. Even more strikingly, this section ends with reference to "a person in Christ who is close to me" whose chastity was being attacked by the devil's temptations and who was resorting to extreme ascetic measures to counteract the assaults. Again, the communal dimension of Elisabeth's visionary life is evident in how her community is part of what she sees and is further strengthened by what she learns.

Other aspects of Elisabeth's piety that are revealed in her works include her devotion to the Virgin Mary and to other saints. Elisabeth has visions of Mary as priest, as queen, and as mother of the infant Jesus. From the beginning of Elisabeth's religious turmoil, Mary is her consoler, her advocate, the one who marks her with the sign of the cross and strengthens her in her struggle against demonic harassment. And although it was others who instigated the inquiry about the nature of the Virgin's assumption, the inquiry was enabled by Elisabeth's sense of herself as receiving the favor of intimate contact with Mary.

Two aspects of Elisabeth's devotion to Mary must be stressed. First, Elisabeth did not perceive Mary's connection to herself to be one of "unconditional love." This phrase, which has become so current in our own day, slips easily into discussions about maternal figures and can too quickly be projected back into medieval devotion to the "Mother of Mercy." In the visions preserved in the *Second Book of Visions*, Elisabeth perceives herself as losing Mary's favor. This is possible in Elisabeth's view because Mary's favor requires service from those devoted to her. The relationship between those living on earth and those dwelling in heaven must be maintained by a service of prayer; in other words, it is a relationship of mutual obligation, not a one-way exercise of power. This holds true with the other saints as well, but it is particularly striking in Elisabeth's devotion to Mary. The other important aspect of Elisabeth's devotion to the Virgin is her affirmation of Mary's role in saving the whole world. Not only did Mary intervene to comfort Elisabeth in her time of need, but at every moment in time Mary is acting to keep the world from being destroyed by the wrath of her Son. Thus the Virgin Mary is understood to have a major role in the economy of human salvation.

The liturgical life that structured Elisabeth's sense of time also offered her the possibility of meditating on the lives of the many saints memorialized in its calendar. Those who particularly caught Elisabeth's attention were John the Evangelist, John the Baptist, and the apostles Peter and Paul. Even though Matthew, Mark, and Luke are not frequently noted, Elisabeth repeatedly sees variations on the vision described in Ezekiel 1, which was understood to refer to the four evangelists. It is possible that Elisabeth's attention to John the Evangelist and the Ezekiel vision reflects some identification with the evangelists and the prophet Ezekiel. She understood herself to share with them the divine grace of seeing visions. Thus her focus on John—who was associated with the explicit claim of visionary experience in the Book of Revelation—rather than the other evangelists makes sense.

Other saints are said to appear to her on their feast days, and Elisabeth usually commends the well-being of her community to their care. When Schönau received relics from the Cologne site reputed to be the graves of Saint Ursula and her companions, Elisabeth's devotion to these saints flowered forth. One might easily expect that the virgin martyrs of Cologne would be an apt subject for Elisabeth to meditate upon, given the positive value she attributes to virginity and martyrdom in, for example, *The Book of the Ways of God*. This is certainly true, but there is something else going on here as well. The stated purpose of this text is to enhance the cult of the Cologne martyrs. Elisabeth begins the text by asserting her willingness to publish her revelations despite potential criticism, because she expects to be rewarded "if this martyrdom shall receive some increased honor from those things which the Lord has deigned to reveal through my labors." Likewise, she ends the text with Saint

Ursula herself praying for God to reward anyone who retells or, literally, refreshes *(renovabit)* their passion. If the goal of the text is the increased devotion to these saints, then the model of virtue here, the example of one to be rewarded, is Elisabeth herself. So the construction of holiness broadens beyond the model of Ursula and her companions to the model of devotion to Ursula and her companions. Here Elisabeth develops a view of virtue that was alluded to at the end of *Regnante domino* when the author exhorted the community of nuns to beseech the patronage of martyred virgins.

For Elisabeth, devotion to the saints can have the very tangible component of direct response from the saints, of a real sensory engagement with them. They can be seen, heard, and if not touched, their presence can be felt in the cures they work upon suffering bodies. And although Elisabeth understood her visionary contact with the Cologne martyrs to be something special, something predestined by God, nonetheless, she did not believe it to be an exclusive privilege. In the book recording her pronouncements about the Cologne martyrdom, the context of which is her peculiar access to those martyrs, Elisabeth affirmed that she was not the only one learning about these saints and their relics. After identifying the body of the martyr Adrian, Elisabeth declared that the name and family background of this martyr had also been revealed to the monk who had transferred the body from Cologne to Schönau. Thus Elisabeth seems to have understood her visions of saints to be part of broad practice of devotion to and therefore actual connection with those who have passed beyond the boundaries of this life. And even though they have crossed that boundary, their visionary accessibility heightens the power with which Elisabeth can evoke them as models for imitation, as she does particularly in her letters and *The Book of the Ways of God.*

Visions, Gender, and Identity

As the religious works of medieval women have increasingly become known in our day, the visionary mode of expression is one feature that has frequently been noted as characteristic of

27

women's writing from this period. While this is in fact a very important observation, it raises many issues. First, it can be stated at the outset that there is no single visionary mode of women's religious works. Noted briefly above were some distinctions between the visionary expression of Elisabeth and Hildegard of Bingen, two women who lived in the same culture and shared the same institutional traditions of Benedictine monasticism. Second, this visionary mode is usually associated with medieval women's need to validate their expression in a culture in which they were not trained or expected to teach or even to have anything to say. Deep traditions of misogyny structured medieval culture, and issues of female credibility and authority can be seen in many women's works. Visionary experience is thus frequently interpreted as the basis of an authority that doesn't rely on the traditional sources of authority (such as education and ordination) unavailable to women. Third, this visionary mode is sometimes dismissed, or at least interpreted, as a mere rhetorical strategy adopted to meet the needs of authorizing women's texts. This point is difficult to argue if the basis of all human activity is seen to be only strategic response to power politics. The claims made in so many of these texts challenge readers to entertain a much more complex view of human activity in which an individual may genuinely feel herself moved by forces outside of herself. That this movement may address real problems of sexism or marginality in her culture need not mean that it is thus revealed to be *merely* strategic or rhetorical. Elisabeth of Schönau and other women visionary writers lived in a world in which belief in a God who intervenes in history was reiterated in many different ways. Also fundamental to that belief was the cherished divine inversions of human power—that God scatters the proud and exalts the lowly (Lk 1:51–52), uses the humble to put down the mighty, the fool to receive revelation (2 Cor 11), or social outcasts and children to recognize the truth that their learned religious leaders ignore (Mt 21:14–17). Thus, within the "logic" of medieval Christian culture were the symbolic resources for structuring a hierarchy of male dominance and for women to feel themselves impelled to act in ways that may seem to resist its hegemony.

But what about Elisabeth? How did her sense of receiving the grace of visionary experience shape her sense of who she was and her place in the world? Elisabeth is a particularly challenging case to examine because the evidence of men's active roles in her career is so clear. This evidence has been interpreted in various ways. F. W. E. Roth, the nineteenth-century editor of Elisabeth's visions, and Kurt Köster, who did extremely important work on the transmission of her texts, assumed that the work they thought was the best—*The Book of the Ways of God*—must have been written by Ekbert.[22] More recently, commentators have tended to emphasize Elisabeth's dependence upon Ekbert and his control of her expression. Part of the challenge in approaching Elisabeth's works is to acknowledge that the very lucid and compelling introductions to her work that Ekbert wrote reflect his interpretation of Elisabeth and should not be assumed to reflect Elisabeth's view or to be the necessarily more accurate view of what happened at Schönau.

For example, both Elisabeth and Ekbert were highly aware of the potentially questionable nature of Elisabeth's claims to divine inspiration and were concerned that her works might be dismissed on the basis of her sex. In his introduction to the *Second Book of Visions*, Ekbert addresses critics of Elisabeth's earlier book by tackling head-on the issue of gender and visionary experience:

> Indeed, [God] is not inhibited by the murmuring of those who think themselves great and disdain whatever they regard as weaker, and who do not fear to mock the riches of His goodness in them. They should be afraid that because of their murmuring they will hear the word of the Father saying, "Is your eye evil because I am good?" (Mt 20:15) It scandalizes them that in these days the Lord deigns to magnify His mercy in the weak sex. But why doesn't it occur to them that a similar thing happened in the days of our fathers? When men were given over to negligence, holy women were filled with the spirit of God so that they prophesied, vigorously ruled the people of God or even triumphed gloriously over the enemies of Israel, like Hulda, Deborah, Judith, Jael and others of this sort.

Ekbert defends Elisabeth's claims of divine inspiration by resorting to biblical precedent. Most significantly, since the criticism was based on gender, that is, the mockery of the "weak sex," gender is foregrounded in Ekbert's defense. First, he tries to make Elisabeth's experience conform to tradition by comparing her to a series of biblical women filled with the spirit of God. Second, he also declares that such female leadership is due to the sinful failure of men to discharge their responsibilities. Thus, his defense of Elisabeth also functions as a criticism of those men whose disdain for Elisabeth is part of a larger picture of male pastoral failure.

This is an eloquent and persuasive interpretation of Elisabeth's experience, yet there is no evidence that this is what Elisabeth believed of herself. She and Ekbert did share a view of her being divinely inspired, and Elisabeth also turned to authoritative, biblical precedent. We have already seen this in the passage quoted above from the *First Book of Visions*, where Elisabeth portrays herself as having bodily experienced a power that overwhelmed her, as having been restored to bodily capacity by an angel who then charged her with the mission of preaching an ominous message of warning to sinners. This vision is followed by several others in which the words she attributes to the angel and to herself are heavy with biblical resonances of prophetic commission. The striking down of the apostle Paul on the road to Damascus, the resistance and claims of verbal inability of Moses and Jeremiah, the assurance that those who listen to the Lord's disciples are in fact hearing the Lord's words are all evoked in these scenes. Thus Elisabeth, like Ekbert, represents her experience in terms that highlight the continuity between Elisabeth and authoritative convention. But the differences between their representations are also striking. Most obviously, Elisabeth speaks the language of experience rather than the language of comparison, which is Ekbert's mode of expression. Elisabeth's language does not stray into the realm of logical comparison. Instead, she proclaims her embodiment of the experience of inspiration: the experience of ecstasy or trance, of overwhelming heat and an incapacity to remain standing, of being forcibly raised up, or of opening her mouth and having somebody else's words come out.

INTRODUCTION

Like Ekbert, Elisabeth also deals with issues of gender in her representation of her prophetic identity, but here the contrast with Ekbert's view is even more striking. Both Elisabeth and Ekbert are aware of the fact that their contemporaries did not generally expect to learn the will of God from the women in their midst. Ekbert's response is to emphasize the biblical precedents for women's active role in religious matters and to account for both the past and present disruptions of expectations about gender by pointing to the failure of male religious leaders. There was a clear sense of the continuity of history and the stability of gender categories for Ekbert. For him, Elisabeth's activity is best understood in light of the roles of other women, and women could play these roles when the historical circumstances were appropriate. But Elisabeth herself does not cite or evoke any biblical model of a woman inspired to do the will of God. In fact, she uses prophetic language that is specifically gendered as male. She describes the angel addressing her as "son of man" and telling her to "act manfully." These passages do not suggest that Elisabeth saw herself as male. But they do attest to her acute sense that what she understood herself to be called upon to do was a male activity. Elisabeth's sense of her own activity is not domesticated within a proper sphere of women's activity in the appropriate circumstances. These passages suggest her view of prophetic proclamation as something "other" to her even as she embraces this vocation.

This difference between Elisabeth's and Ekbert's understanding of her prophetic identity can be linked to other aspects of the visionary texts. Ekbert's inclination to retain tidy gender boundaries and Elisabeth's sense of gender permeability can be seen in the account of the virgin in the sun vision. The representation of the humanity of Christ by a feminine symbol troubled a sensibility in which clear differences between male and female needed to be reproduced. Yet not only did Elisabeth articulate this female image of Christ's humanity, she also articulated a response that pointed again to the blurred boundaries between male and female, that is, the close identity between Mary and Christ.

Interpretations of gender are themselves gendered perspectives in medieval Christian culture, as Caroline Bynum has demonstrated.

31

Women and men did not necessarily understand femaleness and maleness in the same ways; rather, women's views of gender were often more fluid than men's.[23] Ekbert's comparison of Elisabeth to female prophets foreshadows a very similar dynamic in the *Vita Hildegardis*, where Theodoric of Echternach interpreted Hildegard's controversial move to Rupertsberg by citing Origen's comments about the prophet Deborah: "Deborah stands out as a great consolation for womankind. And lest they despair at the weakness of their sex, she challenges them to make of themselves fit for the grace of prophecy; but they must understand and believe that purity of mind, not difference in sex, merits this grace."[24] This passage is sandwiched between autobiographical excerpts in which Hildegard compares her activities to those of Moses and Joshua.[25] Philip of Clairvaux's discussion of Elisabeth of Spalbeek's extraordinary physical experience of divine grace emphasized her appropriateness as a model for women, in comparison to Francis of Assisi as a model for men.[26] This pattern of medieval men's interpretation of women's experience must not keep us from seeing that often women's views of gender did not maintain such neat lines between male and female.

Another way in which Ekbert's "packaging" of Elisabeth's visions may mask some very important aspects of her piety is his insistence on the divine origin of her visions. This is a consistent theme in his introductions to specific books and his general preface. Elisabeth, of course, also believed that her visions came from heaven, and she repeatedly asserts her unworthiness to receive them. Yet, she also portrayed her own effort to receive visions, that is, her prayerful cultivation of her visionary life, and the ways in which her negative actions—or those of her community—could obstruct the course of her visions. In contrast to Ekbert's view, in which divine agency is the only operational force in the visionary experience and Elisabeth is simply a channel of revelation, Elisabeth understood herself actively participating in a complex world with many agencies—that of God, the Virgin Mary, the saints, herself, and her sisters and brothers. And that is why Elisabeth's words are often fraught with the poignant tensions borne of her complicated sense of agency. She felt herself to be engaged in realizing the divine will, and that engagement was sometimes more successful than others. It drew on her resources as a faithful Christian and could not be separated from the dynamics of her religious life, dynamics that included striving and struggling, fear, and even sin. Ekbert's focus on the divine origin of her visions may explain the puzzling fact that he never wrote a *vita* of the woman he knew so well and whose words were so important to him. But Elisabeth knew her life was inextricably linked with her message, and that is why her works can really be seen as spiritual autobiography.

A Classic of Western Spirituality

Elisabeth's works found a receptive audience in her day, as witnessed by their widespread circulation. At least 145 medieval manuscripts are known to have transmitted copies of her works, and her visions enjoyed their first printing in 1513.[27] The books about the Cologne martyrdom and the assumption of Mary were the most popular, attesting to how much Elisabeth's visions spoke to current practices of devotion. But the frequent inclusion of her work in manuscripts that transmit works by writers such as Hugh of Saint Victor and Bernard of Clairvaux also suggests that her works were not tied simply to those devotional focuses. In addition to the existence of her works in many medieval libraries, there are occasional comments about her works that suggest how they were appreciated. About a decade after her death, Roger of Ford, an English Cistercian monk, encountered her works while traveling in France. He sent a copy of them back to his abbot, accompanied by a letter in which he testified that "in these parts it [The Book of the Ways of God] is eagerly copied and read and heard not only by the unlearned but by bishops and our abbots." He also suggested that Baldwin have another copy of her works transcribed to send to the women's community where his mother lived.[28] The same text was selected for reading at collation at the Cistercian abbey of Saint Mary at Himmerod.[29] Within a century of the beginning of Elisabeth's visionary career, a chronicler could testify to the many monastic libraries in France and Germany that owned copies of her works and could matter of factly incorporate even the most surprising "data" from the revelations about the Cologne martyrdom into his history, declaring all previous historians wrong.[30] *The Resurrection of the Blessed Virgin* was translated into Anglo-Norman verse (as yet undated) and Icelandic (1226–34), and in the fourteenth century *The Book of the Ways of God* was translated into French.[31] Yet despite this evidence of the popularity of her work, Elisabeth's concerns about the novelty of some of her visions were well founded. John Beleth, a contemporary Paris theologian, referred to Elisabeth's assertion of the Virgin Mary's bodily assumption forty days after her death. This, he declared "was not approved in the Roman church."[32] This view was repeated two centuries later by Nicholas Trevet,[33] even though there is no known official commentary on *The Resurrection of the Blessed Virgin*, positive or negative. But these two remarks suggest a recognition that Elisabeth's visions were perceived as controversial.

The immediate sphere of Elisabeth's popularity only begins to address the question of the value of her work. As this series of translations continues to redefine the "canon" of Western spiritual classics, it is worthwhile to consider directly the question of Elisabeth's classic status. A classic is a complex phenomenon, for it is simultaneously typical and outstanding—it can typify its class and yet it must somehow be luminescent, not hackneyed or a mere pastiche of traditions. In considering Elisabeth's works, it is first of all necessary to acknowledge that these texts represent a major new direction in religious writing. Elisabeth's immersion in monastic traditions did not provide her with a model for articulating her experience. She was undoubtedly influenced by biblical accounts of prophetic revelation and even hagiographical or didactic accounts of visions. Yet visionary literature before her day was usually comprised of accounts of one-time, "out of the blue," often near-death visions.[34] Even the work of Hildegard of Bingen, frequently cited now as so influential on Elisabeth, is in fact substantially different. Elisabeth's works, unlike hagiographical accounts of visions and the brilliant theological visions of Hildegard's *Scivias*, foregrounded the recipient of divine grace as an agent in the work of divine revelation. There is a great extent of autobiographical narration in these visions, because for Elisabeth, what she experienced in her body (illness, trance, the taste of honey), what she desired (intimate contact with the divine), what she was doing at any particular moment (praying, sleeping, sitting with her sisters), what those around her did (spill eucharistic wine, mortify their bodies for her sake, ask her difficult questions, ignore their religious obligations) was part of what enabled or obstructed the flow of divine grace. These things were also part of the message of consolation that she preached. It was part of her message of consolation for others to learn that God wrenched her body from health to illness and back to health, or that corpses being exhumed belonged to saints who revealed their stories to her, Elisabeth of Schönau. It is, however, the autobiographical idiom of Elisabeth's expression that can be most misleading to modern readers. It is not an assertion of Elisabeth's unique individuality, as the very strong communal dimensions of her piety must remind us. But it is an assertion of embodiment, that the visions are a complex interaction between divine grace and the very human, female subject. This autobiographical innovation in Elisabeth's visionary works would in fact become the idiom or genre for so many women who followed Elisabeth in the thirteenth, fourteenth, and fifteenth centuries.

The value of Elisabeth's works also lies in what we can learn about religious life more generally. Most significantly, they require us to refashion certain modern concepts of spirituality that often implicitly assume the individual as the locus of interaction with the divine. We have already seen the very substantial ways in which her piety and visionary experience were part of a life of communal prayer. So many medieval works come out of settings similar to that of Elisabeth, yet often the dynamics of human interaction and shared aspiration are masked in the resulting texts. Elisabeth's works remind us of the fundamental Christian affirmation, rooted in its Jewish origins, of human community as the partner in relationship with God.

About This Translation

We have already seen the process by which the corpus of Elisabeth's visionary works grew: the composition of new texts and the supplementation and revision of earlier texts. The existence of different versions of individual texts, most notably in the *First* and *Second Book of Visions*, and Ekbert's *Death of Elisabeth*, presents a problem for their presentation in this translation. Throughout this volume, I have generally opted for presenting the longer versions of these texts for two reasons.[35] First, the longer versions offer the reader the greatest exposure to the visionary texts. Second, the longer versions correspond to the texts in the edition of F. W. E. Roth, which although problematic, is still the most comprehensive collection of Elisabeth's works and serves as the basis for this translation.[36] Thus, the longer versions here facilitate a comparison with the Latin for those readers who are interested. Throughout the notes to these translations, I have indicated the disparities between earlier and later versions of the texts. These notes are based on my examination of manuscripts from each of the major redactions of Elisabeth's works.[37] While this practice is not a substitute for a critical edition, it does allow a much more complete view of the collection of Elisabeth's works as reflecting a living process of growth, reconsideration, response to controversy, censorship, and transformation, as well as giving occasional insight into the reception of her work beyond the walls of Schönau.

In the translation I have followed common practices of rendering medieval Latin into modern English such as breaking up very long sentences and introducing paragraph breaks where they seem appropriate. I have chosen to retain some literal expression where commonly recognized modern forms could have been adopted, for example, "liberation" *(liberatio)* and "healing" *(remedium)* rather than "salvation"; "divine sacrifice" *(sacrificium dominicum)* rather than "the Mass"; "service" *(servitium)* for what is rendered to the saints, rather than the somewhat flatter "prayers." Each of these more literal renderings communicates more of the power and nuance of the religious world Elisabeth inhabited.

As Ekbert observed in his introduction to the *First Book of Visions*, the words Elisabeth uttered were often evocations of biblical or liturgical passages. Often these utterances, especially liturgical passages, are not fully transcribed in the texts; instead, only the first words are given, followed by "et cetera." I have followed the text in giving only the abbreviated passages and have included complete quotations where possible in the notes. (Sometimes complete

quotations are given in the text even when followed by "et cetera.")
Biblical passages are indicated parenthetically within the body of
the translation; these references are to the Vulgate. They are rarely
exact quotations of biblical passages; they were probably recited
from memory and adapted to fit the immediate context. I have rendered them as direct translations of the Latin in the visionary text
rather than quoting any modern translation of the Bible. There are
also many passages that "sound biblical," especially in the letters
and *The Book of the Ways of God*, where general pastoral advice
sounds like passages from Ephesians or other New Testament epis-
tles and condemnation of sinful humanity sounds like prophetic
denunciation from Isaiah or Ezekiel. The dividing lines between
biblical quotation, reference, evocation, or expressing oneself
"from a biblical perspective" are matters of judgment. Some bibli-
cally sounding passages are unnoted because the referents seemed
to me too general. Liturgical references, usually citations from
antiphons from the divine office, are indicated in the notes if the
citation gives more information than is already communicated in
the text itself. But if the text already identifies the quotation and its
liturgical context, no further information is given in the notes.

I have included chapter headings in this translation. They are
taken from Vienna, Österreichische Nationalbibliothek Vindob. Pal.
MS 488.[38] In the interpretive act of summarizing the chapter, the
author of the headings sometimes presents a slightly different picture
than the text itself.[39] Occasionally there are headings that occur
within long chapters. These are given in brackets within the text.

The Preface of Abbot Ekbert to the Visions[40]

All who are about to read the words of this book should know without a doubt that some of the speeches that the angel of God is said to have made to Elisabeth, the handmaid of God, were uttered totally in Latin, some in German, and yet others he announced partly in Latin and partly in German. I, Ekbert, brother of the handmaid of God, had been drawn by the marvelous workings of God from Bonn to the monastery at Schönau, where at first I was a monk, but then by the grace of God, was called to the abbacy. I put into writing all these discourses and the other things that are written about her revelations in such a way that where the words of the angel were in Latin, I left them unchanged. Where they were in German, I translated them into Latin as clearly as I could, adding nothing from my own presumption, seeking nothing of human favor nor worldly advantage, with God as my witness, to whom all things are naked and open (Heb 4:13).

First Book of Visions

1. The place of her monastic profession and the year in which she was visited by the Lord.

In the days of Pope Eugene,[41] in the territory of the diocese of Trier, in the monastery of Schönau, under the administration of the Abbot Hildelin, there was a certain young woman of monastic profession by the name of Elisabeth. When she had spent eleven years in the monastery among religious women, at the age of twenty-three, in the year of our Lord 1152,[42] she was visited by the Lord, and His hand was upon her, performing in her works of great wonder and worthy of memory like His mercies of old. For it had been given to her to transcend her own mind[43] and see visions of the secrets of the Lord which were hidden from the eyes of mortals. Moreover, this did not occur without a visible miracle. Frequently and indeed as if by habit, on Sundays and other feast days, around the hours in which the devotion of the faithful was especially inflamed, a certain affliction of the heart came over her and she was violently disturbed. Finally, she became as still as if she were dead. Sometimes this happened in such a way that no breath or vital movement could be detected in her. But then, after a long trance, when her spirit had been gradually restored, she would suddenly utter in Latin certain very divine words that she had never learned from anyone else and that she could not have made up herself since she was unlearned and had little or no skill in speaking Latin. Also, she frequently announced—without any premeditation—testimonies from canonical scripture and other expressions from the divine office that were appropriate to what she had seen in spirit. Since everything that happened to her seemed relevant to the glory of God and the edification of the faithful, they were for the

41

most part written down in this small book. They were written according to her own narration as she expounded the individual events to one of her brothers from among the clergy whom she knew better than the others. Although in fact she hid many things from inquirers because she was very God-fearing and most humble in spirit, she was compelled by familial love and by order of the abbot to explain in intimate detail the whole thing to this cleric who was diligently investigating everything and desirous of handing it down to posterity. She began her narration as follows.

[What Elisabeth said to her brother about the beginning of her visitation by heavenly grace and the many causes of her fear of declaring her revelations.]

You entreat me, brother, and have come so that I would explain to you the mercies that the Lord has deigned to work in me according to the pleasure of His grace. I am entirely ready to satisfy your desire in all things and my soul has long wished for this very thing: that I may be given the opportunity to confer with you about all these things and to hear your judgment on them.[44] But I ask you to pause a moment and consider the multiple afflictions of my heart, which oppress me more than can be believed.[45] If that message, which you have heard, were made public (as when it was already in part made public—God knows, against my will—by certain incautious brothers),[46] what do you think people would say about me? Some perhaps would say I am holy and attribute the grace of God to my own merits, judging that I am something when I am nothing. And indeed, others would think about it, saying to themselves, "If she *were* a servant of God, she would certainly keep silent and not allow her own name to be magnified upon the earth." They would say this, not knowing the goads by which I am constantly urged to speak out! And, of course, there would be those who say that all the things they have heard from me are womanish fictions, or perhaps they would decide that I am deceived by Satan. In these and other such ways, dearest one, I will be tossed about in the mouths of the people. And why is it that I, who chose to be in a hidden place, should become known to anyone? I certainly do not think of myself as worthy for others to lift up their eyes and look at me. It also increases my afflictions not a little that the lord abbot is pleased for my words to be committed to writing.[47] Indeed, what am I that my affairs should be handed on to posterity? Won't this be attributed to arrogance?

But certain wise people say to me that the Lord has done these things to me not for my sake alone. Rather, they say that He also has provided for the edification of others through these works because these deeds to some extent concern the confirmation of the faith and the consolation of those who are troubled in heart for the sake of the Lord. For these reasons they think that the works of God should not be passed over in silence. And in part I believe it is as they say, for the reasons I will now tell you. At various times it happened that although I had planned to hide in my heart the things shown to me by the Lord, such a great torment seized my heart that I thought I was close to death. Yet whenever I revealed what I had seen to those around me, I was immediately relieved. But I admit that I am not as yet totally sure what is best for me to do. For I acknowledge that it is dangerous for me to keep silent about the mighty works of God, and I greatly fear that it is going to be more dangerous to speak out. I understand that I have less discretion than I would need to discern which of the things revealed to me should be spoken and which should be honored with silence. And behold, in all these matters I am put in danger of doing wrong. For this reason, my beloved, my tears do not stop and my spirit is continually distressed.

But, behold, at your arrival my soul has begun to be consoled and a great peace has been produced in me. For many days I prayed for your coming, and blessed be the Lord for He has deigned to receive this prayer of His handmaid! And now, because you have been sent to me from afar by the will of the Lord, I will not hide my heart from you; rather I will reveal those things—good and evil— about myself. Then, the appropriate course of action may be placed in your discretion and that of the lord abbot.

I, the least of His poor ones, give thanks to the Lord because from the day that I began to live according to the monastic rule till this hour, the hand of the Lord has been established upon me such that I have never ceased to bear His arrows in my body (Ps 37:3). My long and varied illnesses have troubled not only me, but also all the sisters who are around me. May the Lord have mercy on them because they have borne with me the burden of my distress with motherly affection. At one point they also administered medicine for my ailments, but I was further weakened by it, and in a nocturnal vision I heard a voice saying to me, "Our God in heaven has done all things, whatever He has willed" (Ps 113B:3). Thereupon I understood that I had been warned not to commit my body to human remedies but to the will of my Creator, and so indeed I did. And when I was frequently overwhelmed by so great a sickness that I could not control any part of my body except my tongue, I remained—I say this without arrogance—no less zealous in meditating on the psalms. But when paralysis subdued even my tongue, I fulfilled with my mind the duty of my tongue.

It would be tedious to recount the lack of necessities that I endured along with my illnesses. You have become aware that the property of our house is modest and people who ought to have taken pity on me were far away. But the Father of orphans (Ps 67:5), the Lord, is anxious for me (Ps 39:18), through whose grace all my grief becomes great joy to my heart.[48] In all things may God, the comforter of the lowly, be blessed. But lest I weary you any longer (Acts 24:4), let me turn now to those issues about which you chiefly inquire.

2. The circumstances of the day on which the works of the Lord began to be manifested in her and the various struggles of temptation that she endured from the Adversary.

On the holy day of Pentecost,[49] when the sisters were gathering for the Eucharist, I was detained for some reason so that I did not partake of that divine and life-giving sacrament. Thus the celebration of that day did not gladden me as it usually did, but instead I remained all day in a certain darkness of soul. On the next day also, and for the whole week, I was sad and went along in the same darkness, unable to shake off that melancholy. All my faults rose up in my heart more than usual, and I exaggerated each of them, and in so doing, piled up sorrows for myself. Gradually, therefore, as this unhealthy sadness grew in me, my mind was darkened so that wherever I would turn, I felt like I was walking in shadows in comparison to the light that I used to experience. Amid all this, I was also afflicted with so great a weariness that there was nothing that my soul did not loathe. The prayers that used to be my greatest pleasure were annoying to me. The Psalter, which had always been a great joy to me, I threw far from me when I had hardly finished reading one psalm. Then, in turn, reflecting upon and wondering about what had happened to me, I picked it up again and read, but again I broke down. Indeed, my Adversary[50] flooded me with all his force. The Betrayer even made me hesitate in my faith so that I pondered our Redeemer with skepticism, saying to myself, "Who was He that so humbled Himself for humankind? Could all those things that were written about Him really be true?" Then I turned around and said, "Yet He was good—whoever He was—about whom so many good things are preached." Likewise, I was thinking skeptically about Mary our blessed Advocate at the same time as the sisters were celebrating her memory. And what surprise is that, my brother? Almost all my senses were topsy-turvy! At times, however, coming back to myself, I understood that I was being tempted. I strongly resisted and urged my friends to pray for me, but my Adversary so much more strongly pressed on, disturbing me in such a way that it even wearied me to live. Because of this weariness, I could only take but the slightest food and drink, and I became weak and my whole body wasted away. Finally, that Betrayer inspired me to put an end to my life and thereby terminate the tribulations I had endured for so long. But at this worst temptation, the one who defends Israel did not sleep (Ps 120:4–5). Indeed, He did not allow this greatest evil to reign over me; instead, He led me to understand the malice of my Waylayer and He quickly diverted me from that thought. How rich you are in mercy, Lord, rescuing from great dangers those who trust in you (2 Cor 1:10)! I confess to you, Father, that if you had not helped me, my soul would have all but dwelt in hell.

3. She saw a phantom clothed in a monk's cowl who laughed at the word Satan when the Passion of the Lord was read over her.

These things continued like this until the feast of the blessed Maximus, which is May 29. On that day at Compline, I saw in our chapel a very small phantom, looking as if clothed in a monk's cowl. As soon as Compline was over, a very grave illness rushed over me, and I asked the mistress[51] if she and the other sisters would come with me into the chapter hall and pour out prayers over me. When I tried to prostrate myself before the crucifix, my bones became so stiff that in no way could I bend my knees. Therefore, gathering force in myself, I threw myself heavily to the ground, and I lay there miserably, trembling and quivering in head and foot and every other part of my body. When I arose from prayer, the gospel was brought and they made me read the Passion of the Lord, and they helped me because I was too weak to read. But while we were reading, that same phantom appeared to me as before. When we read the passage where the evangelist says, "And Satan entered into Judas, who was surnamed Iscariot" (Lk 22:3), it began to leap about and provoke laughter. I told the sisters to drive away that evil figure, and they wondered what I was talking about. When the gospel was finished, it disappeared.

4. She saw the same thing at Matins in a horrible form and also the following day in the form of a dreadful bull.

After this at Matins it was standing before me—in human shape, short in stature and stocky, and dreadful in appearance. Its face was fiery and its flaming tongue stuck far out of its mouth, and its hands and feet were like the talons of greedy birds of prey. It appeared to me seven times that day in this form, and once in the form of a very hideous dog. On the following morning it stood by my bed and threatened me, swearing that it was about to strike me in the teeth with a shoe that it appeared to be holding in its hand. After this, a little before Mass, it appeared to me again, this time in the form of a huge and dreadful bull, opening its mouth above me as if ready to swallow me, and it looked like it was wearing a bell on its neck.

5. On Saturday she saw a wheel of great light like the full moon, in which she saw the Queen of Heaven marking her with the sign of the cross.

Afterward, on Saturday, when the Mass of our Lady the blessed Virgin had begun,[52] I sank into ecstasy and my heart was opened, and I saw above our atmosphere[53] a wheel of great light like the full moon, but almost twice as large. And I looked through the center of that wheel and I saw the likeness of a regal woman standing on high, dressed in the whitest garments and wrapped in a purple mantle. I immediately understood that this woman was the exalted Queen of Heaven, mother of our Savior, whom I had long desired to see. While I looked at her with longing, she prostrated herself three times, worshiping in the presence of the divine light before her. Then, when she had lowered herself for the fourth time, she seemed to lie there for a long time. And when she arose, she turned her face to me and came forward toward me, into the lower atmosphere a little, with two glorious companions, one on her right and one on her left. The one who was on her right seemed to be dressed in a monk's cowl, except that it was dazzling white, and he seemed to carry an abbot's staff in his hand. Thus it occurred to me that this was our venerable father, blessed Benedict. However, the one on her right appeared to be a seemly youth, remarkable for his bright and curly hair. Standing there, my Lady marked me with the sign of the cross[54] and implanted—I don't know how—these words in my mind, "Do not fear, because these things will not harm you at all." In truth, I did not hear the sound of her voice; rather I only clearly saw the movement of her lips.

6. She sees our Lady again, adorned with a glorious crown.

    After this she returned to the inner area of her light and I, most devoutly worshiping, followed her with the praises of thirteen versicles that I customarily recite. And when I had said them, I returned from ecstasy and immediately refreshed my spirit with the salvific sacrifice.[55] Then I asked the priest to invoke the name of the Lord over me. When he began the litany, I again went into ecstasy. Again I saw my Lady, this time standing at the altar in a vestment like a priestly chasuble, and she had on her head a glorious crown decorated with four precious gems, and the angelic salutation, "Hail Mary, full of grace, the Lord is with you," was inscribed around it.

7. The evil spirit again appeared to her as before in the form of a bull, and a dove appeared to her, and she saw a cross.

47

On that same day at Vespers I again saw the evil one in the form of a bull, hovering in the air before me. And a little later I saw Mary my Comforter in the celestial light, defending me as before with the sign of the cross. On the next day, which was Sunday, my Waylayer again presented himself to me in the form of a bull as before. Then, because that vision sorely troubled me, I said confidently to it, "If you are truly the evil one, I order you in the name of the Lord to transform yourself immediately, and never appear to me again in this form." It immediately disappeared, and I saw a horrible valley full of smoke and black flames, and out of it came a very foul herd of she-goats. On that day at Vespers, a great light in heaven appeared to me and from its center a beautiful dove of extraordinary radiance and almost fiery brilliance came down, having something red—I don't know what—in its mouth. And then it suddenly made a circle in the air and withdrew again back into the light. Following it with reverence, I said prayers of the Holy Spirit, because I had heard that the Holy Spirit had appeared in the form of a dove. After this, at Compline, while I was standing before the cross and most devoutly reverencing it, there was shown to me in the heavens a great cross of golden splendor, so brilliant that it even forced me to turn aside the eyes of my heart, the very means by which I was seeing it.

8. The assault of the Adversary and how he harassed her but how she was once more liberated through the grace of God.

In the morning of the following day, while I was standing alone in the chapter hall and praying, my Adversary again presented himself to me. He stood in front of me in the form of a delicate cleric, looking as if he were wearing a white alb. I was very frightened, but nevertheless I persevered in prayer and did it all the more earnestly so as more fully to confound him. However, when I finished my prayer and went up to the dormitory, he followed me there. I withdrew from there and went into the chapel to stand between two sisters who were praying. He followed me even there and stood before me, mocking me with a certain lewd gesture, and I was not able to turn the eye of my mind away from him. Then, not tolerating his vileness any longer, I boldly said to him, "I order you, in the name of the Father, and of the Son, and of the Holy Spirit, to cease this behavior immediately and never show such lewdness to me again." He immediately abandoned his earlier deportment and stood reverently as if clothed in a monastic habit. Then I went out to sit in the nuns' convent, and he followed me there and stood and smiled at me. When he then disappeared, he never appeared to me again. Then, when I had heard Mass and received the Eucharist and had gone to lunch, I hardly touched my food because of a severe distress. Moreover, after lunch I suddenly grew faint and no strength remained in me, and I was so pressed everywhere that no part of my body was not in pain. Then, with difficulty I made a sound to indicate to the sisters standing around me to bring the relics and recite over me prayers and the Passion of the Lord. While they prayed I felt as if my throat were being drawn tight by some strong hand so that my breath was almost totally cut off. However, when that hour had passed, I had a greater peace from my Tempter than before, due to the grace of the Lord who knows how to deliver His people from temptation (2 Pt 2:9). It was, I believe, brought to pass in this way by the Lord.

9. The communal prayer of the brothers and the sisters and how the Holy Spirit appeared to her.

Seeing my difficulties, the sisters and brothers came together and they decided to pour out communal prayers for seven continuous days and mortify themselves in the presence of the Lord for my sake, and to celebrate a Mass each day for my distresses. One of these seven Masses, the Mass of the Holy Spirit, was to be sung on Thursday, so I awaited that day with great desire, hoping that I might then receive some consolation. The longed-for day arrived, and while the brothers were celebrating the divine rite, I was lying prostrate in prayer with the sisters. And my heart was enlarged and I saw a great light in the heavens, and behold, a dove of great beauty, such as I had seen earlier coming from the light, flew to me. With wings outspread it circled around my head three times and then flew to the heavens.

10. The sacred cross that she saw.

After this, on Friday, when the Mass of the Cross was being said and I was lying prostrate, a glorious sign of the cross was shown to me in the heavens, as if at the left side of the divine Majesty.[56]

11. She saw our Lady prostrate in prayer during the sequence "Ave preclara," and she was accustomed to see her every Saturday when the office of our Lady was celebrated.

On Saturday, when the office of the glorious Virgin was being celebrated, I again saw her in celestial brightness worshiping in the presence of the great Majesty. And when the ministers of the altar were devoutly singing her praises with the sequence "Ave preclara," and they came to the versicle, "Pray, Virgin, that we may be made worthy of that heavenly bread," she fell on her face and totally prostrated herself in prayer, and remained like that until the gospel was begun. From that day to the present time, on every Saturday and on other days whenever her office is celebrated, I have usually seen the same vision.[57] On that same day after Nones, I was standing in the chapter hall and weeping very bitterly because of certain dreams in which my Way-layer's evil intensely troubled my soul. At that time I most fervently asked my Lady to deign to offer me some consolation if indeed those vexations were not going to be harmful to me. And behold, suddenly that celestial light flashed and my Comforter came forth from it. And when she had descended a little, she stood facing me. Looking at her, I carefully watched the movement of her lips, and I understood that she was calling me by my name, Elisabeth, and then she said no more. Taking this as consolation, I thanked her and she withdrew from me.

12. The dove that she frequently saw, and how she was assured that the Holy Spirit was being shown to her thereby.

At one point when the dove, about which I have already spoken, had been frequently appearing to me, I began to wonder about it. I inquired of the lord abbot whether Satan could transform himself into a dove (2 Cor 11:14). Although he affirmed that he had never read such a thing, I remained dubious. One day, I looked at the cross that I usually saw, and that same dove came from the other direction and rested on it. Therefore I was assured that this was not Satan, because Satan is the enemy of the cross.

13. She saw the precursor of the Lord in great brightness.

On the vigil of the feast of blessed John the Baptist,[58] while the divine office was being celebrated, I was at prayer saying fifty psalms and certain other prayers in praise of that venerable precursor of the Lord. And when I had almost finished my prayers, suddenly a great light flashed in the heavens and in the center of it there appeared what looked like the form of a glorious man in white garments, standing facing the rising of the sun. After a little bit, he turned his charming and very lovely face to me as if he wanted me to see him. On his head he had a very radiant crown of golden brightness, which was marked in the front with a somewhat purple hue. In his right hand there appeared to be a palm branch of such splendor that I could hardly discern the other things around it due to its great brilliance. Therefore, I understood this man to be the glorious martyr whose feast we were celebrating. After this, at Matins, while we were praying, "We praise you, Lord,"[59] that martyr appeared to me in the same way. Leaning against the wall I barely restrained myself from ecstasy. And when he had disappeared again, that light in which I had seen him suddenly appeared to be cut in two, and it burst forth like lightning, which I couldn't bear to look at. I said, "Your grace is sufficient for me, Lord (2 Cor 12:9). Have mercy on my weakness and relax this excessive brightness, because I am not strong enough to bear it." It was immediately removed and in its place a very bright star appeared. Again during the day, at the time of the divine sacrifice, the man of God appeared to me in the same manner.

14. She sees the blessed martyrs John and Paul.

On the third day after this, on the feast of the blessed martyrs John and Paul,[60] at the time of Matins, while I was reading fifty psalms in honor of these martyrs, I saw them standing together in a very glorious light, facing east with their backs turned toward me. When I finished my prayers, I very diligently entreated them to deign to turn their faces to me. And they did turn to me. Moreover, they also bore the signs of victory and martyrdom, namely, shining palm branches in their hands and on their heads exceedingly radiant crowns, which were decorated with red on the front. Indeed, whenever holy martyrs deigned to appear to me, they seemed to be adorned with such signs.[61]

15. She saw the apostles Peter and Paul with our Lady, and when the lord abbot read about the Holy Spirit, she saw it in the form of a dove.

    At First Vespers on the feast of the blessed apostles Peter and Paul,[62] I sank into ecstasy, and I saw those glorious princes standing in the radiance of a great light with the signs of victorious martyrdom. With their faces turned toward me, they descended into the region of our atmosphere, preceded by the blessed Virgin, mother of our Lord Jesus. Peter stood making the sign of the cross over me, and I greeted him saying, "You are shepherd of the sheep, prince of the apostles," et cetera.[63] Also, looking at Paul, I seized these words of his, "I have fought the good fight, I have finished the race," et cetera (2 Tm 4:7).[64] When they had turned back to the region of light, I recovered from ecstasy. During the day, at Mass while the office was being intoned, I saw a dove descend from heaven and come as far as the right corner of the altar and rest there. Its size was that of a turtledove, and its whiteness beyond that of snow. Among the other collects, the lord abbot said the one that is, "God, to whom every heart is open," and had proceeded up to the part that is, "Purify the thoughts of our hearts by an infusion of the Holy Spirit."[65] At that point, the dove flew to him and circled his head three times and returned to the place where it had rested before. Moreover, when the Sanctus was said, it came and rested on the corporal, and it looked as if something red hung from its mouth. When Mass was over I went forward with the sisters to receive the Eucharist. When I turned my eyes of flesh toward the dove, I was not able to see it. However, when I turned my eyes away, I saw it. Because of my awe, as soon as I received the Eucharist, I came into ecstasy and then recovered. And from that point on, whichever saints we were celebrating, by the grace of the Lord they appeared to me in the celestial light on their feasts, as, for example, Kilian the martyr with his companions and then the Seven Brothers.[66]

16. She sees the blessed Benedict, blessed Margaret, and blessed Alexis.

    After this, our blessed father Benedict seemed to come forward into our atmosphere, toward me.[67] Then I saw blessed Margaret distinguished by her great brightness and glorious with her signs of victory. On the feast of the Division of the Apostles,[68] all the apostles appeared to me, but Peter and Paul seemed to stand apart from the others. After this I saw Alexis the Confessor, who held something—I don't know what—of great beauty from his breast to below his navel.

17. She sees the blessed Mary Magdalen with our Lady.

At Vespers on the vigil of her feast,[69] I saw the blessed Mary Magdalen with a very bright crown and with her was the mother of the Lord. They were standing face to face as if talking to each other, and after a little while, they turned toward the east. At Mass during the day, while I was on my knees in prayer, I saw in the sky but as if close to the ground two shining men sitting facing each other, and in between them a bright thing that appeared to have the shape of a tomb. And behold, a woman like the one I had seen the night before came and stood, looking intently at that same tomb-like shape. While she was standing there, a youth wrapped in the whitest mantle, with black hair and a downy beard and an uncommonly beautiful face, came up behind her. She turned to meet him and stood as if asking him something. Then I began to wonder anxiously to myself who that youth was. I was excited by a great desire to know this, and suddenly a golden cross appeared in his right hand. Thus I immediately concluded that it was He who rose from the dead and appeared to Mary first. On that same day at Vespers, when I could not be with the community because of my sickness, I was sitting in the chapter hall with the mistress, and we were engaged in the Vespers psalms. It was a rainy time, but with my mind's eye, I saw a shining rainbow. When I directed my external eyes to the sky from the place where I was, I could not see it. And I said to the Lord in my heart, "I entreat you Lord, that I may also see with my eyes of flesh what I saw just now with my mind alone, so that I may be more assured of this spiritual vision." Indeed, I did not fully believe it myself. After a little while, the sisters left the chapel and stood together in the cloister looking up at the sky. When the mistress wondered what they were looking at, I said, "I believe they are seeing the rainbow that I saw a moment ago with my mind's eye." So we went out with them, and we saw it too.

53

18. She sees a shining ladder descending to the main altar during a dedication, and a multitude ascending and descending on it.

    After lunch on the feast of Saint James the Apostle,[70] I began to be severely weakened, but not yet to the point of ecstasy. And the light that I usually perceived I now saw above the church of Saint Florinus, where the brothers were.[71] Moreover, on the next day the dedication of that church was to be celebrated there. And I saw a ladder, as it were, glowing like radiant gold, coming down from that light, extending as far as the main altar in the sanctuary. While I was looking at it, I saw two youths descending on it to the altar. The one leading the way appeared to carry a gold thurible in his hand. After them, two others also came down. And then a great multitude descended and then ascended in reverse order (Gn 28:12). They went up and down like this from Nones of the first day till Nones of the following day. Indeed, I remained continuously in this vision for that long. Moreover, blessed James also appeared at the top of the ladder, standing with blessed Christina the virgin, and the Virgin of virgins was with them. During the day, around the time of the Lord's sacrifice, he appeared to come down to the lower region of our dwelling. On the same day, I saw a great brightness around the aforementioned altar and everything that took place there. For I also recognized the type of altar covering, and I indicated this to our mistress. She sent a messenger to that place and ascertained that it was just as I said.

19. She sees Saint Peter and Saint Stephen and Saint Oswald and Saint Afra and Saint Cyriacus and Lawrence in great glory.

    On the feast of Saint Peter's Chains, I saw Peter again in the same form in which he had appeared to me before. After this, I then saw Stephen, the first martyr, on the feast of his invention, then King Oswald, then Afra the martyr with her two servants, and then blessed Cyriacus. Then I saw blessed Lawrence on his vigil.[72] Pouring out all around him was a light so dense that it seemed as if it could be touched. The splendor of his palm branch and crown was so intense that it somehow forced me to turn aside the eyes of my heart, just like the splendor of shining gold deflects the eyes of flesh. He had a bright stole extending from his left shoulder to his right side. I asked the mistress what this could mean, and she told me that this was a sign of Lawrence's diaconate. The blessed Virgin was standing with him, just as she had been with the aforementioned saints, and she sweetly kept her face turned toward me until she had fulfilled my desire. Indeed, they all used to offer this grace to me.

20. A vision that she saw on the Sunday following the feast of Saint James, in which the houses of the saints and the glory of great majesty in three persons and one deity were shown to her.

On the first Sunday night after the feast of Saint James,[73] I grew weak throughout my whole body, and at first the tips of my hands and feet and then all my flesh began to crawl, a sweat broke out all over me, and my heart felt as if it were cut in two parts by a sword. And behold, there flashed forth in the sky a large fiery wheel, whose sight afflicted me with great distress, and then it immediately disappeared. After this, in that same spot, it was as if a door was opened. I looked through it, and I saw a light far surpassing that which I had been accustomed to seeing, and many thousands of saints were there. They were standing around the edge of a great Majesty, arranged in the following order. In the foremost part of that circle there were certain magnificent and truly distinguished men adorned with palm branches and brightly shining crowns, marked on their brows with the sign of their passion. From their number as well as from their exceptional glory, which surpassed that of all others, I understood that these men were the venerable apostles of Christ. To their right stood a large and glorious crowd marked with the same signs. After them, other splendid men stood together, but the sign of martyrdom did not appear on them. To the left of the apostles, the sacred order of virgins shone forth, adorned with the signs of martyrdom. After them there was another multitude of extraordinary girls who were crowned but without the signs of martyrdom. Then appeared other venerable women with white veils, and in this way the circle was filled out by all of them. Within it appeared another circle of great brightness, which I understood to be that of the holy angels. In the center of all of this, there was the glory of immense Majesty, which I cannot fully describe, whose glorious throne was encircled by a shining rainbow. To the right of the Majesty, I saw one like a Son of Man abiding in great glory (Rv 1:13). To the left, there appeared a sign of the cross emitting many beams. While I was looking at all of this with my heart trembling, the Lord also deigned to add this as well. Somehow—I dare not explain—He showed to me, a most unworthy sinner, this about the glory of His ineffable Trinity: that there is truly one divinity in three persons, and three persons in one divine substance. To the right of the Son of Man, the Queen of the angels and Lady of kingdoms was sitting on a throne surrounded by a huge starry light. Also, to the left of the aforementioned cross, twenty-four honorable men sat together in a row with their faces turned toward her. I saw not far from them two large and bright rams standing before the sign of the cross and bearing on their shoulders a wheel of extreme brightness and marvelous size. When I had looked carefully at all these things, I burst out in these words, saying, "Lift up the eyes of your heart to the sacred light, watch closely and see the glory and majesty of the Lord."[74] In the morning after this, at the third hour, I was weakened even more severely than the night before. One of the brothers came to the window and I asked him to celebrate the Mass of the Holy Trinity and he agreed. However, as soon as he began the Mass, I fell into ecstasy. Again I saw the aforementioned vision, but this time more clearly. At the same time, I saw that same brother standing at the altar. He was surrounded by much light and the breath from his mouth ascended on high like white smoke.

21. She sees the same vision and although she wished to hide it, the Lord did not permit it.

On the next Sunday, that is, on the feast of the Invention of Saint Stephen,[75] I was weakened in the same way, and I saw the same vision but more fully, because now I saw standing before the throne of God a very lovely lamb, which looked like it had a golden cross fixed on its back. Then I also saw the four evangelists in those forms that sacred scripture attributes to them.[76] They were arranged in a row to the right of the blessed Virgin in such a way that they had their faces turned toward her. However, for more than seven days, I kept these visions to myself. When I had firmly fixed it in my heart that I would reveal them to no one, I was seized by a very harsh torment in my heart in such a way that I thought I was about to die. And so the sisters earnestly entreated and urged me to reveal to them what I had seen. When they had forced it out of me, I immediately recovered from my suffering. And lest I further repeat what I have already said, know that the visions of this kind that I saw on the aforementioned Sundays, I was accustomed to see either two or three times or even more on every Sunday that occurred thereafter. I would see them before sinking into ecstasy, just as you have already seen with your own eyes.[77]

22. Having poured out prayers to the Lord, her mouth was opened in praise of God.

After Compline on the Wednesday before the Assumption of blessed Mary,[78] I was standing in the chapel and I prayed to the Lord with all my heart saying, "Lord, my God, behold. To your holy and undivided Trinity I commend my soul and my body, joined together by your right hand. To you, Lord, I commit all my distresses, because my spirit has been sorely troubled by these things that you have done to me, for I know that I am totally unworthy of so great a grace. You know, my Lord, that I never presumed to request such things from you. But now, because in your gracious goodness you have magnified your mercy with me like this, I implore you to continue to preserve me in this way so that through no transgression of my own may I deserve to fall from your grace. And may that spirit of sadness, which would have already consumed me had you not come to my aid, take no further hold of me." When I had finished these and similar prayers and then returned to my bed, suddenly these words fell into my mouth: "O virgin, be on your guard lest you fall again, lest something worse happen to you, because the good shepherd takes care of his sheep" (Jn 10:11). On the following day at noon, my heart was struck by a sudden shock and I heard these words, "Do not be afraid, daughter, because the Lord your comforter chastises every child He takes to Himself" (Prv 3:12). On the same day at Vespers, when I had tearfully poured out my heart to my Lady, it again happened that I unexpectedly turned over these words in my mouth, "Rejoice and be glad, because the divine mercy has delivered you from danger of body and soul."[79]

23. She saw our Lady on the vigil of her Assumption with a multitude of women, and she also saw her on the feast day itself.

After this, on the vigil of the Assumption,[80] while I was very devoutly praying, this suddenly rushed into my mouth and thus I declared: "These are words of consolation that a new tongue speaks because it is necessary to comfort the turbulent soul." Then again in my usual way I grew weak and, coming into ecstasy, I saw the vision that I usually saw on Sundays. Moreover, among other things I also saw my Lady rising from her glorious throne and going out from that great light, which I saw as if I were looking through a door. She was accompanied by that threefold multitude of women that I had seen standing in the circle. Those who bore the sign of martyrdom on their brows advanced nearest. After them came those who I saw were crowned, but without the sign. In the third place were those adorned with white veils. To the right of my Lady a certain glorious and lovely man, distinguished by his priestly stole, came forward. After she had remained for a while with her holy multitude in this lower atmosphere, with great praise and rejoicing she was drawn back up into that light from which she had appeared to come. When I was aroused from this vision, I immediately seized these words, "O glorious light in which all the saints, robed in white stoles, continuously stand and give glory for their heavenly reward to the One who sits upon the throne and lives for ever and ever" (Rv 4:9). Again on that day at Mass, while I was in a trance and seeing the same vision as before, I turned over in my soul these words: "O glorious Trinity, sitting in the seat of your majesty, you look into the depths and you enumerate the thoughts of each person." To this I added, "Hail Mary, the glory of virgins, the mistress of nations, the queen of angels."[81] After this, as I awoke, I burst forth in these words: "You holy Lord," et cetera, with the verse.[82] I also added, "The Lord opens for us the gate of life if we are willing to struggle against the most unyielding devil." Moreover, I saw all these same things again on the nativity of our Lady.[83]

24. She pronounced hortatory words after the feast of the Assumption.

On the Saturday after the Assumption,[84] I unexpectedly seized these words, "The Lord is our lawgiver, the Lord is our king (Is 33:22) who called us into His marvelous light (1 Pt 2:9) so that if we choose to do penance for evil acts, we will receive the prize that is won in the arena (1 Cor 9:24). Do not ignore these words because they are profitable for your souls. Listen carefully to how the Creator warns His creature." After this I added, "I will console you, says the Lord, and I will give you a spiritual joy against sadness, and I will place fear together with love in your hearts (Jer 32:40). If you fear Me and keep My commandments, you will be My true disciples. Again I warn you that as you love one another, you are to think about how God loved us first. He did not spare His only-begotten Son, but handed Him over as an offering for us so that the drachma that had been lost could be found (Rom 8:32; Lk 15:8–9). Therefore this saying pertains to us: If we love God and have perfect charity and brotherly love for one another, we will find that drachma which was lost. Again I admonish you to have perfect love for God and neighbor because love is the highest gift, the great good on which depends the whole order of perfections. Furthermore, hold charity above all things, because it is the chain of perfection. And let the peace of Christ spring forth in your hearts, the peace in which you have been called into one body, and be thankful; may the word of Christ dwell abundantly in you (Col 3:14–16). Again, to all those who wish to live according to the world and who do not withdraw their bodies from carnal desires but wish to do everything which pertains to this world, greatly to be feared is the following message: Do not love the world and those things which are in the world, but do penance for your evil deeds because the time is near (1 Jn 2:15). Therefore be watchful because you do not know the day nor the hour when the Lord will come" (Mt 24:42; 25:13).

25. On the Beheading of Saint John the Baptist she saw that precursor of the Lord with our Lady.

On the feast of the Beheading of Saint John the Baptist,[85] I was greatly weakened and I began to see that great light which I was accustomed to see as if through a door. Because of this I was anxious, and I totally prostrated myself in prayer. I came into ecstasy and I saw blessed John in the same manner in which I had seen him before, and in my spirit I said, "May God the Father bless us, may Jesus Christ protect us, may the Holy Spirit illuminate us," et cetera.[86] And I added, "O key of David," et cetera.[87] And I continued, "This is John, whom the hand of the Lord consecrated in his mother's womb, by whose prayers we humbly request to be helped." After this, rising out of my ecstasy, I took something to drink but I did not get any stronger. Leaning on the breast of the mistress, I went into ecstasy again, and I saw the same things that I had seen before. Returning to myself again, I seized these words, "Help me, Lord, my God," et cetera (Ps 108:26).[88] They also told me that I said, "Let not the greatness of the revelations exalt me," and no more (2 Cor 12:7). That day at Terce, again in ecstasy, I looked as if through a door[89] and I saw that great light which I usually saw, and my Lady rising from her throne and coming toward me into this exterior realm of light, and that blessed precursor of the Lord was with her. I then prayed most devoutly and eagerly commended myself and all my acquaintances and our place to their protection. I also asked them to show me a sign if they heard me. Immediately they returned to the light from which they had come and, in the presence of the great Majesty, they fell down on their faces as if praying, together with the vast crowd of those standing by. Then, awaking from this ecstasy, I burst into speech, saying, "Praise to you, glory to you, thanks to you, O blessed and hallowed and glorious Trinity.[90] Pray for us, blessed Virgin Mary, that we may be made worthy of the promise of Christ.[91] May all the holy angels of God pray for us in the sight of the Lord. Among all those born of women, there arose none greater than John the Baptist, et cetera.[92] Show forth your marvelous mercy, Savior of those who trust in you" (Ps 16:7).

26. On the Exaltation of the Cross, she sees the sign of the holy cross.

On the feast of the Exaltation of the Holy Cross,[93] I repeatedly came into ecstasy and I saw that glorious sign of the cross in great splendor, not only in that secret area of light, but it was also openly shown to me in the lower region of light.

27. She sees Saint Michael with a multitude of angels on his feast day, and when the priest was blessing the chalice, she saw the substance of blood in it.

At First Vespers on the feast of Saint Michael,[94] when I was in ecstasy, I saw three very glorious men standing before the throne of the Majesty of the Lord. Of them, the one who was in the middle appeared more distinguished than the others. He seemed to be holding a gold thurible in his right hand. When I returned to myself I said, "The angel stood next to the altar of the temple," et cetera.[95] That day at Mass I saw the same more distinguished man advancing with a prominent banner, accompanied by a large crowd. They went around the throne and when they came before the gaze of the Majesty, they threw themselves down on their faces. They did this three times. During that same Mass, when the sisters went forward to receive Eucharist and I was still sitting at a distance because of my weakened state, I looked into the chalice and I saw the true substance of blood. As they poured out the wine, I distinctly saw the difference between the blood and that which was added, until they were mixed together so that the one color of blood appeared. On another day—I don't know which—a similar thing happened. I was seeing from afar—as was customary for me— everything being done around the altar during the Mass. As the priest blessed the chalice, behold, the dove, which I usually saw on the altar, slowly advanced, dipped its head in the chalice, and immediately the substance of blood appeared. Now indeed it is not uncommon for me to see such things.[96]

28. The body of the Lord appeared to her as true flesh.

One day one of the brothers came bringing the divine sacrament of the Lord's body in a pyx for the benefit of a certain ailing sister. While I and several sisters with me were standing by and speaking with him, I looked at the pyx and thought about the dignity of that sacrament. Suddenly my heart was set free in such a way that I could hardly restrain myself from ecstasy. And behold, a great brightness shone in the pyx and I looked in—even though it was still closed—and the substance of true flesh appeared in it. Indeed, I tremble as I say these things, just as I trembled when I saw them. God is my witness that in saying all these things I have invented nothing nor sought my own glory.

29. She sees the holy martyrs Cassius and Florentius.

Brother, you asked me in a letter about your patrons, namely Cassius and Florentius, the martyrs of the church of Bonn. You asked me to offer some service to them on their feast day so that they might perhaps deign to show themselves to me. Indeed, I did this, as much as I was able. I read fifty psalms in their honor on that day after Matins, at which point my Waylayer blew out the candle I was holding in my hand. After this, around the third hour, I came into ecstasy without pain, and I saw three splendid men in the region of light, adorned with palm branches and crowns marked with red in the front. Two of them were standing together and a little apart from the third. On the following day at Vespers, when, in my usual way I was in ecstasy—indeed it was Saturday—I asked the Lord whether He would show me those two patrons again; I was annoyed that I could not clearly recognize which were the two about whom you asked, since I had seen three. The Lord delayed hearing me for a time, so I became frightened that I might have requested this against His will and, trembling, I said, "Lord, if it is your will that what I asked be done, let it be done; but if not, let it not be done." Immediately I saw two very amiable men emerge from the crowd of martyrs with the signs mentioned above, and they came to stand in the center before the sight of the throne. Awakening with joy, I immediately seized these words, "These are the two olive trees and two candlesticks shining before the Lord, the master of the whole earth."[97]

30. She sees the eleven thousand virgins.

After this, on the feast of the Eleven Thousand Holy Virgins,[98] I saw a vast multitude of virgins who were all distinguished by the palm branches of victory and crowns marked in the front, and they were all striking for their beautiful hair.

31. On the vigil of All Saints' Day she sees a multitude of saints.

At Vespers on the vigil of All Saints' Day,[99] I struggled for a long time in agony, and while I was oppressed with severe pain, I bound an image of the crucified Lord tightly to my chest, and at last I came into ecstasy and became quiet. Then, in an unusual way, it seemed to me as if my spirit was carried off on high, and I saw an open door in the heavens and a greater multitude of saints than I had ever seen before. Also, that which I remember telling you about the holy Trinity was then made known to me a second time. At Vespers on the feast day,[100] when I had again started to get weak and be prepared for ecstasy, I saw standing before me what looked like a very amiable boy, clothed in a white robe and girded, and I said, "Who are you, my lord?" He nodded his head for me to be silent, and I said, "Good angel of the Lord, who was with Jacob, may he be with me on my earthly pilgrimage and may God bless my ways." Immediately after this I was in ecstasy and it seemed to me that I was lifted up on high and I heard voices singing the most delightful song.

32. She sees souls tortured by evil spirits.

On the day after this when, according to the custom of the church, the faithful departed are remembered,[101] at the time of the divine sacrifice, I saw what looked like a very tall mountain facing south and next to it was a very deep, dreadful valley. The valley was full of fires that were dark, as though covered and thus not able to send forth their flames very high. I saw there countless torturing spirits and souls handed over to their power. In a terrifying and lamentable manner the souls were shaken, dragged along, and tormented in countless ways beyond measure. I discerned the appearance of neither the torturers nor of the souls; I understood only that the former were torturing, the latter were tortured. Moreover, at a distance toward the east I saw a very glorious building, surrounded, as it were, by three walls, with various kinds of houses in it, and the splendor of an immense light illuminated the whole thing. A most delightful loveliness of trees and grass and flowers appeared around it. The place that appeared in between this building and the aforementioned valley seemed to be completely filled with very harsh and charred-looking thorns. While I was looking at this, behold a large multitude of resplendent people

63

rose up from the valley. They seemed to head through the midst of those impassable thorn bushes with great speed and much effort, and when they finally arrived at the aforementioned building, they entered it. Some of them, however, chose a path beyond the brambles, and they arrived without struggle. This journey was made many times at intervals.

33. About someone whose soul she saw liberated on the anniversary of his death.

Brother, I also do not want you to be in the dark about one of our friends whom we loved as a father. On the anniversary of his death, when I had done certain things for his liberation that had been shown to me in a vision, I saw him at the time of Mass in a dazzling garment standing before me, and with him was a certain beautiful youth clothed and girded in white. When he had devoutly raised his hands and eyes to heaven in my presence, as if giving thanks, he turned from me and went with the companion of his journey toward that building which I already described to you. And I, observing their path, continued to watch them until they entered there. About the visions of the saints, what more can I say to you except that on each of their birthdays, as they are called,[102] they deigned to comfort my soul, except for one of the apostles, whom I had less attentively served, due to my illness.

34. The building that she saw during Advent.

During Advent I saw a certain magnificent building surrounded by a wall, and in its center was a tower of such height that its top seemed to pierce the heavens (Gn 11:4). After it had appeared to me like this many times, one Sunday, when I had returned to myself from ecstasy, I suddenly seized upon this prayer, "Lord Jesus Christ, gracious and ready to hear, make known to me, your unworthy handmaid, what this city is that you have shown me." Immediately these words of response were placed in my mouth, "This is the heavenly Jerusalem, which is built like a city with its top touching the heavens."

35. On Christmas Eve she was delighted by the brightness of a light, and during the first Mass, at the gospel reading of the book of

generation, she saw the Queen of the world descend on a ray of that light with a great company of angels, and she saw two radiant youths remaining by the ministers of the altar during that Mass and thereafter.

After this, with the feast of the Lord's birth approaching, for two days before the feast I prepared for my impending suffering. Indeed, as often as I thought about the dignity of the upcoming solemnity, I was distressed and all my strength was sapped as if I were about to go into ecstasy. And when Vespers of the solemnity came, after much painful struggle I finally came into the quiet of ecstasy. I felt as if I had been lifted up on high, and I saw an open door in the heavens, and that venerable mystery which I had seen on the feast of All Saints was then shown to me a third time. And when I had taken delight in the abundance of God's sweetness, I finally came back to myself and immediately burst into these words, "Desiring, I have desired to see the Lord God, my Savior, and I have seen and behold my soul has been saved" (Gn 32:30). I spent the night in prayer, and I could not sleep at all because of the extraordinary brightness of the light, which I saw throughout the night. In great delight I saw that door continuously open, which earlier I could not see without being in a trance, and its light appeared as if ten times brighter than in the past visions.

During the preparation for the celebration of the first Mass, which was to be sung during Matins, I saw a beam of great brightness extending from that door to the altar in the oratory. And when the book of generation was begun,[103] behold the glorious Queen of Heaven accompanied by a great crowd of angels came, descending on that beam, and stood at the right hand of the priest. She had a crown of great and most delightful splendor on her head. When the gospel was finished and the antiphon, "O queen of the world,"[104] was being sung according to custom, she was raised up with her retinue and returned to her throne by means of that same beam. Although during that whole time I was overcome in ecstasy, nevertheless, I did not stop invoking her most devoutly. Moreover, there were two splendid youths who had descended by means of that same beam, and they stayed by the ministers of the altar from the beginning of Mass until the end. Also, at the second Mass there were two others. One of them stood at the side of the priest; the other stood next to the deacon while he read the gospel. I thought that the one with the deacon was one of our own deacons who was taking part in the Mass, robed in an alb (which indeed he was not) and standing there to administer the sacrament. But I was even doubtful about this, since this one seemed to have curly white hair, but our deacon had black. Then he turned his face to me as if indignant, and immediately these words were fixed in my heart: "I am the angel of the testament" (Mal 3:1). In the midst of all these things, I also saw a dove stationed above the altar during the Mass.

36. On the following day, she saw Saint Stephen, the first martyr, and on that day at Vespers she saw Saint John the Evangelist.

On the following day at the time of the divine office,[105] I saw blessed Stephen, the first martyr, radiant in supernal brightness and marked with the signs of martyrdom and the diaconate. On the same day at Vespers, I saw blessed John the Evangelist adorned with the brightest robe and a gold stole in the style of a priest, and he was standing in the sight of the throne. Moreover, I looked at that place where I was accustomed to see the four evangelists, and indeed I saw three animals, but the place of the eagle appeared empty.

37. On the feast of the Holy Innocents, she saw a bright lamb and those martyrs following that lamb.

On the feast of the Holy Innocents,[106] at the time of the divine sacrifice, I saw a high and radiant mountain, and on its summit was a bright and very lovely lamb that had an image of the cross on its back. A vast multitude of martyrs with palm branches and crowns marked with red followed it. Indeed, I thought that they were those blessed infants who were killed for the Lord Jesus, but I was astonished that there was no sign of infancy about them. Indeed, they all seemed to possess the fullness of youth.

38. How she saw three kings on Epiphany.

On the feast of the circumcision of the Lord and on Epiphany,[107] I saw Sunday visions, but on Epiphany I saw them more clearly and endured greater distress in ecstasy. Then, at First Vespers, I also saw three crowned kings standing before the throne.

Coming forward, they knelt and worshiped before the Son of Man. Taking their crowns from their heads, they offered them into His hands and received them back from Him. During the day at Mass, I again saw those three worshiping in the presence of the Lord Jesus, and they seemed to place in His hands some shining little gifts.

39. She sees the Lady of the world and her purification with a multitude of young women with shining lamps in their hands.

On the feast of the Purification of Holy Mary,[108] at Mass, before the gospel, I began to languish severely, and when the gospel had been read, I immediately came into ecstasy. Behold, I saw our Lady come, descending on a beam of light. She stood to the right of the priest, and next to her was an aged and venerable man who had a long white beard. When the sisters had offered lamps into the hands of the priest,[109] Mary returned to the heavens, and behold, a vast crowd of distinguished young women with shining lamps came to meet her. After a brief pause in this outer realm of light, they returned with her above, following her with joy. On that same day at Vespers, while I was in ecstasy and saw her again, I most devoutly invoked her help, and with all earnestness commended myself and my loved ones to her. At the end of this prayer, I continued, saying, "My Lady, what shall I expect from you?" And she seemed to respond, "You and all those who trust in me can hope for good favor from me." God has magnified His mercies in me and done these things for me, brother, during your recent absence.[110]

40. On a Sunday in Lent, she saw a rotating wheel and a bird hovering above it barely able to hold steady above it, and she saw a ladder above the wheel and the form of a man standing next to it.

At First Vespers on the first Sunday in Lent,[111] a sudden physical languor overcame me and—as usual—I went into a trance. I saw a bright wheel spinning around in the air with astonishing speed. Also, at the top of the wheel I saw a small white bird maintaining itself with great difficulty lest it be carried around by the force of the wheel. Indeed, several times it seemed to slip down a little from the top and then struggle again to reach the top. It labored in this way for a long time, slipping down and rising again in turn. After this, I saw a lofty and very pleasant mountain and the wheel was brought above it. Again the wheel was moving around in a circle there as before, and the little bird clinging to it was persevering in its struggle. I eagerly wondered what those things could portend, and with great longing I beseeched the Lord for the meaning of this vision. And when I had received a little understanding, I returned from ecstasy and then unexpectedly seized these words, "Narrow and difficult is the way that leads to life (Mt 7:14). Lord, who will go that way?" And I added, "The one who guards his or her life from carnal desires and whose tongue has no deceit." I also added, "Lord, what should I do?" And again these words of response came into my mouth, "If you wish to walk as I have walked, observe closely My footsteps and do not turn away to the right or to the left, but follow Me and in this way you will arrive, because I have said, 'I am the way, the truth and the life; if anyone enters through Me, that one will be saved and will find pasture'" (Jn 14:6, 10:9).

After this, on Monday, I came again into ecstasy, and I saw the aforementioned vision as before, but more fully, because I also saw a ladder standing above the wheel. It was so high that its top seemed to go into the heavens. Its lateral posts seemed to be triangular and made of stone; the rungs differed from each other in their very diverse and beautiful colors. Moreover, I remember that the first of them was white as snow, the second red as burning iron. On the next day I again saw all these things, and standing next to the wheel I saw an image of a man whose head appeared to be gold and his hair was like pure white wool. His eyes were very bright and beautiful, his chest and his arms—which he extended in the manner of a cross— had a certain very pure luster like well-polished silver. He had in his right hand a branch of a tree, green and very pleasing in appearance; in his left hand he held a shining wheel adorned with the variety of a rainbow. His belly appeared to be bronze, his thighs of steel, his lower legs of iron, his feet of earth (Dn 2:32–33; 7:9; Rv 1:14–16). All these things appeared to me many times during Lent. Moreover, on the first Sunday after the feast of blessed Gregory,[112] while I was in ecstasy and was seeing the visions that I usually saw on Sundays, I saw in the heavens that famous doctor full of glory and lovely brightness, like the glory of the most holy bishops Martin and Nicholas.

He had on his head a venerable crown, just as I had seen them wear, the kind said to be worn by popes. In that same hour, I also saw the aforementioned vision, and I burned with a great desire to understand what I was seeing, especially what the image of the man could signify since I already understood something about the other aspects of the vision. Therefore, I very eagerly beseeched that blessed man of God to procure for me from the Lord an understanding of the vision which I desired. He turned toward me and responded with these words, "You are not able to understand what those things signify, but talk to the learned ones who read the scriptures; they know." Now therefore, most beloved brother, I entreat you to take up this task. Examine the divine scriptures and try to discover a suitable interpretation of this vision. Indeed, perhaps the Lord has reserved this for you.[113]

41. On the Annunciation of our Lady, she saw the Lord Jesus with infinite thousands of saints in the realm of this atmosphere, looking as if recently crucified and showing His wounds to the world and making a great complaint.

      Seven days before the Annunciation of our Lady,[114] I became sick and fell upon my bed, languishing throughout my body in such a way that I was able to take almost no refreshment into my body. Moreover, I remained in this sickness until the third day before the feast. On that day, around Nones, I began to have a liquid in my mouth like a comb of honey, and I was as refreshed by its sweetness as if I had taken sufficient food, and I was strengthened throughout my body and emitted a copious sweat, and I remained like that until the following day. Around the time of Mass, I began to be most seriously distressed, and after excessive and miserable sufferings of my body, I went into a trance and it seemed to me as if my spirit was drawn away from my body and lifted up on high. Moreover, in that trance, I saw the heavens open and the Lord Jesus with infinite thousands of saints coming into the realm of this atmosphere. There was neither beauty nor comeliness in Him (Is 53:2); rather, He appeared as pitiable as when He had just been crucified. And when to the whole world He brandished the cross on which He had hung, His wounds flowing as if with fresh blood, He shouted with a great and terrible voice, saying, "Such things have I endured for you, but what have you endured for Me?"

42. She saw two orders of people being judged: The just were rewarded with life, and the reprobate were condemned to punishment.

Two different crowds of countless people were standing by Him, one to His right, the other to His left. An immense light seemed to surround those who were on His right. Outstanding among them appeared the Virgin of virgins, glorious Mary. There I distinctly noted various people of every ecclesiastical level, among whom I was also delighted to distinguish our venerable father blessed Benedict with his monastic retinue. However, those who were to the left were surrounded with such dense and horrifying shadows that I could hardly distinguish the various individuals among them. There was, however, that great prince of this miserable crowd and frightful king of pride, and next to him stood Judas and Pilate and the crucifiers of the Lord. Alas, how many from the clergy, even how many men and women from our order, full of confusion, did I discern there! And when I had looked closely at all this, the Judge of all said to those who were at His right, "Come, blessed ones of My Father, receive the kingdom that has been prepared for you from the beginning of the world" (Mt 25:34). But to those who were on His left, He said, "Go, cursed ones, into the eternal fire that has been prepared for the devil and his angels" (Mt 25:41). At once the former followed the Lord with pleasant speed to the shining mansions. But the others, filled with sadness and confusion, were plunged into the deepest shadows with their prince. Immediately after this I returned to myself and, after copious weeping, burst into these words, "Free me, Lord, from eternal death on that terrible day when heaven and earth will be shaken." And I added, "I believe that my redeemer lives, and on the last day I will be resurrected from the earth and in my flesh I will see God my Savior" (Jb 19:25–26). Furthermore, on the day of the feast when I was again in my trance at the time of the divine sacrifice, the Passion of our Savior was presented to my eyes: how He was stripped of His garments and whipped by the impious ones, and in the end nailed to the cross. However, I did not see everything that was done to Him in the Passion as I would later see one by one on Good Friday. When I ceased to see these things, I saw my Lord standing in heavenly brightness and I received a revelation of a certain thing that I do not yet wish to be made manifest.

43. On Palm Sunday, she saw the Lord hanging on the cross while "Pilate entered" was being sung. She saw the Lord seated on an ass and meeting a crowd of the great and the lowly.

After this, at First Vespers on Palm Sunday,[115] while the sisters were saying the response, "Pilate entered," and they had gotten as far as the verse "Let Him be crucified,"[116] I was standing among them and suddenly I fell into ecstasy with a great convulsion of my body, and I saw the Savior as if He were hanging on the cross. The same thing happened to me again at Matins. That day at Mass, when the Passion of the Lord was begun, I again went into ecstasy. Then I saw in the distance a pleasant mountain, and the Savior was coming down from it, seated on an ass, and He went toward a great city. At the foot of the mountain, a crowd of great and lowly people met Him with verdant branches, and many of them took off their robes and scattered them on the path He was taking, and they rejoiced and went with Him to the city gate. And there was a great crowd there and it made way for Him and He went through its midst up to the Temple. Getting down from the ass, He went into the Temple. I could not see Him beyond that, and I returned to myself.

44. On that day with her mental gaze she saw everything done by the brothers in church at the divine office.

I had earnestly asked our brothers to celebrate the office of Palm Sunday that day in the meadow where we could see them. They were not able to do this because the brooks had flooded; instead, they conducted the service behind the church, where we were not able to see it. And the Lord respected the desire of His handmaid, and with the eyes of my mind I saw everything that they did there.

45. During the canon of the Mass she saw the Lord hanging on the cross and blood flowing down into the chalice.

After this, at Mass on Holy Thursday,[117] I saw—as I usually did—everything that was being done at the altar, and when the priest said the canon and raised the chalice to the sight of God, I saw the Lord Jesus as if hanging on the cross above the chalice and blood from His side and His feet seemed to flow down into it.

46. She saw the Lord sitting at supper with His disciples, eating and washing their feet. She also saw Him praying at the Mount of Olives, with drops of blood running down from His most holy flesh.

When the time for Vespers drew near, I began to languish seriously, and all the strength of my body disappeared, and the sisters laid me in the chapter hall where they were going to celebrate the washing of feet. And when the antiphon, "Before the feast day,"[118] was begun, I suddenly burst into copious tears, and began to struggle, and after great sufferings I became quiet in ecstasy. Then I saw the Lord in that same city which He had entered on Palm Sunday, sitting in a house with His disciples as if to eat. And while I was watching, He arose from the meal, and putting aside His garments He girded himself in a linen cloth, and taking a basin He knelt before Peter. Peter suddenly leapt up and stood looking alarmed. Still bending over, the Lord seemed to speak to him, and after a little while, Peter sat down again. The Lord washed the feet of each of them and, putting His clothes back on, He returned to the table and sat as if speaking to them. After this, He rose and went out with them from the city and went toward that mountain from which I had seen Him descend. Having watched these things, I returned to myself and immediately began to be even more distressed than before, such that the sisters thought I was dying. While they were saying the litany over me, I came again into ecstasy. Then I saw how the Lord withdrew from the remaining disciples, and, kneeling on the ground, He then lay outstretched in prayer, looking as if He was experiencing great distress. I also saw those precious drops of blood running down from His most holy flesh onto the ground. After His prayer, He returned to His disciples, who I saw were sleeping. When He had spoken to them, He again returned to prayer, and this happened three times. Then, returning to myself, I immediately had these words in my mouth, "In agony, Jesus prayed at length, and His sweat was like drops of blood flowing down from Him to the ground" (Lk 22:44). And I added, "On the Mount of Olives I prayed to My father, 'Father, if it can be done, may this cup pass from Me'"

(Mt 26:39). And after a little while, I went back into ecstasy. I looked, and behold, the Lord returned from prayer and, taking His disciples with Him, went into a garden (Jn 18:1).

47. She saw how the Lord was handed over by Judas and how the Jews blasphemed Him with spitting and various mockeries and later lifted Him up on the cross.[119]

After a little while, Judas arrived with an armed band and came forward and kissed the Lord. However, those who were with Judas retreated and fell to the ground (Jn 18:6). Then they rose up, caught hold of Him, and led Him miserably chained to the city. I also saw the disciples run to their hiding places. Then I returned from ecstasy with these words, "My friend betrayed Me with the sign of a kiss saying, 'The one whom I will kiss is the one; take Him'" (Mt 26:48). After this, throughout the whole night, whether asleep or awake I saw how those impious ones blasphemed the Lord by whipping Him, spitting on Him, striking Him with blows and slaps. I did not even come into ecstasy, but all my perception was directed there and I could pay attention to nothing else, with the result that I appeared to be almost insensate. In the morning, at the third hour, with great fatigue I came into ecstasy in which I remained until the sixth hour. Then I saw how they were dressing the Lord in a purple garment and wrapping Him in a scarlet mantle, and, placing a thorny crown on His head, they mocked Him. Then they stripped Him of those garments, dressed Him in His own clothes, laid the cross upon Him, and led Him outside the city into a certain place that looked plowed but without verdure. There, they stripped Him, raised Him up on the cross, and fastened Him to it. They did the same to two others. Then I awoke and with copious tears burst into these words, "Christ the Lord was made obedient unto death" (Phil 2:8). And I added, "Life dies on the wood; hell is robbed of its sting."[120]

48. On Good Friday, during the divine office, she again saw the Lord dead on the cross and His mother with the disciple whom He loved standing by the cross; His side was pierced by a lance, then His body was loosed from the cross and placed in the tomb.

Then, after a little while, the brothers began to celebrate the office of the day, and when they had gotten as far as the reading of the Passion, I began to suffer and be oppressed beyond all measure in such a way that I could not speak to anyone. Truly, brother, if all my flesh were torn into pieces, it seems to me that I could have borne it more easily. Finally, however, coming into ecstasy, I again saw the Lord on the cross, and then in that hour He gave up His spirit, and His neck was curved, His lovely head fell forward, His knees were bent, and His every limb sunk down. And so His dead body hung, worthy of pity beyond every pitiable thing that the human eye has seen. And meanwhile, brother, what do you think was the grief of my soul when I saw such great sufferings and contempt so unworthy of the best and innocent man who did nothing for Himself, but freely endured all this for us?

I also saw the mother of my Lord, full of sorrow and herself worthy of great pity, standing by the cross with the disciple whom Jesus loved. Lastly, I also saw this: how one of the impious ones ran up and drove a lance into His side, and immediately copious blood together with water flowed out. And behold a thick and horrible darkness arose over the whole earth, and rocks seemed to fly about the fields in a terrible manner and collide and break asunder. When that disturbance subsided, behold certain venerable men came and unfastened the body from the cross, and carried it with great veneration to a green and pleasant garden. They wrapped the body in a clean shroud and placed it in a tomb. Then at last, having regained my spirit, with bitter weeping I seized this lament: "Our shepherd, the fount of living water, has departed; at His death the sun was darkened" et cetera.[121] And I added, "Hail Mary, partner of the martyrs when you were stabbed with the blood of your crucified child."[122] And I continued, "When the Lord was interred, the tomb was sealed," et cetera.[123]

49. On Holy Saturday, she saw women carrying perfumes.

After this, at Vespers on Saturday,[124] when I was in ecstasy, certain venerable women who seemed to be carrying perfumes appeared to me.

50. On the holy day of Easter, she saw the rock removed from the tomb and women running to meet the Lord and two disciples hurrying to the tomb. She also saw two of the Lord's disciples going to Emmaus and she saw the other things read about in the gospels on these days.

When the holy day of Easter had just dawned,[125] I was sitting in a place of prayer and reading in the psalms. As I approached the end of the psalms, I came into ecstasy and I saw the garden in which was the tomb, and the stone had been moved from its entrance. Angels were standing there, and behold, a certain woman came to the tomb weeping. She looked in and, not finding the body there, she withdrew a little, looking sorrowful. The Lord came to her and she paused as if asking Him something. And after a moment she turned to go back to the tomb. Suddenly she turned again as if called by Him, and she ran and fell at His feet. After He disappeared, she stood up, ran quickly to the house where the disciples had gathered, and told them. Immediately after this, when I had revived a bit, I saw two women coming to the tomb with perfumes, and when they saw the angels they stopped as if stunned. After this they came closer with fear. After delaying briefly, they left. The Lord also came to them along the way, and they ran up and fell before Him and held onto His feet. By no means had this been shown to me in the case of the aforementioned woman.[126]

After this, when Mass was being celebrated, I saw two disciples hastening to the tomb; one appeared older, the other younger. The younger one, who arrived at the tomb more quickly, did not go in. But the older one went in as soon as he arrived; thereafter, so did the other. And what more do you seek to know, brother? Almost everything that, according to the gospels, happened at this time was shown to me. For I also saw how the Lord, looking like a pilgrim, joined two people going from Jerusalem to Emmaus. When they arrived at the town and He made as if to leave them, they held Him back and led Him into a house. Immediately after He sat down to eat and blessed the bread and broke it, the place where He had been sitting appeared empty. At once those two rose and went with speed to the house in which the disciples had gathered and announced to them. Moreover, while they were announcing it to them, the Lord appeared, standing in their midst. After this I also saw how He ate with them. On the table there was a dish holding fish and another containing a honeycomb. The clothes that I saw Him wearing after the resurrection were very white and the appearance of His face was cheerful and of such brightness that I could hardly discern it.

51. On the day of the Ascension of the Lord, she saw the disciples gathered in a house. She also saw how the Lord led them outside and in their presence was raised up to heaven.

While at Mass on the day of the Ascension of the Lord,[127] I was in a trance and I saw the disciples gathered in a house and the mother of the Lord was with them. And the Lord came in to them, and after He had taken food with them, He led them out from the city and up a mountain. And I saw how He was raised up in their presence, and a multitude of angels came to meet Him and He was carried up into heaven. While they were standing and looking up to heaven, two shining youths appeared above those coming and spoke to them. At once the others returned to the city and gathered in the house from which they had come. Then I returned to myself with words like this: "The Lord led forth His disciples to Bethany" (Lk 24:50), and the other words that follow in the gospel, as well as this: "O king of glory, Lord of hosts, who as conqueror has today ascended above all the heavens," et cetera.[128]

52. On the holy day of Pentecost she saw the Holy Spirit descend from heaven upon the disciples in flames of fire. Later she saw the Spirit in the form of a dove fly above the priest and other ministers celebrating the Mass.

After this, on the day of Pentecost before the celebration of the Mass,[129] while I was in ecstasy, I again saw the disciples gathered in the house mentioned earlier, and the mother of the Savior was with them. While they were seated, something like a flame of fire appeared above each of them, descending from above with a powerful force. Immediately, with one mind, they all rose and went out with gladness and great confidence to proclaim the word of God to the people. After I had surveyed these events, I returned to myself and then I took up these words, "The Holy Spirit, coming forth from the throne, entered unseen the hearts of the apostles," et cetera.[130] When the office of the Mass began, I came into ecstasy again, and I saw a flashing beam of light extending from heaven down to the altar. The beautiful dove that I usually saw came down the center of this beam, carrying in its mouth a certain red thing that looked life a flame of fire, but it was a little larger than usual. With wings outspread, the dove first hovered over the head of the priest and there deposited what looked like a drop from that thing which it was carrying in its mouth. The same thing was done to the ministers of the altar who were vested for reading, and after this the dove sat on the altar. After I returned from ecstasy, I told our mistress that she should exhort the sisters to devotion in their prayers, hoping for the same thing to happen later. When the Mass was finished and we went forward to receive communion, I slipped from the hands of the sisters who were supporting me and fell violently into ecstasy. And while each of the sisters was receiving communion, I saw the aforementioned dove fly to them and distribute to each something from what it was carrying in its mouth.

53. She begins to narrate the visions of the following year and she commences with the words that she—not knowing how—announced on the feast of Saint Lawrence and the Assumption of Saint Mary.

Those are the divine mercies of the Lord, brother, which were done for me in the first year of my visitation. Moreover, in the course of the second year, almost all the same things that usually happened to me on the saints' feasts in the first year occurred again, and also some new things, which I will for the most part pass over in silence because of the unbelievers. Moreover, sometimes words of an unusual kind were placed in my mouth as I returned from ecstasy. Thus when I spoke, I was following not my own will but the will of the Lord, who through my mouth made known the visions that through modesty I had been accustomed to hide from the sisters. For example, on the feast of blessed Lawrence,[131] I made known the vision that I saw in these words: "I saw a certain most noble deacon, Lawrence, standing before the gates and holding a palm and his crown was red. He was turned toward me, looking sweetly at me." Likewise, on the Assumption of our most blessed

Lady,[132] when I was returning from my trance, in the presence of everyone I suddenly made a speech of this kind, saying, "Above the heaven of heaven, I saw in the east many thousands of crowned saints—I reckon more than one hundred and forty-four thousand—who were all crowned with golden crowns, all according to their own orders. In the center was a high and very glorious throne, and I saw the One sitting in the middle of the throne whose face was awesome. From that One and from the throne a great splendor like flashing lightning came forth so that I could hardly lift my eyes because of the extreme light. Around the throne stood many angels and the four animals, and they all fell down and worshiped the One sitting on the throne, saying, 'Glory and honor and blessing to the One sitting on the throne who lives for ever and ever.'"[133] After this I added, "Hail, holy one, hail, pious and noble Virgin Mary, you indeed are gentle, you are sweet, you are helper and comforter to all who trust in you. Help me, my Lady Mary, because my soul trusts in you. Pray for me to your only born Son, our Redeemer, so that He will accomplish in me the work of His mercy."

54. The words she announced on the feast of All Saints.

On the feast of All Saints,[134] after ecstasy my mouth was opened in these words, "The angel of the Lord came to me and snatched my spirit from my body, and suddenly I came with him and he led me into the height before the door that is in the sight of the Lord. I looked in and I saw many thousands of crowned saints standing by and ministering to God, and I saw the four animals around the throne. Indeed, angels and archangels, cherubim and seraphim stood before the throne of God, and throwing themselves down they worshiped Him and in a clear voice they said, 'Holy, holy, holy Lord, all powerful God, who was and who is and who is to come.'[135] Likewise I saw twenty-four elders fall on their faces and worship the One who lives forever and ever" (Rv 4:1–10; 7:9–12).

55. A vision about the consecration of the church at Bonn, where she saw her brother, who was then a canon, reading a lesson at Matins.

I also have something to tell you about the recent consecration of the church at Bonn. Just as you had suggested to me in a letter, I prayed to the Lord to open my eyes in the accustomed way at First Vespers of the feast of the Exaltation of the Holy Cross.[136] Among other things shown to me, I saw a beam of copious light descending from heaven to that church and the whole thing was illuminated by an immense brightness. I also saw a multitude of angels descending on that beam, and they stayed with the ministers of the church for the whole time of the dedication. Everything being done there was filled with such great majesty that I could not look at it without trembling. I was in this vision continuously from the time of Vespers of the preceding day up to that hour in which the office of dedication was completed. Moreover, among other things going on there, I saw you, brother, standing in the pulpit at Matins and reading one of the lessons.

56. A vision about a sister who died at Dirstein.
One of our sisters who had been staying at Dirstein departed from this life. So when her death was announced to us, we undertook mortification for the relief of her soul according to our custom. While we were doing this, I saw an angel of the Lord standing near our mistress, under whose ministry the divine service was being performed. In that same hour I also saw our most blessed Lady, who looked as if she were standing in the realm of the lower atmosphere and watching us. And when we had finished our mortification, the angel was lifted up to her and together they returned to the heights.[137]

57. A vision that she saw on Christmas Eve.
At the time of Matins Mass on Christmas Eve,[138] while I was at prayer, the Lord opened my eyes, and I saw in spirit the man whose presence I had desired, hastening from afar to see to the agony of my passion. Vespers time was already drawing near when he arrived and a powerful and bitter suffering rushed over me, and I was fatigued by it beyond belief. Then, while the sisters were tearfully praying over me, around the end of the prayer, I saw the angel of the Lord coming from above as if to help me. When he was stand-

ing before me, I said to him, "My lord, I am weary of enduring." And he said to me, "Take comfort, be consoled, do not fail on your path." After a little while my flesh became quiet in ecstasy. He carried me in spirit into the height, and, just as I had the year before, I contemplated the delights that God has prepared for those who love Him. After a long trance, I returned to myself and at once these words flowed from my mouth, "Sent from the exalted dignity of the Father, He descended from the heavens, entered our realm through the ear of the Virgin, clothed in a purple stole, and through the golden gate He went forth, the light and glory of all creation."[139] And also, "From that hidden dwelling the Son of God descended and came to seek and save those who longed for Him with their whole hearts."[140] And also, "The angel of the Lord came to me and snatched my spirit," et cetera, just as I have described on the feast of All Saints.[141] After this, I blessed the Lord, saying, "I give you thanks, Lord, for you have sent your angel to me, who has comforted me in my tribulation, for you alone regard my suffering and pain" (Ps 9B:14).[142] At Matins time, at the celebration of each Mass, I endured the same suffering.

58. The words that she announced on the holy day while in a trance and the vision about our Lady and her infant that she saw on the same day.

At the principal Mass of the day,[143] while I was again in my trance, I most earnestly prayed to the Lord for the communal correction of the church. At the end of my prayer, I asked the Lord to deign to indicate to me His will regarding clergy and nuns not walking along the good path.[144] When I had finished this prayer and had begun to return to myself, my angel stood by me and I said to him, "O sweetest and most loving youth, answer me about those things that I asked the Lord." He said to me, "Shout and say to the sinful nation, the people full of sin, 'Woe, woe to you who live under the power of the devil, cease to do evil, learn to do good (Is 1:4, 16–17). But if you do not, behold, I the Lord will send My smiting angel among you (1 Chr 21:15). If you will not be converted from your evil ways and do penance for your perverse deeds, I the Lord will accomplish My indignation upon you'" (Ez 18:30; 6:12).

Now I also cannot keep silent about the great consideration by which my Lady gladdened my heart! While I was still in my trance, I saw her from afar in a certain house, lying in bed, as it were, and touching with her hands a beautiful and very lovely infant. When she had wrapped Him in the whitest swaddling clothes, she laid Him in a manger that seemed to be near her. After a little while, she took Him to her breast and lay down.

59. The exhortation by which she admonished a certain friend to ascend to the priestly office and the response of our Lady.

Immediately after this I saw her like a queen and ruler in the kingdom of brightness. Therefore I invoked her in my usual way and prayed to her especially for a certain friend of mine. He was in the order of the diaconate, and I had frequently exhorted him to not delay rising to the sacred order of the priesthood. But he, offering various excuses for his fear, said that he did not yet dare to enter so difficult a state. While I was referring to this matter in my invocation in the presence of my Lady, she responded to me in these words, "Tell my servant, 'Do not fear; do what you are going to do and calculate the service that you owe me but have not done.'"[145]

60. A vision that she saw on the feast of Saint John the Evangelist about the four animals in the Book of Ezekiel.

At the time of the divine office on the feast of Saint John the Evangelist,[146] while I was in bed because of illness, at that very moment the hand of the Lord was upon me, and I saw that lovely priest of the Lord standing in the presence of the throne. So I poured out my prayers to him and asked if he could bring it to pass that I might be allowed to see some of those things which had been shown to him while he was on earth. At once I saw four animals standing in that same place, just as they are described in Ezekiel, and the quadriform wheel was with them (Ez 1:4–21). After this, when I was just about to return to myself, I saw two angels, terrible and with faces full of indignation, standing in the lower atmosphere. One of them had a terrible sword in his right hand, extended as if ready to strike. And I said to my guide, "My lord, who are they?" He answered, "They have power to destroy the earth" (Rv 7:2).

61. About the Innocents she saw on their feast, and about the circumcision of the Lord.

After this, on the feast of the Innocents,[147] I saw a great crowd of shining young people marked with the signs of martyrdom descending from a high mountain. Before them went a bright lamb carrying a sign of the cross. I said to my guide, "Lord, who are they that I am seeing here?" He responded, "They are the innocent and the unstained who follow the Lamb wherever it goes" (Rv 14:4). I said, "Lord, why these more than others?" And he said, "They are not alone. There are others as well who are innocent and unstained and chosen virgins of Christ who follow the Lamb wherever it goes." In response, I said, "Why the lamb more than another animal?" He replied, "Because the innocent Lamb, unstained and elect, was slaughtered for the salvation of humankind." On the feast of the Circumcision of the Lord,[148] I experienced around me much grace from the merciful Savior.

62. She saw three kings with gifts on the Epiphany of the Lord and the marriage at Cana in Galilee and the baptism of the Lord.

On Epiphany[149] as well the Lord multiplied His grace in me and I saw in spirit my Lady and her little one staying in a certain house that seemed far away. And behold, three men of regal bearing entered there, and they knelt and worshiped before the child. Then one of them, holding out a large gold coin that appeared to be stamped with a royal image, offered it into the hands of the child. Likewise, the other two also came forward and reverently offered their gifts in small vessels. After this, the marriage that took place in Cana of Galilee was shown to me, and again I saw there the Savior with Mary, His mother, reclining at table among the guests, and I saw the six urns placed in that same spot (Jn 2:1–6). Moreover, the Lord did not disdain to show to His handmaid the washing of His virginal body, which was performed in the Jordan. I saw how He went down into the waters of the blessed river with the holy Baptist and was baptized by him, and how a dove descended from heaven and rested on His head. Awaking from this vision, I opened my mouth in these words: "The Holy Spirit appeared in the form of a dove and the Father's voice was heard, 'This is My beloved son, in whom I am well pleased; listen to Him'" (Mt 3:16–17; Lk 9:35).

63. About what happened to Elisabeth on the Purification of Holy Mary.

After this, at First Vespers on the feast of the Purification,[150] God did a certain new and unusual thing to me. I was in a trance in my usual way, praying in spirit to the Lord and greeting my Lady, whom I could see in spirit, and pouring out fervent prayers to her. During this time, the sisters who were standing around me plainly heard the whole course of my prayers. But when I returned to myself and they told me this, I would not believe it until they repeated in order the same words I had used in prayer.

[About a certain sister among us who had died, whose soul Elisabeth saw the angels receive.]

It came to pass that a certain elderly sister among us was weak with an illness from which she died. However, on the third day before her death, her illness suddenly worsened to such an extent that we thought she was then about to die, and we hastened to begin the litany over her. Then a very serious suffering rushed over me, and I fell to the ground, and the sisters gathered around me with prayers. When I had been lying as if dead for a short while, suddenly I was aroused and said, "Anoint her." She had not yet been anointed with oil. Having said this, I immediately went into a trance. Again, after reviving a little but before I had fully returned to myself, I announced to the others the vision that I seen, saying: "Our Lady descended with our father, the blessed Benedict, and immediately—I don't know why—they returned to the heavens. And then so many evil spirits were present here—some of which like dogs are still circling around us, and some like vultures are sitting on the roof. But standing near the bed of our sister were two angels who said to those spirits, 'Leave this place; this sister has just received a respite.'" After I had said these things and had returned completely to myself, I was not aware that I had revealed this vision.

Calling to the mistress, I began to tell her privately what I had seen. She, however, admitted that she had heard all these things from my own mouth.

On the third day after this, when that same sister departed from this life, at the hour of her passing away, I saw in spirit those two angels standing by her and receiving her soul as it departed from her body. Where they took it, however, was not revealed to me. And while we were praying in the funeral procession, I saw a beautiful, apparently small angel sitting on the top of the bier. He was not shaken off when it was carried to the brothers' church, and he remained until the time of the burial.

65. How Elisabeth was invaded by a fever and what happened to her.

After this, a high fever gripped me, and I desired the sacrament of anointing. At that time, however, the lord abbot had gone to neighboring places and I was awaiting his return. That same evening around dusk, while the mistress was sitting with me, a certain venerable man arrived and stood within my sight. I thought that he was the lord abbot, and I was cheered. And while I was reproving his lateness and the harshness of his ways, he kindly received this reproach and comforted me, saying that I was not yet about to die. So I asked him to recite the Lord's Prayer and the Creed in my presence and then to anoint me. When he had done this and I had responded at intervals to each of his words, then it seemed to me that he had completed the whole rite of anointing and, having blessed me, he left. Then the mistress, who had heard all my words, asked me with whom I had been speaking. I said, "Wasn't the lord abbot present and didn't he anoint me?" She, however, declared that she had seen no one there. It was then that I first understood that I had seen a spiritual vision.

66. How she was freed from her illness on the Annunciation of our Lady and the vision of Mary that she had.

After this, when the feast of the Annunciation was near at hand, I fell into a very serious languor and for two days before the feast day I lay in weakness. On the morning of that feast,[151] my languor was so aggravated that the sisters came to my bed to say the litany over me. When they were about to depart from me, they asked if I wished to take communion that day since they were about to do so themselves. I, however, declined saying that, unlike them, on account of my bodily sickness I had not prepared for this by doing any worthy acts. They were saddened by this and left. Then an angel of the Lord came and stood by me, placed his hand on my head, and said, "Rise and stand on your feet; you have been freed from your infirmities. Go and take communion; be fortified and you shall be strong!" At these words, all the languor suddenly fled from me and I was most sweetly relieved throughout my whole body. He also added this: "Indeed, it was possible for the Lord to have alleviated the passions that you have endured so far, but He willed for you to be afflicted in this way so that you would believe it better." So at once I grabbed my clothes, rose from my bed, and with strength restored and vivid color I went down and joyfully came into the gathering of sisters, and with everyone marveling, I did what he had commanded me. On the same day, the annunciation was also presented to me. Indeed, I saw in spirit our Lady as if standing in prayer in a certain room and suddenly an angel of great brightness appeared in front of her as though he were speaking to her. She seemed to be frightened by that sight and, after a discussion, she reverently bowed to him and then he disappeared.

67. The words she announced before the feast of Palms.

On the day before Palm Sunday,[152] when the time for Vespers was drawing near, I was standing alone in the oratory, concentrating on my prayers. And behold, a ray of abundant light from heaven suddenly poured over me, making me warm like the sun when it shines in its strength (Rv 1:16). And I fell flat on the ground with a violent force and went into a trance. Then the sisters came running to me, wanting to raise my head from the ground so they could put pillows under it, but with no effort could they lift it. After a little while, the angel of the Lord came, and quickly raised me up and stood me on my feet saying: "O person, rise and stand on your feet and I will speak with you, and do not be afraid, because I am with you all the days of your life (Ez 2:1–2; Is 43:5). Act manfully and let

85

your heart be strengthened and wait for the Lord (Ps 26:14). And say to the apostates of the earth, 'Just as once the people crucified Me, so I am daily crucified among those who have sinned against Me in their hearts.' Indeed, they turn their faces from me and their heart is far from Me lest they see, lest they acknowledge how I have suffered and how I have freed them by My blood. Say to them, 'Return, sinners, to the Lord, your God, because He is kind and merciful, who wills not the death of a sinner, but rather that the sinner be converted and live'" (Ez 33:11). When he had spoken these things, he departed. I made a sign to the sisters to bring tablets so that these words might be captured in writing. Indeed, I was not able to speak of anything else until all these things were written down according to my narration.[153]

68. The words she announced on Palm Sunday.

Again on Palm Sunday,[154] at the time of the divine office, when I had fallen down again in the same way, the angel raised me up, saying: "O person, think about what you are; that you are dust and ash, and a paltry creature. Hear me, who speaks with you. The Lord says these things: 'The earth is full of iniquity, and this people is not My people, but a people turned away from Me. Their heart is hardened and they do not grasp—they are not able to understand—the words that I have spoken; rather, they withdraw from Me. Woe to them, because they are overwhelmed by the devil and obey him. They dishonor My face with their depraved works and have forgotten God their Creator.'" And I said, "My lord, I do not know what I should say or do, because I am unlearned in the divine scriptures." And he said to me, "My grace is sufficient for you (2 Cor 12:9). Truly, to the one who has, it shall be given, and from the one who has not, what is already held will be taken away" (Mt 13:12).

69. The words she announced on Monday.

After this, on Monday,[155] while I was at Matins, the Lord placed His word in my mouth. And suddenly I said, "Woe to you hypocrites who hide gold and silver. This is the word of God and the divine law, which is more precious than gold and silver. To humans you appear pious and innocent, but inside you are full of evil inclination, and with your pollutions you come to the holy of holies, which is the altar of God, to take the sacrament of the Eucharist. Truly the Lord turns His face so that He does not see your burnt offerings and sacrifices. You then are more miserable than those who look to you as if to a mirror, and when they see your evil works, are scandalized by you. Know beyond doubt that the law shall perish first from the priests and elders of the people in this time" (Ez 7:26).

70. The words she announced on Wednesday.

Again on Wednesday,[156] when I was alone in the chapter hall, I fell into ecstasy. And the angel of the Lord said to me, "And you, son of man,[157] speak to those who inhabit the earth. Listen people! The God of gods has spoken: 'Repent, for the kingdom of God is at hand (Mt 4:17), and turn to Me with your whole heart (Jl 2:12), and I the Lord will be turned to you and will be reconciled with you. But if you will not and if you provoke Me to rage, you will die in your sins and death will devour you suddenly in your ignorance. You will be more miserable than every creature, even brute animals, because when they die, at least they suffer no more evil. You, however, will be tormented in eternal fire, where there will be weeping of eyes and gnashing of teeth without end'" (Mt 13:42). And I said, "Lord, I don't know how to speak and I am slow of speech" (Jer 1:6; Ex 4:10). And he said, "Open your mouth and I will speak, and the one who hears you, also hears Me" (Lk 10:16).

71. The words she announced on Holy Saturday.

On Holy Saturday before Easter,[158] I was going to the chapter hall and collapsed on the threshold of the chapel. A light shone around me (Acts 22:6), and an angel of the Lord stood by me and said, "O most miserable ones who hoard up treasures for yourselves in infernal punishments (Mt 6:19; Jas 4:3)! Don't you know that the noble, the powerful, will perish on the Day of Judgment; that the rich and the wise will wail? Oh, the glory of world is a miserable thing; woe to those who love it! I have shouted, says the Lord, and again I shout, and who will hear Me and consent to My counsels?

And when I shouted, I shouted and said, 'If anyone thirsts, come to Me and drink, and the waters of life will flow from your belly' (Jn 7:37–38). O person, whoever you are, say, 'Here I am' (1 Sm 3:4), and it will be said to you, 'Deny yourself, and be obedient and of humble heart; come and follow Me, and I will test whether you be true or not. And you, unshaken and persevering, do not fail in the struggle. Indeed, the one who will struggle well until the end will be saved'" (Mt 10:22).

72. The words she announced one day in Easter week.

One day in Easter week at noon while I was hoping to rest, the angel of the Lord stood by my bed and said to me, "Do not be sad about these things that are wont to happen to you. My grace is sufficient for you, because I will not desert you if you are willing (2 Cor 12:9; Heb 13:5). Strive to be obedient with all humility of heart and with gladness. Be patient with your enemies; do not raise yourself up in pride, but always be humble, so that you will be lifted up (Lk 18:14). Despise nothing; disdain no one; show a good example in all things (Ti 2:7). Love the Lord your God with your whole heart, and love your neighbor as yourself (Mt 22:37, 39), and what I have given to you, give to others, so that they too may be refreshed, because you have nothing but what has been given to you from above" (Jn 19:11). He added many other things beyond this, like a father kindly instructing his daughter, but alas, because of the intervening sleep, they have slipped from my memory!

73. The vision she saw on the feast of Saint Mark the Evangelist about the four animals that the prophet Ezekiel saw.

On the feast of Saint Mark the Evangelist,[159] I saw an open door in the heavens, and a great splendor poured out from it upon me, and I fell suddenly to the ground. While I was in a trance, I saw four animals before the throne of God, just as I had seen on the feast of blessed John the Evangelist. Each of them had four faces arranged in this way, which I carefully examined. The face of a person was on the front part, which looked at the throne; in the back was the face of an eagle. On the right was the face of a lion; on the left, the face of a bull. They each also had six wings, of which two were joined together above their individual heads. Two other wings were extended, so that the wing of one touched the wing of another; and two wings covered their bodies. They were, moreover, full of eyes in the front and the back. There also appeared a large and bright wheel standing in their presence before the throne. It seemed to encircle four wheels that were linked together in such a way that one partially overlapped the two next to it. Each of those inside also touched the larger wheel with its own rim. In the middle of the four wheels, in the center point of the larger wheel, there was a certain red space like a flame of fire, and from it certain sparkling things seemed to emerge. And all the wheels seemed to be scattered by it, as if made alive. Whence at that moment this came to mind, "The spirit of life was in the wheels." While I was looking at them, the animals separated from each other in four directions, and each of them went before one of the wheels (Ez 1:5–21).[160]

74. She saw Satan in the form of a black bull next to a certain man.

On a certain Sunday, while Mass was being celebrated among the brothers, by chance I looked through the window, hoping to hear the brothers singing the glory of God. However, a certain man stood in the way, crying aloud to another and saying, "You devil, why are you delaying so much now?" And immediately I saw Satan in the shape of a black and deformed bull standing next to him. Let the faithful be warned by this to refrain from evil speech of this kind.

75. The light she saw on Pentecost above the pyx where the body of the Lord was.

On the day of Pentecost,[161] the liturgy of the Mass was suspended at our place because of the excommunication of the count,[162] but nevertheless the Lord did not suspend His consolations from His handmaids. One of the priests came to us, bearing the sacrament of the body of the Lord in a small box, from which, according to custom, we were about to take communion. When he had been let in and had placed the box upon the altar that is in our place, I saw a great light coming from heaven and it was aimed at the box like a ray of the sun, and it lit up the whole thing. Then a snow-white dove seemed to fly through the center of that light and settle next to it. And the angel of the Lord came, and, like a witness to our devotion, stood beside the altar until we had all taken communion in order.

76. The scales that she saw and the books of her righteous deeds and transgressions placed there by a good and an evil angel; at first the book of transgressions seemed to weigh more and later, because of holy communion, the book of righteous deeds weighed more.

On Sunday night before the feast of the apostles Peter and Paul, I was standing in a place of prayer and beginning to feel my usual pains. I was thoroughly frightened because I had been so worn out on the feast of the nativity of Saint John the Baptist, who appeared in glory to me after the three-day languor and severe fatigue I had endured in awaiting him. I was hoping, therefore, to avoid it this time if I somehow could, so that the suffering would not come over me. I withdrew from the place where I was standing, wanting to leave the oratory. And when I had gone forth a bit, the pain worsened so that I could go no further. I barely returned to my place and then collapsed on the ground. Immediately the angel of the Lord stood by me and said in our language, "O miserable one, why do you suffer this so unwillingly? There are many who would freely endure these things if they were allowed to perceive the things that you perceive. If you do not suffer these things in the present, you will surely suffer in that place where you must suffer more severely before you would be worthy to see what you are about to see."

I said, "My lord, this unwillingness to endure stems from my great fragility. And if you wish to encourage me, lord, what will you show me?" He said, "Come and see and contemplate the sweetness that will come to you from your God." At once he raised me up on high into the celestial atmosphere, and I looked through a door of brightness, and I saw in my usual way the glory of the blessed city of God. I was led back again to my pitiable body and recovered a little. Again, however, I went into a trance, and in front of that aforementioned door I saw a scale hanging. My angel stood there, holding a book, and Satan was there holding another book. Then I understood that the book that the angel held was the book of my acts of righteousness; but the other was the book of my transgressions. Each of them placed the book he was holding on the scale, and the book of transgressions seemed to weigh more. Standing there as if in sorrow, the angel said, "It shall not be like this because she has endured many and great pains for her transgressions and has often undertaken harsh flagellations." After enumerating more things of this kind, he said, "This must be deferred until tomorrow." Then I returned to myself and with copious tears exclaimed, "Do not enter into judgment with your handmaid, Lord! (Ps 142:2). Rather, I entreat your mercy: Forgive my sins before you come to make judgment!" While I was constrained by excessive anxiety, the angel presented himself again to me, and I said to him, "Lord, what should I do? Instruct me, my lord." He said, "Be completely obedient, humble, patient, and loving. Willingly endure those things that happen to you; embrace with love those things that the Lord brings about in you; offer prayers for those who love these things, and for all those who have commended themselves to your prayers and to whom you have bound yourself by a promise." When he had said these things, he withdrew.

I, however, no less restless in my heart, began to reflect upon these things to myself, saying, "Haven't I always had great trust in the body of my Lord, Jesus Christ? Isn't this the remission of all sins? Indeed, let me take refuge there." Therefore, I asked the mistress to request—via a messenger quickly sent—that the lord abbot celebrate the Mass of the Holy Trinity and bring the divine sacrament to me on the next day. Indeed, I feared that I was about to die on the next day because of the angel's words, "This is to be deferred until tomorrow." When the Mass was celebrated as I had requested, at the time of the sacrifice I went into a trance and again I saw the scales I had seen in the evening, and the books placed on it. Then the angel, my faithful protector, came bearing something like a small piece of bread such as priests use in the celebration of the Mass, and he put it on top of the book of righteous deeds, and right away, as if he had placed a huge bulk on it, it quickly seemed to outweigh the book in the other tray. At that, waking up with great gladness, I exclaimed, "Holy Trinity; Father, and Son and Holy Spirit, into the hands of your power, into the hands of your mercy, I commend my spirit, my sense, my judgment, my thoughts, and all my body, my life, my end, and all my acts. May your blessing always be upon me, day and night, and may your mercy lead me into eternal life." Because I was about to take communion, I also added this: "Lord, I am not worthy that you should come under my roof, but make me whole and I will be saved, since you are my praise (Mt 8:8). May I be worthy to receive your body and blood not for judgment, but for the remission of all my sins." At the same time I also saw in spirit the lord abbot in the church of the brothers piously confecting the salvific sacrament, and a dove attending upon the sacrifice and a brightness of light shining all around. After this he came to me bringing what I had desired, and I comforted my soul with holy communion.

77. On the vigil of the apostles Peter and Paul, she saw the same scale and the books placed on it seemed to be of equal weight, and she did not cease to implore the apostles and other saints until the book of righteous deeds appeared to weigh more.

Again, at Vespers on the vigil of the feast of the Apostles,[163] after much anguish, I saw in spirit the apostles and the mother of the Lord in the area of brightness. I also saw the same scale I had seen earlier, and the books placed on it. There was a multitude of demons around one tray, and a multitude of angels around the other, and the trays appeared to be of equal weight. Then I invoked my Lady and the apostles with great distress because I thought that surely I was about to die. They withdrew a little further within. When they appeared again and I ceaselessly invoked them and very many other saints, the book of righteousness appeared to weigh more. After this, when I was catching my breath, my angel came to me and said, "A respite has been given to you; make your life more perfect." And I said, "My lord, what more can I do? Don't you know my fragility and that I cannot struggle more than I do?" Then he instructed me and exhorted me to a certain bodily mortification that I had often practiced on myself. Returning to myself, I said, "Peter, as God commands, loose the chains of the earth,"[164] and other prayers to Peter. And I added, "Holy Paul the Apostle, preacher of truth and teacher of the Gentiles, intercede for us to

God, who chose you."[165] And I added: "Lord, do not judge me, a miserable sinner, according to my acts; I have done nothing worthy in your sight. Therefore, I pray to your majesty, that you, God, wipe out my iniquity, because you formed me from the earth." And this: "Do not hand over to the beasts my soul, which trusts in you. And forget not the souls of the poor forever" (Ps 73:19). At Mass during the day, the apostles appeared to me again, and our Lady together with them. Then in spirit I saw the brothers ministering in the church, and the lord abbot standing at the altar, and I indicated to the sisters what kind of chasuble he was wearing. On the same day, when the divine sacrament was brought to us, I saw the same vision I had seen on the day of Pentecost.

78. The angel lifted her up into the height so that she could see all the ends of the earth and fiery arrows falling from heaven; he whipped her for wanting to hide the word of God that the Lord had delivered through her; she was not able to speak until she had shown to the lord abbot what the Lord had deigned to reveal to her.[166]

On the feast of blessed Ciriacus,[167] which was on Sunday, after I had been sick for six days with that languor that usually comes to me before visions of great things, I dragged my feeble limbs from my bed and went to a secret place to pray. While I was intent on my psalms, I was overwhelmed by a violent pain, and I went into a trance. This was around the third hour. And behold the angel of the Lord came and lifted me up into the height so that I could see all the ends of the earth.[168] I saw what looked like fiery, hooked arrows falling to the earth from every part of the sky as thick as snow. Then I was severely troubled inside, fearing that this was the fire that was about to destroy the whole world. The angel said to me, "This is not the fire you are thinking of. Rather, it is the wrath of God, which is about to come upon the earth." Moreover, I continued to see it until the sixth hour. Then I caught my breath a little and I began to return to myself. Again, however, the angel came to me and stood in front of me saying, "Why do you hide gold in the mud (Mt 25:25–26)? This is the word of God, which is sent to earth through your mouth, not so that it would be hidden, but so that it would be made manifest for the praise and glory of our Lord and for the salvation of His people." Having said this, he lifted a whip above me and five times he struck me sharply with it as if in great anger. Each time I was so shaken throughout my body that all the sisters who were around me were amazed at my convulsion. After this he placed a finger of his shining hand over my mouth, saying, "You will be silent and will not be able to speak until the ninth hour, at which time you will announce the things the Lord has worked in you." Then, when he left, I remained as if half dead until the time for Nones. Finally, however, when I had lifted myself up, I could not speak at all. I made a sign to the sisters to call the lord abbot. When he arrived, already the bell for Nones was sounding, and my tongue was not yet loosed. I made a signal to our mistress, who alone was aware of my secret, to bring to me what I had secretly hidden under my bed, namely, the part of the present book that you, brother, had left with me. Indeed, just as we had agreed, I had most firmly intended to hide all these writings until the end of my life. When the book was brought to me and I offered it into the hand of the lord abbot, the chain was loosed from my tongue with these words, "Not to us, Lord, not to us, but to your name give glory" (Ps 113 B:1). Moreover, for three days after this I severely languished throughout my body because all my flesh had been struck by the harshness of the whip. On the fourth day, however, I was strengthened by a profuse outpouring of sweat.

79. On the Assumption of our Lady she received consolation from the angel and the Enemy harshly attacked her until she was liberated from his assault by the grace of the Lord and intercessions of the glorious Virgin.

On the feast of the Assumption of our most blessed Lady,[169] after the celebration of the divine sacrament, I began to tremble violently all over, and all my powers failed. I fell into ecstasy and I saw the same vision that I had seen last year at this time. Then I greeted my Lady, saying, "Blessed are you, Virgin Mary, mother of God. You believed in the Lord and the things that were said to you were brought to pass in you. Behold, you are exalted above the choirs of angels."[170] And I added, "You are loved by the Lord over every beauty, and you are worthy to be called the Queen of Heaven, for the choirs of angels are your partners and fellow citizens."

At that moment, the angel of the Lord stood by me and, looking kindly at me and as if with a compassionate expression, he spoke to me, saying, "Do not be sad and let not your heart be disturbed. The sacred visions, which you see and have as if by habit, you will no longer see until the day of your death. But always look to and contemplate continuously the holy light, the heavenly light. It has been given to you until the end of your life. Then, after this life, may God, who lives and reigns for ever and ever in perfect Trinity, deign to grant you perpetual light." And I responded, "Amen." And I said to him, "Lord, is this happening because of my failings?" And he said, "No. Rather, the Father of orphans has taken pity on you, and has worked with you according to the grace of His compassion." When I then began to grieve to myself at these words that he had said, that I would no longer see my customary visions, my Waylayer took this occasion and began to trouble me through dreams. In my dreams I appeared to be fleeing from him, and calling out for the help of the Lord and my Lady, and holding up before him the sign of the salvific cross. But nonetheless, he seemed to press in eagerly upon me. After being troubled like this for three straight nights, on the third night, I awoke from that torment and sat up in my bed and with profuse tears took up this lament, "Lord, omnipotent God, I make this complaint to your Majesty, to your most holy Trinity, about this one, my most impious Waylayer. May he, who shows no reverence for your holy name, which I always invoke whether waking or sleeping, cease to disturb me when adjured by your name. Your most holy cross, Lord, which I raise above him, he does not so revere as to flee from its sight. But also to my most holy Lady, the perpetual virgin Mary, whom I always invoke, and to all the saints of God I make my complaint, since he also shows no honor to them nor is he frightened away by my invocation of them." When I had made these and other similar prayers, I read fifteen psalms to the honor of our Lady along with certain other of her praises. When I had finished, I earnestly begged her to persuade the Lord to take this impious one from me and give peace to His handmaid. I had hardly finished this prayer, and behold, I saw him in the form of a goat fleeing from me and crossing through the house of prayer with a violent force, and he escaped through the window with a great and horrible roar. Excited by this, the dogs of our house rushed together and, as if they were detecting something strange, they chased him far, barking loudly. From that time on, therefore, through the grace of the Lord, who knows how to deliver His people from temptation, I did not feel his malice. And now, wish me joy, O handmaidens of Christ, because for your consolation the Lord has magnified His mercy with me in these and so many more things of this kind, not as one who judges merits, but as the most generous distributor of His grace and consolation to all who hope in His mercy. Therefore, my soul, glorify Him with all your strength, love Him, praise Him for this, now and forever. Glory and honor to the celestial Trinity, praise to the compassionate Christ reigning with God the Father and the Comforter Spirit for ever and ever. Amen.

Here ends the first book of Elisabeth's visions.[171]

Second Book of Visions

1. An exhortation to all readers of this book urging them not to be scandalized at the marvelous and unheard of divine goodness.[172]

Rich is the mercy of our God, and abundantly does He bestow grace upon grace on those who love Him. In accordance with the greatness of His goodness, He has multiplied His consolations in His handmaid, as the words of the preceding book declare, and behold, His hand is still outstretched in consolation. Indeed, He is not inhibited by the murmuring of those who think themselves great and disdain whatever they regard as weaker, and who do not fear to mock the riches of His goodness in them. They should be afraid that because of their murmuring they will hear the word of the Father saying, "Is your eye evil because I am good?" (Mt 20:15) It scandalizes them that in these days the Lord deigns to magnify His mercy in the weak sex. But why doesn't it occur to them that a similar thing happened in the days of our fathers? When men were given over to negligence, holy women were filled with the spirit of God so that they prophesied, vigorously ruled the people of God, or even triumphed gloriously over the enemies of Israel, like Hulda, Deborah, Judith, Jael, and others of this sort. And now, because it is hoped that these things will edify the minds of the humble, what the Lord has deigned to work in His handmaid after the end of the first book is added here, according to the narration of her own mouth.

2. How to understand that in the first book the angel said to Elisabeth, "The holy visions that you see, you will no longer see until the day of your death."

Perhaps it will disturb the reader that it was written earlier that the angel said to Elisabeth, "The holy visions that you see, you will no longer see until the day of your death,"[173] and yet after that point she still saw visions like the earlier ones. As I understand it, when he said, "holy visions," he meant particularly those visions of celestial secrets that she had been accustomed to seeing through an open door in the heavens on the greatest feast days and frequently on Sundays. Indeed, from the moment he said this to her, visions of this kind stopped completely. However, at the place where the image of the door had appeared, a light of great brightness has not ceased to appear to her. This is in accordance with the message the angel had given her, saying, "Contemplate always and look to the holy light, the heavenly light. It has been given to you until the end of your life."

3. When the following visions were shown to her.

On the vigil of Pentecost,[174] which was at the beginning of the fourth year of her visitations, the handmaid of the Lord saw a vision that she narrated in this way.

4. She saw a marble column extending from the abyss to the height of heaven, and she announced the significance of its shape.

I was in a trance and was transported as if to a green and very pleasant meadow, and the angel of the Lord was with me. I saw an image of a marble column extending from the abyss up to the height of heaven, and it was triangular in shape. One angle was white as snow, while another was red, and the third had the appearance of marble. Moreover, ten very brilliant rays appeared encircling its lower part, descending obliquely from it to the earth. Each of them seemed to be supported by many white and red rays. While I was wondering about this vision, the angel said to me: "Study carefully what you are seeing." I said to him, "My lord, show me, I implore you, what these things mean." He said, "The column that you see descends from the throne of God into the abyss, and its three angles signify the holy Trinity. You discern three colors in it: white, red, and marble. The white color represents the humanity of Christ; the red, the Holy Spirit; and the marble refers to the divin-

98

ity of the Father. The ten rays that you see with it are the Ten Commandments. From these, as you see, innumerable rays come forth,
some white, others red, by which the observers of the Law are represented. The white ones signify those who have preserved themselves pure and spotless for the Law of God; the red are those who
have chosen to pour out their blood for Christ rather than transgress the Law."

After this he said to me, "Look up." And around the top of the
column I saw other innumerable rays, part white and part red, coming forth from it in all directions and even more rays clinging to
them. While I was silently marveling at this, he said to me, "These
are my companions and fellow citizens; white for their purity and
red for the love with which they always burn for the Lord. Clinging
to them are the saints who enjoy their blessed company." After this,
he added, "Pay close attention to these things. Behold, you are
already beginning to care little for these things. And why are they
not committed to writing as they used to be?"

When I was beginning to return to myself from ecstasy, and
was just drawing a breath, the Lord placed a message in my mouth
and I said, "Lord, your mercy is in heaven and your truth reaches to
the clouds. Your justice is like the mountains of God; your judgments are a great abyss. They shall be inebriated with the fullness of
your house, and you shall give them to drink from the torrent of
your delight. Lord, with you is the fountain of life, and in your light
we will see the light. Stretch forth your mercy to those who know
you, and your justice to those who have an upright heart" (Ps
35:6–11). I also added these words, "I give you thanks, Lord Jesus
Christ, because you have shown to me, your unworthy handmaid, a
great and marvelous thing full of mysteries."

5. She sees the blessed precursor of the Lord on the vigil of his
nativity and at his intervention she became worthy to see the face of
our Lady, whom she had not seen for a long time.

After this was the solemnity of the blessed precursor of the
Lord, and again he did not forget to show his usual kindness to me.
Indeed, on the vigil of his birth,[175] around the ninth hour, after a
very serious weakening of my body, he appeared to me in that same

99

glory in which I was accustomed to see him. With all my might I asked him whether, with his help, I might be able to see the face of our Lady, who had been hidden from me longer than usual. Immediately after these words, he disappeared, and I, returning to myself, broke into praise of him, saying: "From the sublime powers of heaven, he is the one whom the hand of the Lord consecrated in his mother's womb, by whose merits we suppliants beg to be helped."[176] I then began to experience greater agony than before, and I heard this response from the angel, who was standing by me: "You will remain in this torture for a long time unless you receive absolution from your spiritual father." But I was by no means able to announce these words to the sisters who were around me. Thinking that my death was imminent and acting on their own judgment, they announced it to the lord abbot, who came and said litanies and prayers over me. Then, with great difficulty, I finally pulled together these words and said, "Forgive me, father!" Thereupon, once I had received absolution from him, I immediately relaxed and went into ecstasy. And behold, our most glorious Lady came forth from the heavens with the blessed precursor and she deigned to show her desirable face to her handmaid. Indeed they had a very long conversation with me, but their words have slipped from my memory, driven out by my failings.

6. How the precursor of the Lord appeared to her again on the holy day.

On the feast day,[177] after the reading of the gospel, the man of God again deigned to present himself to me. When I had earnestly commended myself and the whole congregation of brothers and sisters to him, he responded to me in this way: "Convince them that through these things that the Lord has worked with you, they have been warned to strive to correct themselves in all things. The Lord has had compassion on them and will have yet more compassion, and I will be their willing helper." Having said these things, he was withdrawn from my sight.

7. How the angel of the Lord transported her to a pleasant meadow where she saw three girls walking. She learned from them

that they had been detained thirty years in that place of punishment and how they could be liberated.

Immediately the angel of the Lord transported me, and we came to a verdant and pleasant meadow. And behold, three pretty girls appeared there, walking near a river. They were in clothes not quite white, had no shoes on, and their feet were very red. As I wondered to myself who they might be or what they were doing here alone, they said to me, "Do not marvel. We are souls and had lived under the discipline of a rule, one of us from childhood, the other from adolescence, and the third from advanced age. Because we seemed to everyone to be of some goodness, when we departed from life we were aided by prayers less than was necessary. Although we could have been liberated within the course of one year if the services owed to us had been offered, now, behold, we have been detained here for thirty years. We do not endure any punishment other than the great fear we have of three frightful dogs who constantly seem to threaten to bite us. But if you would ask your abbot to offer the divine sacrifice to the honor of God for our liberation and that of all the faithful departed, we expect that we would very quickly be liberated and be able to cross over to the delights prepared for us." When I had disclosed this to our sisters, with devout intent they agreed to undertake together corporeal mortification for them and, having divided the Psalter among themselves, they prayed to the Lord with great diligence for the liberation of those women.

8. On the following day, the aforementioned girls appeared again to Elisabeth at the time of the sacrifice offered for them and they were led happily to the house prepared for them.

On the next day when the office of vigils was over, the lord abbot came and, at my advice, diligently celebrated the divine office for the faithful departed. At the time of the sacrifice, I was again transported to the place mentioned above, and those women again appeared there and looked as if they were going up the river with great speed against the current. Joining them, I inquired where they were from and what their names were. One of them answered for all: "It is too long to tell you all about ourselves, so let me briefly respond. We are from Saxony; I am called Adelheid. This one next to me is Mechthild, my sister in flesh as well as spirit. That one, Libista, is only our spiritual sister." Seeing that they did not want to delay, I didn't want to detain them any longer, but I did eagerly commend myself and our whole congregation to them so that when they would be received into the fellowship of the saints they would remember us. When they graciously promised this, they quickly proceeded on. And behold, on the path they were traveling, an angel of the Lord appeared before them in the likeness of a seemly youth. He went before them with great speed as if guiding them. When they had approached the building in which I frequently see blessed souls received, three venerable men came out, each holding a gold thurible in his hand, and they offered incense to each of the women. Soon their faces as well as their garments had been made whiter than snow by the smoke of the incense and they were led happily into the interior of that building.

9. Before the sacred Vigils of the apostles, she saw the prince of the apostles and she saw him a second time with Saint Paul; also, the kind consolation that she received from him.

After this I remained in continuous infirmity until the feast of the Apostles.[178] On the night preceding the sacred Vigils, the great extent of my illness so oppressed all my senses and I was so fatigued that the sisters around me expected nothing other than my death. But the angel of the Lord stood by me the whole night, and the prince of the apostles appeared to me adorned with great brightness. I was taking such delight in the vision that I forgot to think about the distress of my whole body, which those around me could not look upon without great sorrow. I remained in that bodily torment until about the sixth hour of the following day. The lord abbot was apprised of my sufferings, and he came to visit me. After he had invoked the Lord upon me and blessed me, I finally went into ecstasy and thus found rest. In my trance I saw the blessed apostles Peter and Paul gloriously crowned and enveloped in inestimable brightness, with palm branches in their hands. Looking at me, the prince of the apostles said, "What is more pleasing to you: to be tormented thus and enjoy our vision or to be free from vision as well as torment?" I said to him, "My lord, if it were possible with God's grace and yours, I would rather endure these sufferings than be deprived of your sweet consolation." "You have spoken well," he said, "Therefore from this time you will be troubled with less suffering in your visions." I asked him, "Lord, why did I undergo such great suffering now?" He responded, "You have been so gravely weakened for no reason other than that the miracle of sudden health may appear even more gloriously in you. Rise, therefore, and be healthy. Speak and guard your tongue from idle talk, and the Lord will give you wisdom and understanding."

When he had said this, I immediately drew my breath and said: "With God commanding, loose the chains of earth, Peter, you who make the celestial realms open to the blessed.[179] Saint Paul, apostle, preacher of truth, intercede for us to God who chose you."[180] And I added, "The Lord sent His hand and touched my mouth and filled it with the spirit of wisdom and understanding" (Jer 1:9; Eccl 15:5). Immediately after this, I rose from my bed and went out, healthy, with all my strength restored.

10. On the holy day at the canon of the Mass, she saw the sacred host changed into the true substance of flesh and blood and she saw the same princes of the apostles.

On the holy day at Mass, less tormented than usual, I again saw the apostles of Christ, and when the lord abbot was blessing the sacred host, I saw it changed into the true species of flesh and blood. When everyone had taken communion and the solemnity of the Mass was finished, one of the two angels whom I saw standing by the altar with a gold thurible in his hand was raised up to the apostles, whom I saw on high. Looking at blessed Peter I said, "Lord give us some sign by which we may understand if you deign to care anything about us." He immediately raised his right hand and blessed our place with the sign of the cross, and then he disappeared.

11. Again on the octave she saw the same apostles and the blessed mother of the Savior, whose face was averted, and she learned why from St. Peter.

Again on the octave of the feast of the Apostles[181] at the time of the sacred mystery, those glorious princes appeared to me. The blessed mother of our Savior appeared with them but not in her usual way. Indeed, she held her face away from me as if in indignation. Saddened, I spoke to blessed Peter, saying, "My lord, what is my iniquity that I am not worthy to see the face of my Lady?" He said, "Behold, you have become tepid in her service; and you do not devote yourself to the ministry owed to her like you used to. Now then, fulfill as devoutly as you can the vow that you swore to her. Also, ask your abbot to commemorate Mary in the divine office as he did on the preceding Saturday, so as to obtain that which you, together with your sisters, requested. He should do this a second and third time before the solemnity of the Assumption. In this way you will be pleasing in her sight."

Fearing that we had offended our Lady's benevolence with our communal negligence, we began to beseech her with our communal prayer. We prayed that she, who frequently used to show me her glorious face even without torment of my body but now had withheld it from me for many days, might not refuse me her customary grace. Also on this occasion I vowed that I would read seven Psalters to venerate her.[182] When these things had been said and the apostles had disappeared, I began in my usual way to look at and pay attention to the signs that the lord abbot was making above the sacred host during the canon, and I was expecting to see its transformation. The angel of the Lord said to me, "What you wish, you cannot see at all, but make confession of your sin, and you will see." He said this on account of the vanity of the nocturnal vision.

12. She saw our Lady again as before, with her face averted, and she received consolation about this from the angel.

After this, on the feast of the Translation of Saint Benedict,[183] when the principal Mass was beginning in the church of the brothers, I went into a trance and in the region of light I again saw our Lady with her face turned away as before. With her was that venerable father of our order. Looking at him, I earnestly called upon him so that by his intercession my Lady might deign to be reconciled to me. But at this I received no response from him. The angel of the Lord, however, stood by me and consoled me sweetly, saying, "Look—do not be sad about these things, because you will soon receive consolation from the Lord. Beg your abbot not to quit this undertaking, because it will be beneficial not only for you but for him as well. And the next time he celebrates the Mass of blessed Mary, you should receive holy communion from him." Having said these things, he departed, and I returned to myself.

13. She saw our Lady appeased and received a response from her about having offended her grace. Our Lady also pronounced a word of consolation about the lord abbot.

On the Saturday after this, when the lord abbot was celebrating the divine office with us, around the beginning of the Mass I was led into ecstasy after the struggles of my agony. And behold, my Lady deigned to look from the heavens at her handmaid with a serene and very pleasant face. I greeted her, saying, "Hail Mary, full of grace, the Lord is with you." And I added, "Most holy Lady, most merciful Lady, Queen of Heaven, may you deign to show me, a sinner, how I have offended your grace. Behold I am very willingly prepared to correct it and to please your mercy with every satisfaction." She responded, saying, "You have too greatly neglected me in your heart, and you do not strive to serve me with the devotion that you owe me. You have quickly laid aside that little bit of special service that you used to offer me." I replied, "Most merciful Lady, from now on if there is anything you might care for, how gladly would I offer it to you!" I also added, "Most pious Lady, is there anything troubling to you in the present worship service?" She responded, "Truly, I say to you, today there is the sweetest odor in the sight of the Lord." While she was saying these things to me, the ministers of the altar were singing with great devotion the chant "Ave preclara." And when they came to the versicle, "Pray, Virgin, that we may be made worthy of the bread of heaven," she seemed to turn to the east and pray on bended knee, and she remained like this until the beginning of the gospel reading.[184] After this again she turned to me, saying, "He is my chosen servant and for the service he has offered me on your behalf, he will receive recompense with you. And if he is ever in any need and cries out to me with his whole heart, he will find my help because he has carried out my service with a contrite and humble heart."

14. She saw the three liberated girls and spoke with them about their liberation.

On August 1, the feast of blessed Peter, at the time of the divine office, I was transported in spirit to that mansion of the blessed, which I was accustomed to seeing frequently. The three sisters mentioned above came to meet me, together with a splendid and very venerable youth. They looked at me with pleasant and glad faces, as if rejoicing in my arrival, and they repeatedly turned their faces to the companion of their journey as if asking him for permission to speak with me. He kindly nodded to them and said, "Speak with her and thank her for what she has so well negotiated with her abbot on your behalf." They said to me, "May the Lord God repay you because you have well fulfilled our request to your abbot. May the Lord grant him favor since he has helped us so much, for it seems to us that we could have been suffering distress forever." And I said to them, "Then in turn, repay him and the women of our monastery, by whose intercession you have been helped, so that at the time of their deaths they may deserve to come to the place of refreshment and peace." They replied, "Most gladly shall we entreat the Lord at all times for this."

15. The angel of the Lord bore her to a pleasant place and she rested under a tree where she saw Saint Peter and two beautiful virgins. From Saint Peter she received the message that Saint Lawrence expected a service from her abbot and then, borne away, she saw a certain monk in a quiet place.

Immediately after this, the angel of the Lord bore me to another place of most pleasant loveliness and set me under a tree that was completely covered with very pretty flowers. I said to him, "My lord, let's rest a little in this place." He said, "It's pleasing to me that you rest." Then I sat down in the grass and filled my hands with flowers, which were lying all around me. I held them close and inhaled their fragrance of marvelous sweetness. Although I was hoping to linger there longer, I saw at a distance a very venerable man coming toward us, accompanied by two most beautiful virgins. My lord, who was standing next to me, said, "Behold our lord, blessed Peter, is coming." I rose immediately and went to meet him.

Falling down before him, I humbly committed both myself and my loved ones to his protection. He kindly acknowledged this and said, "Tell your abbot that blessed Lawrence expects a service from him." I said to him, "And what can he expect from you, my lord?" He replied, "He can have considerable expectation from me and my fellow apostles for that devout service that he customarily offers us." After Peter had been borne away from me, the angel said to me, "Come and I will show you one of the brothers from your monastery." Then, in a place of refreshment, he showed to me a certain monk who was called Erminricus, and he said that another of our brothers, Gerard by name, would be coming soon to that same place.

16. The angel showed her a horrible place of punishments where there were souls of those who had brought death upon themselves.

Again the angel transported me from there to a place between two mountains, and he said to me, "Up till now you have seen the delights and the mansions of the just. Now look below—such is the place and punishments of the impious." And behold, I saw a great abyss where there were such dense shadows that I could not recognize anyone who was there. But I did note this: Their punishments surpassed all estimation. When I asked him who they were and if they could ever be liberated from there, he responded that they had brought death upon themselves and could never be liberated from that place. Repulsive-looking people were lying miserably around that mountain. I learned that they were souls who had been permitted to leave that abyss occasionally and rest there a little while. When I asked what would finally have to be done about them, the angel responded, "It belongs to the Lord alone to know what He might wish to do with them on the day of judgment."

17. He brought her to a high mountain with an extraordinary brilliance at its peak.

After this, he carried me up extremely high along the mountain and stationed me on the mountainside. While I was looking up to the summit, a brilliance of such great light appeared that I could hardly endure the sight of it. He said, "You began to climb this mountain three years ago, and you have come this far now. You will climb what is left and when you arrive at the summit, you will not regret all your struggles."

18. She heard a frightening voice from heaven on the feast of Saint Lawrence.

On the feast of blessed Lawrence,[185] I was led up to an incalculable height, and I heard a great and frightening voice from heaven saying to me, "I have visited you with My spirit, wishing to fulfill My will in you. I have begun and I will finish, never fear, because I the Lord have known from the beginning those in whom I delight to dwell. I have chosen you so that you would be insignificant in your own eyes because of your weakness, and I have established you as a sign to those who are stronger than you. I worked a great miracle in you and nobody recognized that I am good and show no partiality (Gal 2:6; Jas 2:9). But those who seek Me with their whole heart and love Me, I will love and manifest My very self to them. Alas, what shall be done about those who scandalize the ones in whom I must dwell? Indeed that ancient Deceiver has inspired certain people to be envious and disparage those whom I love, with the result that he entraps and ruins them. Truly I say to you: The more they have been harassed, the more splendid are they before Me. No one can grasp the words I speak and have spoken except one who is from Me. I the Lord created human beings in My image and likeness and I made them conscious of Me so that they may be wiser than all creatures. But they did not wish to remain like that; rather, inflated by the advice of the venomous serpent, they disdained Me and took his advice. Thinking that what he proposed looked good, they agreed. He taught them to rise higher, while he descended lower. And what then? What was lost by human disobedience one person regained by obedience to His Father. O human, hear and understand the words that you hear. Rejoice with Me because I found you and established you so that you could be My servant. I consecrated you and illuminated you and opened your eyes so that you could see by no other vision other than the knowledge that I have revealed to you. Now, therefore, pay attention to how you should repay Me because you have received unheard-of grace from

Me. You have seen, I declare. How have you seen? You have looked into My secrets, which are beyond human vision. And what have I hidden from you? Nothing. You have seen in your vision as if on a high throne three persons in one essence and power. And what else? In the midst and around the throne you have seen the holy ministers of God rejoicing in His secrets and blessing God in perfect praise. When you beheld that vision, to the right of the throne you saw the glorious Queen of Heaven, crowned with purest gold and robed in many colors; to the left, the holy cross by which you were redeemed, and the twenty-four elders sitting in their seats and falling prostrate before the throne of the one who lives forever. Then the holy apostles, martyrs, confessors and virgins, monks and widows, at whose sight you were frightened and even disturbed. Now do not waver any longer, but have faith in the Lord your God that all things indeed are possible for the one who trusts in God. You have seen these and many other visions at this time for no other reason than because of the unbelief of many and for the confirmation of the faith, and thus they were revealed to you during the divine mysteries. Therefore it is appropriate and necessary to reveal such visions, which appropriately contribute to the confirmation of the Christian faith. For many are called Christians, but few wish to follow the one from whom they have taken this name."[186]

19. Elisabeth saw the lord bishop Ekbert and her uncle Theodericus, and the uncle of her father, lord Helid, and the punishments in which they were being held.

Then he transported me to that great and delightful building that I was accustomed[187] to seeing very often. Among the many venerable bishops there, he pointed out one and said, "This is the lord bishop Ekbert, the uncle of your mother.[188] It has not been long since he has come to this place." On another day while I was in ecstasy, the angel showed me certain places of punishment. Among other things I saw what looked like a certain underground cave filled with fire and smoking horribly. While I was looking at it, what appeared to be a figure of a man came forth from it. Standing in the cave's entrance, he was burning from the violent fire blazing from within. I said, "Lord, who is this?" He said, "This is Theoderic, your uncle." Terrified, I said, "Can he ever be liberated?" And he said, "He can be liberated from the punishments that he now suffers if in memory of him and of all the faithful departed thirty Masses and thirty vigils are celebrated and thirty times alms are given." I asked if he could ever be fully liberated, and he nodded. The angel also showed me my father's uncle, lord Helid, whose mouth was violently tormented. The angel told me that he was being tortured in this way because of his habitual undisciplined speech. For although Helid was a God-fearing person, nonetheless he frequently used jesting words. When I became sorrowful over this, the angel said to me, "Why is it a surprise that they are tortured like this? They have no one to offer them a drink." And I said, "Lord, what kind of drink do they need?" "Hot tears," he replied, "must they drink."

20. She saw the two aforementioned souls and learned from her uncle how to liberate him.

Seven months after that vision, the angel showed me the aforementioned people who were now liberated from their torments. One of them, the last mentioned, was attractive in appearance and in a pleasant place, but not, however, in that perfect refreshment of blessed souls. The other, Theoderic, wasn't there. After many days he showed me my uncle Theoderic, who was now lying in a dry plain, looking as if he were very wearied and resting there. Examining his appearance, I asked my lord if I could have permission to speak with him, and he agreed. I said to him, "O sweetest soul, speak to me, I ask, and tell me what punishments you are now enduring." He responded, "I am tortured by the most severe hunger and thirst." Again I inquired, "Tell me, I beg, how can this torment be relieved?" He responded, mixing Latin and German words, "If someone would offer the bread of life and the cup of salvation for forty days on my behalf, I would be liberated from this torment and everything else would be more tolerable for me." Again I spoke, "Don't prayers other than the Mass that are dedicated for you come to your aid?" And he said, "Whatever is dedicated for me other than the bread of life and cup of salvation offers me as much value as when a starving person is refreshed not with bread and wine but with other foods."

21. On the feast of Saint Michael she saw an island where souls walked about and had a respite through the intercession of Saint Michael, and she inquired about the liberation of the soul of Count Rupert.

On the day before the feast of blessed Michael,[189] the angel lifted me up to a certain pleasant island, which appeared to be surrounded by burning water. I saw a countless multitude of souls walking on that island, and I asked the angel about them. He said, "These are souls who rest here for the whole night through the intercession of blessed Michael." I also heard a great wailing and extremely miserable moaning coming from the water surrounding the island. I asked where the soul of Count Rupert was.[190] My guide responded, "In such a place where he endures the most intense punishments." When I asked about his liberation, he gave me no response. However, I heard a voice from the side, coming from I don't know where, crying out and saying these words, "Frequent prayer very quickly liberates the soul. Seek this and give alms." I turned to my lord and said, "Do you have anything to say to me, my lord, that I may report to his wife, who is very concerned about him?" He responded, "Tell her what you have heard."

22. The announcement of her angelic guide about the liberation of the young cleric Gerard and the master Adam.

One day while my guide was with me, I questioned him, saying, "May it please you, lord, to make known to me about a certain young cleric, Gerard, who was a companion of my brother in Bonn. Where is he and what should be done about him?" Immediately he said to me, "He has been liberated. Do you wish to see him?" As soon as I nodded, he raised me up and led me to the blessed mansions of holy souls and there he pointed him out to me. He looked radiant and joyful. He also showed me that famous master Adam among the blessed souls, full of glory and joy, whom he said had been liberated in less than five years: "At the time he was liberated, one of his friends was promoted to the order of the priesthood."[191]

23. On the feast of All Saints, at the order of her guide she received holy communion although she had already decided against it.

After this on the feast of All Saints,[192] after a great bodily discomfort during the silent part of the Mass, the angel carried me away. While he was showing me certain hidden things in the customary way, I spoke to him in that trance and said, "Lord, why did I endure greater discomfort than usual?" He responded, "This was the cause: You were not intending to receive holy communion today." I said, "Lord! I was afraid to take communion because I had not sufficiently prepared myself. Moreover, I had recently taken communion on the feast of the apostles Simon and Jude."[193] Again he spoke, "And how are you ever able to do anything so good that you are rendered worthy of such a thing, unless you are made worthy by the grace of God? Therefore, we will now speedily return and you will go with the sisters to take communion." Immediately I returned to myself and it was already the time of communion. I took some water, arose, and did just as he had commanded me.

24. She saw the abyss and the holy hermits, Saint Paul the first hermit, and abbot Antony in great glory.

One day in Lent the angel carried me to a high mountain and stationed me on the mountainside. When I looked down from there, I saw a huge precipice and shadowy waters lying below. He said to me, "Here you see the abyss." As we proceeded toward the summit of the mountain, we came to a certain very beautiful door. Going through it, we found one even more beautiful than the first, and a third one more beautiful than the others. Crossing through the third, we found a great multitude of very beautiful people ardently rejoicing and praising God with a loud and joyful voice. At the arrival of my guide, they all appeared to bow their heads toward him. Of the song they were singing, these words alone have remained in my memory: "Praise and glory be to glorious God." I said to my guide, "Lord, whom are we seeing here?" He said, "They are the holy hermits who lived in the days of old." I asked where blessed Paul, the first hermit, was, and he pointed him out to me as the one having special glory among all the others. He also pointed out blessed Antony to me, and he declared that all of these people gaze at God face to face.

112

25. The carelessness that occurred one day in Easter week when the blood of the Lord was spilled, and how the priest was consoled most kindly by our Lady, the Mother of Mercy.

I will narrate the affair that disturbed us with great sorrow, but with the Lord being merciful, it had an ending full of consolation. One day in Easter week, we had gathered for the Lord's Supper and were about to come forward to take communion. It happened by chance that the priest who was at the altar, with a careless push of the chalice, poured out some of the Lord's blood upon the corporal. At that same moment I fell into ecstasy and saw the outcome of the whole thing. There were two angels standing near him, one to his right and one to his left. When the priest dissolved into most bitter weeping and stood there awaiting the arrival of the lord abbot, the angel that was at his right looked at me and said, "Comfort this brother because it was not his sins but another's that led this to happen." But he, not wanting to receive any solace, persevered in abundant tears for three days and withdrew himself from any consolation. On the morning of the third day, while it was just beginning to grow light, I went into a trance with great physical pain, and our Lady, the Mother of Mercy, appeared to me in the celestial light. When I had earnestly prayed for that brother, she said, "His groans and tears have ascended to me. Console him and tell him that he should straighten himself up for he has bent over too much. I know that he is my servant because he loves me and I love him. I will be his support in any need for which he invokes me with his heart." And I said, "Lady, what should be done with the corporal that is tinged with the Lord's blood?" She said, "It should be placed among the relics." This had already been done according to the mandate of our written customs.[194] I continued, saying, "What then if in the future someone secretly seizes the box of relics and treats that altar cloth disrespectfully, not knowing that it was suffused with the sacred blood?" She responded, saying, "Because it is His, the Lord will protect it."

26. The following year she had a vision about that corporal.

After many supplications had been offered to the Lord for this negligence, a year passed and Easter time was approaching again.

On Palm Sunday at the time of the divine office, I saw what looked like a linen cloth shaped like a corporal stretched out in the air above the altar. It was completely white except that in one spot it seemed to have a reddish stain about the size of a person's fingernail. I saw this vision each day of that week while Mass was being celebrated, but I saw that stain diminish more and more from day to day. In fact, on Easter day, that same linen cloth appeared whiter than snow and gleaming just as clothes that have been pressed with glass shine when they are illuminated by the sun, and I saw no trace left of that earlier stain. Therefore I asked the angel, who was standing by me at that moment, what he thought this vision might mean. He said, "Just as the little cloth that you see looks beautiful and clean, likewise the sin of carelessness that occurred here last year is purged in the sight of the Lord."

27. A vision on Easter day in which she saw our Lord Jesus.

On that same Easter day at the time of the divine office, I went into a trance and was led in spirit to a place where I met three men of great splendor and divine beauty. One of them, clothed in a very white garment, spoke to me, saying, "Do you believe that on this day I rose from the dead, true God and true human?" I responded to Him, saying, "I do, Lord, but if I do so less than perfectly, help me to believe more fully." Again He repeated the same words, saying, "Do you believe that on this day I rose from the dead, true God and true human?" A second time I responded as before, saying, "I do, Lord, but if I do so less than perfectly, help me to believe more fully." When He had asked the same thing a third time and I had responded to Him for a third time as before, He added, "Because you truly believe this, know that you will have a share in My resurrection."

28. On the feast of Saints Peter and Paul, the passion of Saint Peter was shown to her and she saw him glorified in great glory. A bird was also shown to her as a symbol of people who have the gift of tears.

On the feast of the blessed apostles Peter and Paul,[195] the passion of blessed Peter was shown to me in a vision of my spirit. I saw how he was hung on a cross with his feet pointed up and his head cast

114

downward. The angel of the Lord said to me, "Behold, you have seen what he suffered for Christ, and now you will see with what kind of reward he was repaid." And instantly he showed me that same person wonderfully glorified in heaven. With the attention of my heart turned toward him, I began to humbly pray, calling to mind two people close to me to whom God had given the gift of tears in their prayers. Among other things I said, "Help them, lord, that their tears may have the same effect that yours had in the sight of the Savior."[196] He immediately responded, saying, "I will use a comparison to show you what their tears have obtained and how they will be beneficial for them." Immediately I saw a lovely little bird, which was white except for its dust besprinkled wings. It was flying here and there by a small stream of water. After it had done this for a short while, it totally immersed itself in the water and washed itself with great care and was made as white as snow. Then it flew away and settled in a beautiful tree planted by the stream.

29. On the feast of the holy martyrs John and Paul, St. John the Evangelist and other martyrs appeared to her and he revealed the true day of his death.

On the feast of the blessed martyrs John and Paul,[197] a certain brother was celebrating the divine rites with us. Among the other collects, he said one about blessed John the Evangelist, because on that day his death is marked on the calendars. Then, during the secret of the Mass, that holy evangelist appeared to me with those two martyrs. Just as I had been advised by that brother, I questioned him about what it meant that his death was being proclaimed on this day. He responded to me with these words, "This is the day on which I entered by myself into the tomb, and it was an extraordinary miracle."[198] He did not say more. No one, however, on account of these words should judge that the church errs in celebrating this feast in the winter, since perhaps that change was made on account of the honor of the Lord's birth.[199]

30. All the apostles appeared to her on the Division of the Apostles, and it was revealed that on that day the bones of the apostles Peter and Paul were separated from each other.

On the feast of the Division of the Apostles,[200] all the apostles together appeared to me according to their usual kindness, but blessed Peter and blessed Paul appeared to stand apart from the others. I asked the angel, who was standing in my sight at that time, what that segregation of the two signified. He said, "On this day their bones were separated and this feast pertains especially to them." And I said, "Why is it then, lord, that they all appear to me?" He replied, "From their kindness they do this for you because the divine office is celebrated today for all of them together."

Third Book of Visions

1. The great vision that Elisabeth saw about a celestial city with a golden wall surrounding it, twelve doors, a tower, and a river flowing through its center, with two trees nearby. She also saw bright multitudes of holy angels all along the top of the wall, singing praises to the Lord.

The angel of the Lord took me in spirit to a place of great height and showed me the likeness of a certain marvelous and glorious city. This happened for the first time on the feast of Pentecost, a second time on the octave of that feast, and a third time on the feast day of the precursor of the Lord.[201] The city that I saw was encircled on every side by a golden wall and it was quadrangular in shape. It had twelve gates, with three on each of the four sides of the city wall. Each gate was made of four stones of the following variety: The lintels were of a heavenly color like sapphire, the thresholds were shining like crystal, and the door posts between the thresholds and lintels were red like fiery stones. But one gate, which was the center one of the three facing east, was different from the others because its door posts were not red but dazzling white and sprinkled all over with little bloody drops. I looked closely and saw certain letters delineated on the lintels of the gates. I asked my guide what they signified. "The names of all twelve apostles," he replied, "are written over each of the gates." All the gates were open, and I saw no doors in them.

Within the ambit of the wall there stood a certain magnificent tower, very tall, and it seemed to be nothing other than the purest light. Its brightness was just like the splendor of gold when struck by the sun, and I could not endure its sight for the profuse light flashing forth from it. The illumination of that city was not from the sun or the moon or from any other heavenly body; instead, the whole thing was richly illuminated by the splendor of the tower. At the top of the tower was seated a certain great and venerable Majesty, which in some ineffable way showed itself to me as single in substance and threefold in persons. A river of not great size ran down from the top of the east side of the golden wall beside the middle door, and with a gentle flow it wound through the center of the city. Next to the wall where the river descended stood two extraordinarily beautiful and lofty trees facing each other with the river between them. The angel of the Lord who was with me called them both the tree of life. The banks all along the course of the river were planted here and there with other trees of various species. They were lovely to look at, but the beauty of the twin trees of life surpassed all others.

I lifted my eyes to the height of the wall and behold, all along the top of the wall bright multitudes of holy angels were singing the praises of the Lord with earnest jubilation, and their harmonies resounded like all kinds of musical instruments together. I looked closely and took note of the beauty of the wall inside and out. Both on the inside and the out, from top to bottom on all sides, it was adorned with precious stones well arranged in rows and the gold of the wall shone forth between the rows of stones. The stones were of diverse kinds and great thickness, and their arrangement was thus: In the first row along the top of the wall were placed stones having a fiery redness, bright and flashing just like fire. In the second row down, the color was reddish but somewhat dark, like the red of blood. Those located in the third row had the appearance of pure heaven, like sapphire, and their color appeared a little brighter than those that were in the fourth row—just as the look of amethyst is in comparison to sapphire—and many of them looked as if they were scribbled in various places with little white lines. The lovely stones in the fifth row were of a most pleasing green, and there was a sixth row of stones that were white and glistening like precious pearls. In the seventh row under all of these were placed stones adorned by a variety of three colors so that they were a not uncomely black on the lower part, white as snow in the middle and red as blood in the upper part.

2. Elisabeth is taught by the angel and the precursor of the Lord about this vision of the city and the interpretation of everything she saw in it.

Having surveyed all these things, I was hoping to understand the mystery of this vision. I was instructed in the interpretation of all that I had seen in part by the angel, my guide, and in part by the precursor of the Lord. "The city that you have seen," said my guide, is a symbol of the Lord Savior. The golden wall is a sign of His most precious humanity; the tower of bright light from which comes all the light of the city represents the majesty of His divinity, which has deigned to be encircled by the constraints of human nature.

"The twelve gates are the twelve apostles through whose teaching the elect have access to knowledge of the truth that is in Christ Jesus and the communication of His blessed grace. There is no bar to hinder those who wish to enter through them. Thus these gates are perpetually open, and no doors of enclosure appear in them. The lintel stones in the gates shining with a heavenly color are a symbol of the pure contemplation by which these men of God were lifted up into heaven and spoke with God in heaven while they still sojourned on earth in the body. The radiance of the thresholds is the unstained life they lived among the people without quarrel and the shining examples of innocence they offered to many. The redness of the doorposts is the sign of the passions of soul and body that they endured in great patience. But the one that differs from the others in the whiteness of its posts is the beloved of the Lord, the evangelist who was not consumed by the passion of martyrdom like the others but was worthy to be set before the eyes of all the people of God for the example of his unbroken virginity. Yet the spirit of that saint did not fall short of martyrdom—he exposed his body to various kinds of death and many tribulations on account of the word of God and the testimony of Jesus, just as is indicated by the drops of blood besprinkling the whiteness of the posts. That you see the names of all twelve apostles written together over each door is a sign of their unanimity and harmony of teaching."

I turned toward the river of the city and the two high trees between which it descended and hoped to learn what significance they might have. Soon I received this response about them: "These things signify the distinction in the holy Trinity, since all the fullness of divinity dwells corporeally in Christ Jesus, whom this city represents. The twin trees of life are the two persons, Father and Son, and the river flowing down in the middle between them is the Holy Spirit, which is the shared pouring forth of both. This river waters and makes fertile all the children of the kingdom of God so that they may bear the fruit of good works, and the children of the kingdom are the verdant trees that you see planted everywhere along the banks of the river." Looking at the angels who were joyfully settled at the top of the golden wall, I wondered what could be the cause of such exaltation and so much joyful acclamation, and again he responded to my thought: "These are the ministering spirits who once were active around the humanity of the Lord Savior and busied themselves with diligent running about so that the work of human redemption could be performed. Now that their ministry is fulfilled, they rejoice in the Lord Jesus and in the salvation of His people."

After this, the precursor of the Lord was with us for a while on his feast day while I was seeing this vision for the third time. He began to speak to me saying, "Commend to memory everything that you have seen and heard, and tell the man who has been appointed to you in this matter to write down these things, for the Lord has not shown them to you without cause. More things like these will still be revealed to you in their time." Then he also began to interpret for me all the rows of gemstones that I saw set into the golden wall and with great diligence he instructed me, saying, "These are the diverse orders of the faithful who either adhered in faith to the Lord Savior while He lived in flesh upon the earth, or who faithfully awaited Him before His coming, or who after His departure from this world and up until the end of time have joined or will have joined in the union of His body. You see the stones positioned in the highest row that are fiery red and pour forth flashing light; these are the apostles of Christ and His holy disciples who loved Him with the greatest burning of charity and spread the rays of illuminating teaching throughout the whole world. As witness to the truth their lives were consumed in the outpouring of blood. Those that you see in the second row—red but less brilliant—are the holy martyrs who were not commissioned for the office of preaching in the church but who, worn away by countless sufferings, strengthened many souls in Christ by the example of holy endurance." Pointing to those that were of sapphire color and most like the clear sky, he said, "These are the holy patriarchs and prophets, servants of God, to whom the Lord spoke intimately in the Old Testament and abundantly revealed His celestial secrets. They walked in His presence with a perfect heart, sighing all the more for the celestial dwelling place, having gotten a fuller sight of it through the Holy Spirit." Looking at the stones that were similar to them but somewhat brighter and inscribed with white lines, he said, "These are the holy priests of the New Testament and the great confessors in spirit and life. Their color is also celestial, but their teaching is brighter than that of the prophets who came before. The inscribed lines marking them here and there designate their various writings, which have instructed the people of God and filled the church with a wealth of books." Under these were arranged, as was said, stones of pleasant greenness, which were agreeable to look at. The man of God said, "These are the ones who for love of eternal delight preserved uncorrupted the greenness of their virginity. Those who are right after them and have a whiteness like that of pearls," he continued, "refer to the faithful who, living in fear of the Lord, have soberly made use of this world, and those who through faithful penance have earned expiation from the pollutions of the world." He also gave the interpretation of those distinguished by three colors and positioned after the others. "Many," he said, "have been converted from shameful infidelity and criminal life to the catholic faith and have walked praiseworthily in the newness of holy life. They are clothed in such virtue that they do not even hesitate to pour out their blood for the testament of Christ. Thus these stones, variegated by three colors, namely, black, white, and red, are well suited to designate those people." After these words, the holy precursor of the Lord withdrew from me and, having received his blessing, I returned to myself.

3. After the course of a year, she again saw a vision of this city and
how it was constructed by the angels of the Lord, and again she
learned from the angel the meaning of the vision.

When the course of one year had elapsed, on the day of Pentecost I again saw in spirit a vision of the aforementioned city, just as
it was described above, and certain things in the area around it that
I had not seen earlier were shown to me. Facing the twelve gates in
the four city walls, I saw a countless multitude of angels who were
all diligently tending to a beautiful structure. With marvelous labor
they were building, as it were, twelve streets, one facing each of the
twelve gates. Some of them carefully and quickly carried stones
intended for the structure, and others received the stones and fitted
them into it. Some of the builders decorated those streets with
beautiful pavement, while still others constructed walls in such a
way that on both sides, that is, the right and the left, each road had a
high wall. All the stones used for the structure were bright and shining and variously colored according to the different kinds of precious stones. That variety in the walls as well as the pavement was
extremely delightful in appearance because the great light in the
city came out through the gates and suffused each stone with
immeasurable splendor. The structure was begun from the city
gates, and the roads that were being built inclined downwards
toward the lower paradise, but they did not yet reach it because the
work was still incomplete. I asked the angel of the Lord, who was
with me while I was seeing these things, what the meaning of this
vision might be. He said, "The souls of the elect are daily and constantly transferred by the hands of the holy angels from the places
of purgation to a place of rest where they are fitted into the supernal
city. Each is assigned its place there according to the order of the
blessed spirits that has been appointed by God, and each soul has a
brightness according to the quality of its merits. This is that structure, and the master of this whole operation is the archangel
Michael." I said, "Lord, when did the work on this building
begin?"[202] He replied, "On the day on which our Lord Jesus Christ
despoiled hell." He continued, saying, "Those streets will be built
as far as the lower paradise and will be finished on the last day and

then the lower paradise will be one with the higher. Glory and honor to God and our Lord. Amen."

4. On Christmas Eve and Christmas night, Elisabeth saw a vision about a virgin in the sun, crowned with the most splendid gold and holding a golden cup in her right hand, and she learned the meaning of this vision from the angel.

While we were celebrating the vigil of the birth of the Lord, around the hour of the divine sacrifice, I came into a trance and I saw, as it were, a sun of marvelous brightness in the sky. In the middle of the sun was the likeness of a virgin whose appearance was particularly beautiful and desirable to see. She was sitting with her hair spread over her shoulders, a crown of the most resplendent gold on her head, and a golden cup in her right hand. A splendor of great brightness came forth from the sun, by which she was surrounded on all sides, and from her it seemed to fill first the place of our dwelling, and then after a while spread out little by little to fill the whole world. However, next to that sun appeared a great and very dark cloud, horrible to see. While I was looking at these things, the cloud suddenly rushed upon the sun and darkened it and blocked out the sun's splendor from the earth for some time. Then the cloud receded from the sun and the earth was again illuminated by the sun. Moreover, I saw this happen repeatedly so that in this way the world was in turn darkened by the cloud and again illuminated by the sun. As often as that cloud approached the sun and blocked its light from the earth, the virgin who was sitting in the sun appeared to weep copiously, as if grieving much on account of the earth's darkness.

I saw this vision continuously throughout the day and all the following night while I remained awake in prayer. On the holy day itself, while the solemnity of Mass was being celebrated, the holy angel of the Lord appeared to me and I asked him what kind of vision it could be and what meaning it might have. About that virgin whom I most wanted to understand, he responded and said, "The virgin you see is the sacred humanity of the Lord Jesus. The sun in which the virgin is sitting is the divinity that possesses and illuminates the whole humanity of the Savior.[203] The dark cloud that intermittently blocks the brightness of the sun from the earth is the iniquity which reigns on the earth. This iniquity blocks the kindness of omnipotent God, which, with the mediating humanity of the Lord Jesus, provides for the human race. This iniquity also brings forth the shadows of God's anger on the earth. The fact that you see the virgin crying is similar to what you read about before the destruction of the first world. Because of the extent of human iniquity, God was touched inwardly with grief of heart and said, "I regret that I made human beings" (Gn 6:6). Just as it was in that time, so also in these days; the sins of humans have increased to the utmost and they do not consider how much God has done for them through the incarnation of His only begotten Son, whom they dishonor with the worst deeds. They vilely trample upon the benefits of His redemption and they do not give the thanks due to Him for all the pains that He suffered for their wicked deeds. Hence is the bitter accusation against them before the eyes of the terrible God. There is no joy now in the Son of Man for this generation of those who have enraged Him, and great is His regret about those who do not give thanks for His benefits. This is the lamentation of the virgin who cries in the face of the cloud. What you see illuminating the earth when the cloud withdraws from the sun is this: In the abundance of His mercy, God does not completely cease watching over the earth on account of His blessed seed, which is still preserved on earth. The golden crown that is on the head of the virgin is the celestial glory which through the humanity of Christ has been acquired for all who believe in Him. The cup in her right hand is the font of living water that the Lord offered to the world, teaching and refreshing the hearts of those who come to Him, saying, 'If anyone thirsts, let them come to Me and drink and from their belly shall flow living waters'" (Jn 7:38).

On the third day after this, the elect of the Lord, John the Evangelist, appeared to me in his usual way when the office of his Mass was being celebrated, and with him was the glorious Queen of Heaven. I questioned him, as I had been advised, and said, "Why, my lord, was the humanity of the Lord Savior shown to me in the form of a virgin and not in a masculine form?" He responded to my question, saying, "The Lord willed it to be done in this way so that the vision could so much more easily be adapted to also signify His blessed mother. For truly she too is the virgin sitting in the sun because the majesty of the most high God illuminated her fully, beyond all others who lived before her, and through her divinity descended to visit the shadows of earth. The golden crown that you saw on the virgin's head signifies that this illustrious virgin was born in the flesh from the seed of kings and rules with royal power in heaven and on earth. The drink in the golden cup is the sweetest and most plentiful grace of the Holy Spirit, which came upon her more abundantly than upon the other saints of the Lord. And she offers this drink to others when, at her intervention, the Lord makes His faithful ones sharers of this same grace in the holy church. The weeping of the virgin, moreover, is the constant appeal of this most merciful mother who always importunes her Son for the sins of the people of God. What I say to you is true, because if she were not restraining the wrath of the Lord with her constant prayer, the whole world would already have passed into perdition due to the abundance of its iniquity."

5. In the following year on Christmas night she had another vision in which she saw two stars and received a revelation about Origen, doctor of the church.

I saw another vision in the following year on the night of the birth of the Lord at the time of Matins. First, I saw two large and brightly shining stars standing a little distance from each other. They came together from their separate places in such a way that it was as if one body was made from them, like the sun shining in its strength (Rv 1:16), and around it was a bright tri-colored circle of red and green and sapphire. In the middle of this shining body I saw a woman sitting, gloriously crowned like a queen of great majesty, and she held a very beautiful and lovable young child in her lap. It was made known to me that this was our blessed Lady, the Virgin Theotokos. Throughout the whole time while the divine office was being celebrated that night, I saw this vision and so many others, but what was revealed to me in them must now be passed over in silence. In the third Mass our blessed Lady deigned to present herself to me nearer and more clearly than before, but without her child. Then, as

I had been advised by my brother, who was at that hour celebrating the divine office with us, I spoke to her, saying, "I beg you, my lady, may you deign to reveal something to me about Origen? He was a great doctor of the church, who honorably and lovingly wrote your praises in many places. Is he saved or not, since the catholic church condemns him for the many heretical things found in his writings?" To this she answered in this way, "It is not the will of God that much should be revealed to you about this. However, you should know that the error of Origen did not come from malice, but from the excessive fervor by which he immersed his thought in the profundities of holy scripture, which he loved, and in divine secrets, which he wished to scrutinize too much. On account of this, the punishment in which he is detained is not grave. Know indeed that for those honors that he offered me in his writings, a special light shines on him among the other souls on those special feasts in which my memory is celebrated in the church. However, what will be done to him on the last day is not to be revealed to you now, for the Lord wishes to keep this among His secrets."

6. She saw two women run toward each other and she described their comportment.
   One day at Vespers time, I was sitting and confessing to the Lord in psalms. My eyes were opened and I saw two women approaching each other on a plain. One of them walked humbly, with her gaze lowered to the ground, in very modest garments that barely touched the ground. The other, however, walked pompously with her neck extended (Is 3:16), wearing luxuriant and flowing garments that trailed far behind her footsteps. She held a drawn bow and, with a blunt arrow in place, she shot it with great force at the breast of the other woman. However, it turned back upon the one sending it with the same force with which it was shot. Again she shot a sharp arrow with greater force to the other's heart. This one stuck briefly, then was reversed, but with less force. On the third time, with the greatest force and all her strength she shot a hooked, flaming arrow at the area of her kidneys. This one stuck for a longer time, then fell slowly to the ground. The other woman, looking badly wounded, completely doubled over and seemed to indicate

the violence of her pain by her external bearing. After this, she seemed to strengthen gradually and finally, with all her strength restored, she attacked her adversary, and, lifting her heel, she strongly dashed her flat to the earth and victoriously trod her underfoot.

7. One Saturday, at the foot washing, she saw a snowy white dove circling throughout their house.

On a certain Saturday, while we were washing each others' feet according to the command of the Savior (Jn 13:14), I collapsed in ecstasy. I saw a white dove circling with a gentle flight throughout the whole house where we were sitting.

8. A revelation about the three heavens, which she received from the angel.

On Christmas, during the hour of the very solemn office, the angel of the Lord visited me according to his custom, and stood before me. Just as had been suggested to me by a more learned one, I questioned him, saying, "I pray, lord, that you may deign to point out to me the specific distinctions in the three heavens which the apostle indicated in scripture when it says that he was rapt up to third heaven" (2 Cor 12:2). And he responded to me, "I will say nothing about this to you now." After saying this, he immediately turned the conversation to something else.

On the third night after this when it was the feast of blessed John the Evangelist,[204] I was with the sisters who were chanting psalms at Matins. By chance it occurred to me to think about the words of the apostle about which I had questioned the angel. I began to pray to the Lord in my heart, saying, "Lord, if any benefit could come from this, I ask you to deign to make manifest to me that divine understanding that I have begun to seek." While I was turning this over in my heart, I suddenly conceived in my mind the whole understanding of the thing I had been seeking and I pondered within myself many words that I had previously not known. While I was greatly marveling at this to myself, I went into a trance and collapsed. And behold the angel of the Lord stood in my sight and said to me, "What you were seeking, I spoke to your heart."

When I asked him to repeat in order those things that he had made known to me, he said, "If you seek a spiritual understanding in your interrogation, then I will give it to you. Every just person who is filled with the Holy Spirit, just as Paul was, is the heaven of the Holy Spirit. Indeed, all just people may be compared to one heaven because there is one heart and one soul in them and one spirit rules them. Paul was the heaven of the Holy Spirit, who lived in his heart and worked this in him so that he would be the throne of God, and the same Spirit led him to the heaven of heaven. What was this heaven of heaven? The Son of Man. Who was this Son of Man? Our Lord Jesus, who is the fullness of heaven, to whom Paul was led by the Holy Spirit so that he might believe in Him with such strength and cling to Him with such love that he would even give his body over to death for His name. That same Spirit, whom I just referred to, carried him up to the third heaven. What was that third heaven? The divine majesty. He so deeply immersed his heart and mind in it that he was even worthy to hear secret words that a person may not speak. It is impossible for a person to hear and speak them, but the Spirit of God can speak and hear them."

I said, "Lord, explain to me his words, 'Whether in the body or out of the body, I do not know; God knows'" (2 Cor 12:2). He said, "The Holy Spirit led Paul's spirit to such a profundity of divinity that his body was immobile at the time." Then I said, "My lord, I would like for you to put this more clearly." He said, "What I have said, you yourself have frequently experienced. Sometimes it happens to holy people that their spirit, which vivifies the carnal senses for sensing those things that are external, is swept inward to spiritual things with such great force that it leaves the body without sense or motion, and then one cannot discern whether one's spirit is in the body or out of it. In such a way was Paul rapt when he ascended in spirit to the third heaven."

Again I spoke, saying, "He also attests, lord, that he was rapt into paradise (2 Cor 12:4). What is that?" He said, "Paul was rapt to the paradise of paradises and the heaven of heavens. This is the sublime majesty of God and in the shadow of His wings every pure heart can have hope (Ps 56:2). Indeed, He has four wings. Two are grace and justice. Justice, which came under the time of the Law, orders and harshly reproaches. And what is grace? The Son of God, whom the Father sent into the world, not so that He might judge the world, but so that the world might be saved by Him (Jn 3:17). There are also two wings that are still to come: truth and judgment."

When he had said these things, he was withdrawn from my sight. When morning had passed, I sat apart with a sister who wrote this down. And when I was doubtful about certain words, he again came, and standing in the same spot as before, he called everything back into my memory.

9. The revelation she received from the apostle Paul about the Greek people who do not believe in the procession of the Spirit from the Father and the Son.

On the feast of Saint Paul the Apostle,[205] when he had appeared to me, I addressed him saying, "My lord, I would like to ask you something, if with your grace I may." He said, "Ask and I will tell you what you wish." Just as I had been advised, I said, "Lord, we have heard that the Greeks, whom you taught, do not believe in the procession of the Spirit from the Father and the Son—is this their damnation?" And he said, "Without doubt, those who do not believe this and remain in this infidelity till the end cannot be saved. Nevertheless, this is mostly done through ignorance. Many, however, have been converted from this infidelity and many will still be converted since the Lord has His seed among those He is disposed to save. I taught them the catholic faith, but they have given themselves over to error."

10. Elisabeth is taught by the apostle about the saying in his Letter to Romans that in the gospel righteousness is revealed from faith to faith.

On the feast of Paul's Conversion,[206] I was planning to ask—if by chance the apostle should deign to reveal his presence to me— how to understand when he said in the Letter to Romans, that in the gospel, righteousness is revealed from faith to faith (Rom 1:17). While we were celebrating Vigils and singing the morning praises to the Lord, the scripture passage I wanted to inquire about came into my mind by chance, and immediately God placed these words on my lips: "Abraham believed, before the Law was given through Moses, when he saw three and worshiped one (Gn 18:2). Abraham believed in God and it was reckoned to him as righteousness (Gn 15:6; Rom 4:3); the prophets believed and they were justified when they proclaimed to the people that Christ would be born of a virgin. But when He came, what did it avail most of them? They saw Him enclosed in mortal flesh; they saw and nailed Him to a cross. They did not see Him as He had been before, and as He was after, when the Father gave Him every power in heaven and on earth (Mt 28:18). Blessed are those who saw and believed. And we believe that we will see Him, just as He is. We are justified by faith and assured that we will enjoy eternal beatitude and reign with Christ without end and behold the face of God.

"Paul wrote in his letter that in the gospel the righteousness of God is revealed from faith to faith. Understand this according to what I tell you. In the gospel it is proclaimed: 'Unless one is reborn by water and the Spirit, one cannot enter into the kingdom of God' (Jn 3:5). This is the beginning of the Christian faith and its righteousness. It also says: 'Whoever believes in the Son of God will have eternal life. But whoever does not believe in the Son will not have life'" (Jn 3:36).[207] And this was added in conclusion: "These things have been written so that you might believe that Jesus Christ is the Son of God and that believing, you might have life. This is the righteousness from faith that is revealed in the gospel. Through this will one live who is righteous by faith, as it is written: 'And the righteous shall live by faith' (Rom 1:17). And those who live that righteousness which is from faith will live a perfect life, since they will see eye to eye what they now believe as if through a glass (1 Cor 13:12). We are in faith now, but when we see what we now discern as if through a glass, then we will be from faith to faith."

After these words, that doctor of the Gentiles showed his face to me and I asked him about the aforementioned scripture passage because I did not fully trust my own understanding. He responded to me, saying, "What you seek from me, you do understand." At the same hour my lord also stood by me and he said to me, "I am not worried that the apostle may contradict those things that I have spoken to your heart." I added this question, saying to him, "Lord, is that certainty which we shall have in the future also to be called faith?" He responded, saying, "The faith you have now is commingled with hope. In that final peace, where you will reign with Christ, you will have faith with knowledge."

11. Elisabeth sees the lord bishop Ekbert and confers with him about the souls of the dead.

It was the commemorative anniversary of lord Ekbert of venerable memory, the bishop of Münster.[208] While we were celebrating the office of the faithful departed for him, he appeared to me wearing the insignia of episcopal dignity, and shining with great brilliance. I addressed him and said, "Lord, are you aware of the kind of grace that the Lord has bestowed upon me, and how He has deigned to work in me?" He answered me, saying, "I know these things, most beloved, and meditate upon them even more deeply than you yourself." And I asked him, "Lord, do souls already taken into peace receive any advantage from the prayers and Masses celebrated by the faithful in their memory?" He said, "They are most grateful that these services are offered for them and their joy is further enlarged because they know that these things help the healing and liberation of souls still detained in punishment. For divine services offered by the living for any soul already at peace are more pleasing to those who are already consoled, and they do more for the common improvement of the souls who are in purgatory than those intended for any soul who is not yet released." I responded to this, saying, "Do the souls who are at rest pray for their loved ones and family who are still in the world?" "They do," he replied. I said, "I ask you, most beloved lord, to remember me in your prayers, as well the other kin you have in this dangerous world." And he responded, "I do this unceasingly."

12. The angel shows her a pit full of fire and the souls in it, which she learns are the souls of those killed in the excommunicated army.

At a certain time the angel showed me a great pit, full of horrible fire, and there I saw certain souls most severely tortured. I asked him who those souls were, and why they were so harshly tortured.

He said, "They are the souls of those who were killed in warfare while excommunicated."[209] I asked him, "Lord, should any prayers be offered for them?" He said, "No prayers should be offered especially for them, but anyone who wants to come to their aid may offer pious assistance for all the faithful departed together. And when for their sake all faithful souls are gladdened, these souls will have something more tolerable."

13. She receives a revelation from the angel about the proper understanding of the high orders of Seraphim, Cherubim, and Thrones, who, when the work of our redemption was completed, met the Lord Jesus at His ascension, saying, "Who is this who comes from Edom," etc.

A certain brother proposed a question to me that had this form. "It is written," he said, "in the book of the theologian Dionysius the Areopagite that those celestial beings who are higher than all others, namely, the Seraphim, Cherubim, and Thrones, are called the first hierarchy. They are introduced in scripture alone first, but afterward with Jesus. Questioning Him, they gained knowledge of His divine action for us, saying, 'Who is this who comes from Edom, with dyed garments from Bosra?' (Is 63:1). After His response, they said, 'Why then are your garments red and your clothes like those who trample in a winepress?'" (Is 63:2). Then the brother who raised this question inquired closely about these words, saying, "If, as Dionysius asserts, those high orders were asking such things as if eager for knowledge and desiring to be instructed by the Savior about the action of human redemption, it follows that they were at first ignorant of what they desired to learn. But how could it be that, with the work of redemption already done, they still would not have had knowledge of it, when they were closest to the divine majesty and drank from it the full plenitude of knowledge, and poured out their knowledge to all the lower orders? How could this be, when it may be seen from the scriptures that many spirits of the lower orders knew about the Son of God in flesh and long since foreknew the grace of redemption? And how could the Holy Spirit hide such business from them for so long which even the prophets, who were human, had made known many times before?"[210]

Therefore, on the feast of the Annunciation,[211] I presented this question to my lord when he appeared to me, and I received this response from him. "Those high orders about which you ask were aware of the secrets of the Lord from the beginning; they knew that He would be made flesh and suffer for the redemption of humankind. But those things that they first knew by instruction of the Divinity, they also were pleased to ask about and learn from that sacred Humanity of the Savior as He was received into heaven, and to have that Humanity as teacher of religious truth. And what they had learned in mysteries, they also wished to have expressed in words." He continued, saying, "They are the ones through whom the secrets of God are made manifest to us who visit this lower world. They receive every illumination of teaching from the Lord without any intermediary and communicate this knowledge to us." He further added, "Recently, when you asked me origin of the words of the letters that you have been spontaneously uttering, do you remember what I responded to you? I said that I received them from the heart of the living God and spoke them to your heart. You should therefore understand it in this way: Those higher spirits received them from the heart of God, and I received those things from them, and thus I received them from the heart of God through intermediaries."

14. On Easter day she received a revelation from the angel about whether the bodies of saints who arose with the Lord remained with Him or returned to the state of death.

On the day of the Lord's resurrection, I addressed my lord with this question: "Lord, in the gospel it is written, 'Many bodies of the saints who had gone to sleep arose' (Mt 27: 52). Did they arise immediately at the hour of the earthquake that occurred at the time of the Lord's death, or on the day on which the Savior rose from the dead?" (Mt 27: 51–53) He said, "When the Lord arose, they also arose from the dead." Then I said, "And did they again return to death?" He responded, "The Lord deigned to honor them by raising them up with Himself. He likewise honored them by preserving them immortal."

15. It was revealed to her how those angels, who were invisible spirits by nature, could be seen by human beings with their bodily eyes.

I continued to question him in this way: "Lord, how could it be that you, who are a spirit of invisible nature, can also be seen by human beings with their bodily eyes? For example, we read about the holy women who went to the tomb of the Lord and testified that they saw visions of angels there" (Lk 24:4). He responded in this way, "Just as once the Lord was able to transform himself so that Abraham could see Him in three persons—when he saw three and worshiped one (Gn 18:2)—likewise, it is also possible for us, who are spiritual creatures, to take on such forms that enable us to be seen by human beings when it is pleasing to the Lord. For just as God in His divine nature can in no way be seen by human beings while they are in the flesh, so it is also for us. In our spiritual essence we can in no way be seen either by the physical or the spiritual eyes of human nature unless we take on such a form that your weakness can recognize."

16. She narrates the revelation she received from the angel about the first apostate angel, who for a long time had stood out in the glory of his creation. Also whether one order of angels fell with him or if some angels who stood out in each of the nine orders fell with him and about the dignity of Saint Michael the Archangel.

As we were celebrating the memory of Saint Michael on his feast day,[212] while we were standing to listen to the divine office, I, Elisabeth, grew somewhat faint and, losing my strength, sat down. And behold the angel of the Lord, in his customary kindness, made himself visible to my sight, and I said to him, "I would like to ask something from you, my lord, if it could be done with your favor." Looking at me with a cheerful expression, he immediately said, "I know what you are going to ask. Ask, and I will answer you." Just as I had been advised beforehand by a more learned one, I said, "I would like to know, my lord, about the angel who first apostatized. Did he immediately fall at the moment of his creation, or did he remain in the glory of his state for some period of time and then lose it by falling?" He responded, "Know that among all the creatures fashioned by God, that angel was created of the highest beauty and dignity so that after God, he alone surpassed all creatures in glory. Indeed, he continued in this dignity for some time, until he considered his own excellence and understood that there was nothing like him in creation. On this account, he lifted himself up in pride and reckoned that he was even equal to God. But when that pride arose in his mind, immediately he was cast down, because pride could not last for even a moment in heaven, nor will it ever be able to get close to it. Moreover, as lofty as he was over all other creatures, so much the lower was he thrown down below them and made more vile than the rest."

Again I questioned him, saying, "My lord, did one whole order of angels fall with him or did some from each of the nine remaining orders fall so that a tenth order was created?" He responded, saying, "One choir of angels, which was especially devoted to him because of the outstanding glory of their prince, rose up against us and judged themselves to be worthier than the other brothers. For this reason, they deserved to be thrown down together with their prince. We, however, who stood apart from those falling down, were inflamed with such a fire of love for the Creator, that we did not wish, nor were we ever able, to dissent from His will in anything." Again I continued, saying, "And who has primacy among you?" He answered, "Michael the Archangel."

Since I was unclear about this response, the next day, when the angel was present with me, again I questioned him, "Lord, does Michael the Archangel have primacy over all nine orders of blessed spirits or only over some of them?" He replied, "He has authority over the two orders of angels and archangels." When I again queried him about primacy, he said that the Cherubim and Seraphim are the most excellent of all and the closest to God. Then I asked whether, as the Church thinks, Michael the Archangel is the universal prince and defender of the people of God, and he affirmed that such is the case.

17. She received an explanation of the words Moses spoke, "When the Most High divided the people."

I also asked the angel to explain to me those words that Moses spoke, saying, "When the Most High divided the peoples, when He separated the children of Adam, He established the boundaries of the peoples according to the number of children of Israel or of the angels of God" (Dt 32:8). He responded to me with these words, "The children of Israel, about whom you ask, were created by God to be as numerous as the angels. When the angels fell through pride, God established the boundaries, that is, the numbers, of people according to the number of children of Israel who had fallen."[213] He also added, "Tell this to your brother, and then tell me whatever he asks." Therefore, I inquired another time about the above verse, which is, "When the Most High divided the peoples, when He separated the children of Adam." How should it be understood in light of the meaning that he had explained? He immediately said, "God also did this. When the first person was thrown out of paradise for disobedience, and when Cain killed his brother Abel, God separated the children of Adam and divided the peoples by separating the sheep from the goats. And then He established the boundaries of the peoples according to the number of the children of Israel." I immediately replied, "Lord, isn't it written that on the last day He will separate the sheep from the goats?" (Mt 25:32). And he said, "He already began it then, and He will finish it on the last day."

18. She was taught by the angel that angels didn't fall from each order, and he said that every person has his or her own angel.

It was reported to us that a certain brother wanted to oppose the message of our angel that one whole order of angels fell. This brother tried to prove that such was not the case. Instead, he believed that some from each order fell, based on the words of the apostle in the Letter to the Colossians about our Savior, "Despoiling the Principalities and Powers, He confidently led them out of hiding, triumphing in himself" (Col 2:15). Because the apostle here calls certain principalities and powers evil spirits, it seems that they had fallen from the orders of Principalities and Powers. When I consulted my lord about this, he said that there are very many diverse kinds of evil spirits and some are more conspicuous and more powerful for doing harm than others, and for this reason they are called by different names. Moreover, he added, "Let no one for any reason convince you and make you believe that some angels fell from each order. If indeed that were the case, then, when the fall of the lapsed angels is finally restored by the elect human beings, humans would have to be intermingled among the individual orders of angels. But this will not be, because the order of elect human beings will reside separately in its own place in heaven."

I also asked about the truth of the opinion by which we believe that all human beings have their own angels as guardians of their lives. He responded to my question by saying, "On the day on which the grace of holy baptism is received, a person gets two angels: one good and the other evil. A person is always attacked by one but defended and helped by the other." I responded by asking, "Lord, is an angel who is now the guardian of one person who is dying, made the guardian of another person who is about to be born?" He said, "Sometimes it happens in that way, but sometimes not." And when I referred to the souls of the dead, he elaborated by saying, "Twice a year, a soul, which at some time is going to obtain mercy even if it is still suffering punishment, may be visited by its own angel and receive consolation from it, namely, on the feast of Saint Michael the Archangel and on the day on which the common memory of all the faithful departed is celebrated."

19. A letter of Elisabeth sent to lady Hildegard, mistress in Bingen, in which she relates how she has been visited by divine grace and tells about the vengeance to come upon the world, which the Lord revealed to her.[214]

To lady Hildegard, venerable mistress of the brides of Christ who are in Bingen, devout prayers with all my love, from Elisabeth, humble nun. May the grace and consolation of the Most High fill you with joy, because you have had kind pity for my disquiet, as I have understood from the words of my consoler, whom you earnestly reminded of my consolation.[215] Just as you said that it had been revealed to you about me, I truly confess that I have recently harbored in my mind a certain cloud of anxiety on account of the many senseless, untrue words people are saying about me. Now the words of the public I could easily endure if also those who walk in the habit of religion would not also bitterly afflict my spirit. For they too, spurred by I don't know what goad, mock the grace of the Lord in me and do not fear to judge rashly about matters of which they are ignorant. I also hear that certain people are circulating letters of the same spirit written in my name. They declare that I have prophesied about the Judgment Day, which indeed I have never presumed to do, since its coming eludes the knowledge of all mortals. But let me reveal to you the circumstance of this rumor so that you may judge whether I said or did anything presumptuous in this matter.

As you have heard from others, the Lord has magnified His mercies in me beyond what I deserved or could ever deserve in that He has deigned frequently to reveal certain celestial mysteries to me. Indeed, through His angel He has frequently indicated to me what would happen to His people in these days unless they do penance for their iniquities, and He ordered me to announce this publicly. But to avoid arrogance and not look like an author of novelties, I tried to hide these things as much as I could. Therefore, on a certain Sunday while I was in a trance, the angel of the Lord came to me in his usual way and said, "Why do you hide gold in the mud (Mt 25:25–26)? This is the word of God, which was sent to earth through your mouth not so that it would be hidden, but so that it would be made manifest for the praise and glory of our Lord and for the salvation of His people." Having said this, he lifted a whip above me and five times he struck me sharply with it, as if in great anger. Thus for three days my whole body languished from that beating. After this, he placed his finger on my mouth, saying, "You will be silent until the ninth hour, at which point you will make manifest those things that the Lord has done to you." Therefore I remained mute until the ninth hour. Then I signaled to the mistress to bring to me a certain little book that I had hidden in my bed and that contained in part those things the Lord had done to me. When I placed this in the hands of the lord abbot, who had come to visit me, my tongue was loosed in these words, "Not to us, Lord, not to us, but to your name give glory" (Ps 113B:1). After this, I also revealed certain other things to him that I had not wanted committed to writing, namely, about the Lord's great vengeance, which I had learned from the angel was soon to come upon the whole world. Then I most earnestly begged him to keep this conversation to himself. Instead, he ordered me to pray and to seek from the

Lord an understanding about whether or not He wished me to cover with silence those things I had told him.

When for some time I had been prostrating myself in constant prayer about this matter, during Advent, on the feast of Saint Barbara,[216] at first Vigils of the night, I fell into ecstasy, and the angel of the Lord stood by me saying, "Shout strongly and cry 'Alas' to all the peoples, because the whole world has been transformed into darkness. And say, 'Go! The One who formed you from the earth has called you and He says, "Do penance, for the reign of God is at hand"'" (Mt 4:17). Excited by this message, the lord abbot began to spread the word in the presence of the magistrates of the church and religious men. Some of them heard the words with reverence but some did not, instead speaking perversely about the angel who is close to me, saying that he is a mocking spirit and has been transformed into an angel of light (2 Cor 11:14). Therefore, a teacher bound me through obedience to adjure him—if he should appear to me again—through the name of the Lord to reveal to me whether he was a true angel of God or not. But I thought this was presumptuous and received the order with great fear. Then one day, while I was in a trance, the angel presented himself to me in his usual way and stood in my sight. Trembling, I said to him, "I adjure you through God the Father and the Son, and the Holy Spirit, to tell me directly if you are a true angel of God and if the visions I have seen in my trance and the things I have heard from your mouth are true." He responded, "Know for certain that I am a true angel of God and the visions you have seen are true and the things you have heard from my mouth are true and will truly happen unless God is reconciled to the human race. And I am the one who has for so long worked with you."

After this, on the vigil of Epiphany,[217] while I was praying, again my lord appeared to me, but he stood at a distance with his face turned away from me. Understanding his indignation, I said to him with fear, "My lord, if I annoyed you when I adjured you, do not, I beseech, blame me. I beg you—turn your face to me and be merciful, since I was bound by obedience to act and I did not dare transgress the command of my instructor." After I had poured out many tears with words like this, he turned to me and said, "You have acted contemptibly toward me and my brothers by your lack of trust in me. From now on, know for certain that you will no longer see my face nor hear my voice unless you placate the Lord and us." I said, "My lord, how can you be placated?" He said, "Tell your abbot to celebrate devoutly the divine office in memory of me and my brothers." So when the solemnity of the Mass had been celebrated for the honor of the holy angels, not once but many times by the lord abbot as well as by the other brothers, and likewise when the sisters had honored them by reading psalms, my lord again appeared to me with a calm face and said to me, "I know that you acted in charity and obedience. For this reason you have found mercy and from now on I will visit you more frequently than before."

After this, the lord abbot arranged to go to a certain place at the request of the clergy staying there. He was to preach the Lord's word of warning to the people so that perhaps they might do penance and avert the wrath of God from themselves. But first he set about to pray to the Lord, together with all of us, that He might deign to reveal to His handmaid whether or not that sermon which he had already begun to make public should be further divulged. While he was celebrating the divine mystery and we were most devoutly praying, suddenly the joints of all my limbs were loosened and I languished and went into a trance. And behold, the angel of the Lord stood in my sight and I said to him, "My lord, remember what you said to me your handmaid, that the word of God was sent to earth through my mouth not so that it could be hidden but so that it would be made known for the glory of God and for the salvation of His people. Tell me now what should be done about that word of warning that you have spoken to me. Has it been made sufficiently known or should it still be preached?" Looking at me with a severe expression he said, "Do not test God (Mt 4:7); indeed, those who test God shall perish. And say to the abbot, 'Do not fear, but finish what you have begun. Truly blessed are those who hear the words of your exhortation and keep them and are not scandalized by you.' Moreover, advise him not to change the form that he has used so far in his preaching. Indeed, in this I have been his counselor. Tell him that he should in no way pay attention to the words of those who, out of envy, speak with doubt about the things that were done to you. Rather, he should attend to what is written, that nothing is impossible with God" (Mt 19:26).

Encouraged by this speech, the abbot went to the place he had planned to visit. He exhorted the people, who were awaiting his arrival, to do repentance, announcing the wrath of God about to come upon them unless they tried to prevent it by works of penance. In some of his preaching he did describe what kind of plagues were threatening the earth, but not at all like he was said to have done. Therefore many people among whom that sermon was proclaimed afflicted themselves with penance in great fear throughout the whole time of Lent, and zealously persevered in almsgiving and prayers. At that time someone, led by I don't know what zeal, sent letters to the city of Cologne in the name of the lord abbot, although—God knows—he was ignorant of it. In these letters, certain terrible threats were read with everybody listening. Thus, although it may have been a joke from our own foolish ones, nevertheless, prudent people, so we have heard, reverently heeded the sermon and did not disdain to honor God with works of penance.

It happened moreover that on the Wednesday before Easter, when I came into ecstasy with great bodily struggle, the angel of the Lord appeared to me. I said to him, "Lord, what will be done about that message that you spoke to me?" He responded, "Do not be sad or disturbed if the things I predicted do not come to pass on the day I had indicated to you, because the Lord has been appeased by the amends made by many." On Friday after this, around the third hour, I went into a trance with severe pain. Again the angel stood by me and said, "The Lord has seen the affliction of His people and has turned the wrath of His indignation from them." I said to him, "But then, my lord, won't I be scorned by everyone to whom this message was revealed?" He said, "You must endure patiently and with good will everything that will happen to you on this occasion. Take diligent heed of that One who, although He was the Creator of the whole world, endured the mockeries of human beings. Now the Lord is testing your patience for the first time."

Behold, my lady, I have explained to you the whole order of the affair so that you may know the innocence of both myself and our abbot, and so that you can make it known to others. I beg you, moreover, to make me a partner in your prayers, and that as soon as the Spirit of the Lord prompts you, write back to me with some words of consolation.

20. Another letter sent to Hildegard.[218]

Rejoice with me, my lady and venerable daughter of the eternal king, since the finger of God writes in you so that you may proclaim the word of life. Blessed are you and may it be well for you forever. You are the organ of the Holy Spirit because your words enkindle me like a flame touching my heart and I burst forth in these words.

21. She greatly commends Hildegard and expounds to her about the leaders of the church and the Cathars.

My lady Hildegard, rightly are you called Hildegard because the stimulus of God works well in you with marvelous fortitude for the edification of His church.[219] Be strong in the Holy Spirit. Blessed are you, for the Lord has chosen you and has appointed you like one of those about whom He said, "I have appointed you so that you may go and bring forth fruit and your fruit will endure" (Jn 15:16). In this way you enter the path of contemplation of the Lord like a dove in the clefts of the rock, in the hollow in the wall (Sg 2:14). The One who chose you will crown you with the crown of gladness. The way of the Lord is made straight in your presence. O lady Hildegard, carry out the work of the Lord, just as you have done so far, because the Lord has placed you as worker in His vineyard (Mt 20:1). Indeed, the Lord sought workers in His vineyard, and He found them all idle because no one leads them. The vineyard of the Lord does not have a cultivator; the vineyard of the Lord perishes; the head of the church languishes and its members are dead. Alas, what should be done about this, since the Lord finds few in His church who contemplate this with a blazing mind, but instead finds only those who wish to rule themselves and follow their own will. The Lord has tested them and found them sleeping. On account of this a thief has come and broken in and destroyed the foundation stone, and thrown it in a cistern that had no water and was not irrigated. The foundation stone is the head of the church that was thrown away. The church of God is arid, having no moisture, and it is cold in love for God. But I also recall to myself that once there appeared to me poisonous serpents about to come into the church of God, secretly hoping to destroy God's church.[220] I understand this to refer to those Cathars who are now secretly beguiling the church of God. Expel them, Lord, our protector! And blessed is the one who will not be scandalized in this time. The patriarch David said, "Will those who sleep not rise again?" (Ps 40:9). Arise and be stirred and keep watch because the vengeance of God shouts to you! Shriek, pastors, and cry aloud! Sprinkle yourselves with ashes and repent (Jer 25:34)! Don't give place to the devil (Eph 4:27), because like a roaring lion he circles, seeking what he may devour (1 Pt 5:8). Blessed is the one who fears the Lord of all creation and thus agitates the high priest so that he will remove the opprobrium from his people (Is 25:8) and all Israel will be saved.

22. She expounds to Hildegard about their contempt for the Lord and His saints.

Now, moreover, My people are perverse to Me, and stiff-necked they walk in My presence, and they do not think about how to bear My judgment: with flagellation and offerings to Myself and My saints who daily cry before My throne, saying, "Lord, king of eternal glory, in your speech all things are ordained and there is no one who can resist your will. Avenge our blood (Rv 6:10), because the earth oppresses us with their contaminations." I the Lord, Creator of all creatures, have sent My incarnate Word from the heights of the heavens into the dark valley so that it would illuminate those who were in shadows and who thought they were something but were nothing. And the people loved the shadows more than the light. But this was the true light and like the morning star in the midst of fog (Eccl 50:6), and like the sun shining in its strength in the middle of the day (Rv 1:16), so did He shine in the midst of His people, full of wisdom and fortitude, and the whole earth was filled with His teaching, yet you have forgotten Him. I swear by My right hand and My throne that this will no longer be.

23. She turns her sermon to the people of God.

O human, whoever you are, what reason can you use to excuse yourself? You have eyes and you do not see, and ears for hearing and you do not understand. What more shall I do for you? If you lose Him, who do you think is going to redeem you? Remember that the only Son of My heart died once for your sins and arose and ascended into heaven and sits in His glory and left you a model so that you could follow His footsteps. How, by what heart, or by what knowledge, do you follow Him? Far indeed are His ways from your ways. If you will not walk like He walked, how can you come to Him? Do not turn aside to the right or the left, but follow His footsteps and in this way you can come to Him. But now you are slipping from sin to sin, from damnation to damnation. Walk, while there is light in you, lest the shadows surround you, for that ancient leviathan thinks that he is about to swallow the whole world. But there is still time for grace. Do penance, seek the Lord your God while He may be found; call upon Him while He is near (Is 55:6). Turn to Me with your whole heart, and I the Lord will be turned to you and will be reconciled with you and I will not abandon you in the time of tribulation and distress (2 Mc 1:5). And that ancient serpent will fall into such a ruin that even his guts will be poured out.

24. Again she speaks about the Cathars.

What is this that I have said about the guts of the ancient serpent? There are some people who are now swallowed up in his gut and later will be cast forth. They are murderers, adulterers, plunderers—the unjust who have hurled their souls into death. They are also the wretched Cathars, who are more abominable than all creatures and utter their blazing words in sulfury tongues. The earth is contaminated by their abominable faith. Just as once the peoples crucified Me, so daily I am crucified among them because they cultivate such practices. Oh, what devilish insanity! They know that I am the Creator of heaven and earth and all things in them, and I see into the depths. They tear at My wounds, dismissing the body and blood of My sacraments, offered for the salvation of all believers. And if they provoke Me to wrath, I the Lord in My anger will wipe out the earth and its offspring all the way to hell. Cease, sinners against justice! Cease this insanity! If you do not, I will order you to be tortured beyond belief by hellish worms without end, in sulfur and fire inextinguishable. And there is no faculty that can comprehend this hellish punishment except that great leviathan who has stretched out and is seducing the whole world.

25. She turns her sermon to those who have undertaken to govern the church of God; they should destroy the various errors of the heretics in the catholic church.

Lest I strike you with the sword of My mouth, I the Lord, through My right hand, order you kings and princes, bishops and abbots, priests and everyone who is in power, to use all fortitude and the catholic faith to expel and destroy all the heresies that make schisms in My church, which I gave birth to in pain and suffering. Oh, most miserable and wretched hypocrites! In the presence of the people you appear to be pious and innocent, yet within you are full of evil inclination. Tell me how you believe in almighty God if you do not believe that all things are possible with almighty God (Mt 19:26)! Indeed it was possible for God to send the Holy Spirit from the seat of His great majesty into the virginal womb and for the Word of His incarnation to spring forth. Do you believe that God the Father created human beings in His own image and likeness and established them in the paradise of delight so that they would work and guard it? And that ancient serpent deceived them and they fell into sin and were thrown out for their disobedience? Oh, unhappy hypocrite: How long do you think you will remain in your sins, not believing in the Son of God who proceeds from the Father? And therefore you don't believe He was incarnate and truly suffered, or was buried and resurrected, or ascended into heaven and will come to judge the living and the dead.

You, however who are learned, study the books of the New Testament and remember their words and you will find great fruit. Be renewed in the Holy Spirit and revive your souls in the structure of the church, which has been sanctified in Christ Jesus and illuminated by the holy gospel and whitewashed of its ancient rust. The holy church was united with and betrothed to the celestial bridegroom, the Son of the eternal king, who washed her crimes in the

Jordan so that there would be one faith, one baptism, one church, and a single dove, and one elect of Christ Jesus. Therefore you, a chosen race, a holy people, a royal priesthood, a people of purchase (1 Pt 2:9) must remember the freedom with which I have freed you from the yoke and captivity of the devil (Gal 4:31). Indeed, for some time you were the darkness, but now you are the light. Walk as My beloved children, the children of light (Eph 5:8), says your God. And again that same Truth spoke: "My chosen vineyard, I have planted you and made known to you every way of truth. How could you have turned away, walking not along the straight path, but following your own sinful ways? You seek peace according to your own will and you say, 'There will be peace' but you seduce yourselves—this is not the Son of peace!"

26. She delivers a sermon to them about avoiding simony.

So I have been driven out, and there is no place where My feet may rest. I stand at the door and knock, and there is no one who lets Me in. My head is full of dew (Sg 5:2); My bed, in which I was hoping to rest, has been violated by various vices. Those who enter into My sanctuary with their impurities stain My bed with their perverse works. My pastors are weighed down as if in a heavy sleep, and what should I do to awaken them? I will raise up My right hand above them. I have been patient and have waited for them from day to day, and they have consigned Me to oblivion. Indeed, the Law disappears first from the priests and elders of My people (Ez 7:26) because they seek to sell the sacrifices of My sacraments. Those who sell, sell judgment unto themselves. And those who buy, buy a double-edged sword.

Again with fatherly chastisements I warn My pastors who know My secrets: "Be imitators of Me and not of the devil; there are some who do not enter My fold by the door, but climb in by another way, through a different path, like thieves and robbers (Jn 10:1), thieves because of their avarice and robbers because they lose the souls commissioned to them.[221] Indeed they cover their depraved works lest they be seen by the people. On account of this, those who are reprehensible in their own ways do not boldly speak out against every heresy." Again I say to you, "Know beyond doubt that as many of the souls which you have received to govern and guard that are lost from My sheep because of your negligence, that many will I seek from your hands. At the dreadful judgment you shall render an account and all the evils that I spread over them will flow back upon you.

27. She makes an exhortation to those pastors of the church.

"Now, therefore, be revived and think about your predecessors the apostles and the other holy doctors of the church who did not fear the threats of the people and the scourges of the executioner, but carried My word before kings and leaders. They were beaten and suffered many torments, but they endured all on account of My name. Therefore they stand before My throne in glory and honor that no one can reckon. There they see Me not in mysteries, but eye to eye, face to face, in great brightness and majesty. Blessed is the one who reads and hears the words of this text and preserves them because they are true and have been sent from My throne through My angel for the edification of many."

28. How to understand her earlier comment about the Cathars, "They utter their blazing words in sulphury tongues."

While I was thinking about the meaning of the phrase I had spoken, "They utter their blazing words in sulphury tongues," the Lord placed these words in my mouth: "The nature of sulfur is such that its flame does not ascend on high but it burns with obscurity in bitterness. This signifies heresies, which so obscurely offer poisonous words from which the blackest flames come forth and ignite the hearts of the faithful and make them hesitate in the catholic faith."

29. She describes a vision that she saw in Lent about a bright wheel in the sky, a bird above the wheel, and the form of a man next to it.

God has magnified His mercies in me and done these things for me, my brother, during your recent absence.[222] At First Vespers on the first Sunday in Lent, a sudden physical languor overcame me and—as usual—I went into a trance. I saw a bright wheel spinning around in the sky with astonishing speed. Also, at the top of the wheel I saw a small white bird maintaining itself with great difficulty lest it be carried around by the force of the wheel. Indeed, several times it seemed to slip down a little from the top and then struggle again to reach the top. It labored in this way for a long time, slipping down and rising again in turn. After this, I saw a lofty and very pleasant mountain and the wheel was brought above it. Again the wheel was moving around in a circle there as before, and the little bird clinging to it was persevering in its struggle. I eagerly wondered what those things could portend, and with great longing I beseeched the Lord for the meaning of this vision. And when I had received a little understanding, I returned from ecstasy and then unexpectedly seized these words, "Narrow and difficult is the way that leads to life (Mt 7:14). Lord, who will go that way?" And I added, "The one who guards his or her life from carnal desires and whose tongue has no deceit." I also added, "Lord, what should I do?" And again these words of response came into my mouth, "If you wish to walk as I have walked, observe closely My footsteps and do not turn away to the right or to the left, but follow Me and in this way you will arrive, because I have said, 'I am the way, the truth and the life; if anyone enters through Me, that one will be saved and will find pasture'" (Jn 14:6, 10:9).

After this, on Monday, I came again into ecstasy and I saw the aforementioned vision as before, but more fully, because I also saw a ladder standing above the wheel. It was so high that its top seemed to go into the heavens. Its lateral posts seemed to be triangular and made of stone; the rungs differed from each other in their very diverse and beautiful colors. Moreover, I remember that the first of them was white as snow, the second red as burning iron. On the next day I again saw all these things, and standing next to the wheel I saw an image of a man whose head appeared to be gold and his hair was like pure white wool. His eyes were very bright and beautiful, his chest and his arms—which he extended in the manner of a cross— had a certain very pure luster like well-polished silver. He had in his right hand a branch of a tree, green and very pleasing in appearance; in his left hand he held a shining wheel adorned with the variety of a rainbow. His belly appeared to be bronze, his thighs of steel, his lower legs of iron, his feet of earth (cf. Dn 2:32–33; 7:9; Rv 1:14–16). All these things appeared to me many times during Lent.

30. She exhorts her brother to try to find an interpretation of this vision in the holy scriptures.

Moreover, on the first Sunday after the feast of blessed Gregory, while I was in ecstasy and was seeing the visions that I usually saw on Sundays, I saw in the heavens that famous doctor full of glory and lovely brightness, like the glory of the most holy bishops Martin and Nicholas. He had on his head a venerable crown, just as I had seen them wear, the kind said to be worn by popes. In that same hour I also saw the aforementioned vision, and I burned with a great desire to understand what I was seeing, especially what the image of the man could signify, since I already understood something about the other aspects of the vision. Therefore, I very eagerly beseeched that blessed man of God to procure for me from the Lord an understanding of the vision that I desired. He turned toward me and responded with these words, "You are not able to understand what those things signify, but talk to the learned ones who read the scriptures; they know." Now, therefore, most beloved brother, I entreat you to take up this task. Examine the divine scriptures and try to discover a suitable interpretation of this vision. Indeed, perhaps the Lord has reserved this for you.

31. The response of her brother and the exposition that, with God's help, he expressed most clearly.

What is this, my lady, that you have said? You should have announced these things to the doctors of the church and sought an interpretation from them, but now you come to me? I am not a doctor; nor am I a steward of the mysteries of God. Rather, I am an insignificant person of little capacity, so puny for understanding the secrets of God. There is too little oil in the flask for me, if there is even any, and I fear lest it not be enough for me and you. Therefore go rather to those who sell and buy for yourself (Mt 25:9). I refer to those who have increased in their fruit of grain, wine, and spiritual oil (Ps 4:8) and who cry out in the church. You who have no money, come, buy, and eat (Is 55:1). But lest I wound your love, I will undertake what you urge, not, indeed, in a venture of daring but of love, which banishes fear. You, in the meantime, pray that the one who makes the tongues of infants fluent (Wis 10:21) may fill my mouth with blessing.

First, let me analyze the mystery of the wheel and the bird and ladder, since you have already extensively given the beginning of its interpretation. If there is anything missing in your understanding, I will take care to address it. Then I will turn to what you have requested, according to how the Lord will prompt me.

I believe that you discerned correctly when you stated that the way which leads to life is positioned as if on a wheel going round. What, indeed, is this world if not a wheel going round? Look at everything that is of the world and you will not find anything that is not subject to mutability, and mutability, by its turning, rolls down its subjects from one state to another. Now, indeed, through certain advances one is lifted up to better things, but then through various failings one sinks down to worse. In this state of changeableness, the good and the evil walk on the wheel, but in different ways. Encountering the wheel, the good rise as long as they do not chase after temporal things with greed but turn the mind against such greed and strive to be above temporal things, trampling them in contempt. Thus they can be compared to the white bird rising on the wheel. Indeed, only those who are white in their innocence and winged with various virtues are strong enough to do this. But even they are like the aforementioned bird and are driven down somewhat by the force of the wheel, but by the grace of God they again return to the top, just as it is written, "Seven times the just person falls and rises" (Prv 24:16). On the contrary, however, the evil ones, embracing with their whole mind the things that are of the world, necessarily walk the circuit with those things, in the manner of Samson, who through his love of a harlot was destined to be blinded at the millstone (Jgs 16:4–19). They fall into that curse. My God, think of them like a wheel! Indeed, one who with extreme greed seizes hold of some part of the wheel, that is, of this world, then is drawn by it away from the state of rectitude, lifted up in pride, and carried around to many useless and depraved desires, and finally is rolled down into the depth of perdition, and is damned together with this world—isn't such a person like a wheel? Thus, if we do not want to be carried around on this wheel and plunged into ruin, we must just barely touch it, like the bird rising against the wheel, using temporal things with the greatest restraint and extending the wings of our virtue in constant motion by continually exercising them. Because the ascent of the just is exceedingly difficult, and those who strive toward the kingdom of God must necessarily embark upon it, seeing it in your trance, you rightly said, "Narrow and difficult is the way that leads to life" (Mt 7:14). It is truly narrow in that it presses in with great hardship on those entering it. It is truly difficult in that it admits few. In contrast, the path that is going down is called wide and spacious for the opposite reason. Why is it that the wheel which you saw appeared white unless this world, to which we are comparing it, appears beautiful and desirable, and is thus so much the harder to be spurned and overcome by the just? Thus also in the Apocalypse the world is compared to a splendid woman having a golden cup in her hand (Rv 17:4).

I will now analyze the mystery of the ladder that you saw above the wheel, according to what I have been instructed by you, adding a few things from my own understanding. As you say, the two persons of the Father and Son could not unsuitably be understood by the two stone posts of the ladder. The solidity of their indissoluble substance is often designated in scripture by the word "rock," as in the words of the Lord saying, "All who hear these My words and do them I will liken to a wise man who dug deep and laid his foundation upon a rock" (Lk 6:47–48). And in the psalm, "The rock is refuge for the hedgehogs" (Ps 103:18), and elsewhere. "The stone that the builders rejected," et cetera (Mk 12:10). And in Zechariah, "Seven eyes on one stone" (Zec 4:10). Moreover, that a triangular form appears in both posts doubtless signifies that through the differences in personal properties the person of the Father and the person of the Son can be distinguished from each other and each of them from the person of the Holy Spirit, yet they come together in such a union that whatever the nature of one is it is completely shared by all. Indeed, it is the property of the Father alone to be one who begets, and of the Son alone to be begotten, and of the Holy Spirit alone to proceed from both. Yet the Father is God omnipotent, wise, good, eternal, boundless, and whatever else can likewise be said without specifying person, and this, I say, He has in common with the Son and the Holy Spirit, and the Son has in common with the Father and the Holy Spirit. For the Father with the Son and Holy Spirit, and the Son with the Father and Holy Spirit is one divine substance.

The stairs between the two posts you have aptly compared to the Holy Spirit, which is the love of the Father and Son and by which, like an entwining in the middle, they embrace each other inseparably. The Holy Spirit, being sent by the Father and the Son, descends to us from above in diverse charisms and offers us an ascent to heaven. Thus in the Book of Wisdom the Spirit of God is called manifold (Wis 7:22). The multiple gifts of the Spirit are represented by the different steps in the ladder. The first step is white, signifying faith, which is the foundation of all virtues, and the cleansing in baptism, which offers the brightness of innocence. Thus Peter said, "with faith purifying their hearts" (Acts 15:9). Since, moreover, faith without works is dead (Jas 2:20), it is necessary that the works of faith proceed from charity. After the step of faith it was appropriate for there to be a fiery step, which signifies the burning of charity to which true faith sends those who ascend. Rightly did that multi-stepped ladder seem to have its foundation in those two stairs since no virtue can be reached without faith and love. Once these two stairs that have been established as the foundation have been surmounted, then there may be that blessed progression from virtue to virtue until the God of gods is seen in Sion. Also, you have accurately seen this ladder located above the wheel, since only one who has mentally overcome the mutability of this world can climb it.

It remains for me now to unfold the interpretation of that which you originally asked. According to what I am able to infer from scripture, it seems to me that the image of a man which you saw has the form of Christ and the church: Christ is called its head and the church is called His body (Col 1:18). The golden head is the divinity of Christ, according to that word of the apostle: "The head of Christ is God" (1 Cor 11:3), which the bride in the Canticle referred to, saying, "His head is the best gold" (Sg 5:11). The hair of His head like very pure, white wool refers to the angels. From the beginning of their existence they remained in purest innocence, clinging to the highest divinity in inexhaustible contemplation and fixing their roots of unceasing love in Him just as hair planted in

His head. Like white hair are those immaculate thoughts of divine wisdom about which the prophet said, "'My thoughts, indeed, are not your thoughts,' says the Lord" (Is 55:8). The thoughts of the Lord, moreover, are most rightly called His dispositions by which He disposes all things in great tranquility.

And what are those beautiful and flashing eyes if not the mercy and truth that come from His face (Ps 88:15) and run through all His works, according to this verse: "All the ways of the Lord are mercy and truth" (Ps 24:10). They are also referred to here: "The eyes of the Lord gaze upon the good and the evil" (Prv 15:3). But it seems that His eyes close over the good and evil, now one, now the other, now both. The eye of mercy seems to close over the reprobate when He sentences them to eternal punishment. Then truth, that is, justice, appears more than mercy. But it should be known that even in condemning the impious He does not forget mercy, because He does not condemn them as seriously as they deserve; otherwise, how would His mercies be upon all His works? Again the eye of truth, that is, of justice, seems to close when He permits them to prosper in all temporal things and in this way has mercy on them temporarily. Such mercy is more like a refuge from celestial anger since they deserve that God, in His just judgment, should instead let them be disfigured by temporal things. Thus He says through Isaiah, "We could have mercy on the impious yet they would not learn to do justice. In the land of the holy ones, they do iniquities and will not see the glory of God" (Is 26:10). Likewise, both the eye of justice and the eye of mercy seem to close upon the just, as when sometimes He, as if angry, permits those who seem to deserve little or no evil to be afflicted. But even in that—if we attend carefully—He shows them mercy and exercises justice. He offers mercy to the soul that He enriches in patience and humility and other virtues through adversities, and He inspires in it the sweetest consolations. And He exercises justice in grinding the flesh. Indeed, it is just to afflict the flesh. The flesh is inimical to the image of God, that is, the rational soul, which, through the tinder of sin, the flesh always attacks, burdens, weighs down, and tries to turn away from its Creator. Therefore, that kind Father chastises His children by mixing the sweetness of mercy—by which He consoles the soul—with bitter justice—which avenges the insolence of the flesh. This is just like an oxymel, which is a mixture of honey and vinegar, that one drinks so that the core of sin, if it is already in the soul, is dissipated, or if it is not, will not be allowed to arise. I could also illustrate the mercy and justice of God in the chastising of the just in other ways, but it would make a major digression from my proposed task. Why I have chosen this mode, my sister, you know because you have been the cause of this whole digression![223] Now, let's return to the main point.

The chest and the arms and the hands of the person whom you saw have a certain very pure whiteness. Here I think the perfect cleanness of our Savior is to be understood: He was innocent in hands and clean heart, alone among human beings to be free from the blemish of all impurity. Furthermore, in that they had a certain likeness to silver, I understand that they were infused with the riches of wisdom and knowledge overflowing from the font of divinity to His sacred chest. From there these riches were distributed in all His works, according to the words of the apostle, "In whom are hidden all the treasures of wisdom and knowledge" (Col 2:3). That He seems to hold a verdant branch of a tree in His right hand and in His left hand a shining wheel adorned with the variety of a rainbow can be indisputably correlated to that scripture passage that, speaking about the Wisdom of God, says, "The length of life is in Her right hand; in Her left are riches and glory" (Prv 3:16). The right hand of God is called celestial blessedness in which the length of life, that is, the eternal life, is reserved for the elect. And what, indeed, is eternal life other than He who says of Himself, "I am the way, the truth, and the life" (Jn 14:6)? Truly He is the life of the living and the tree of life for those who lay hold of Him. The tree of life in Paradise could preserve human life from death forever by its fruit and protect it from external heat by its leaves. Likewise Christ refreshes those who feed on His sweetness in heaven with such satiety that they live forever. And He shades them so that they are fatigued by no further heat of tribulation either in body or soul. This refreshment and protection are declared in the Apocalypse by the voice of the angel saying, "The One who sits on the throne dwells over them; they shall hunger and thirst no more, nor shall the sun or any heat fall upon them"

(Rv 7:15–6). Thus also the bride, led into the joy of her Lord, exalts saying, "I sat under the shadow of the one I desired, and his fruit was sweet in my throat" (Sg 2:3).

Furthermore, that He appeared to stretch out that branch toward the bird struggling on the wheel could be understood as if He were saying to the soul struggling against the world: "Do not fail in the fight; think of the never-fading reward of your labor. Behold the delights in My right hand till the end. Whoever shall be victorious, I will give to eat of the tree of life, which is in the paradise of My God and that person will dwell in the protection of the God of heaven."

Now we must attend to the wheel that He is holding in His left hand. The left hand of God is called this temporal life that we have received from the Lord. He established a shining wheel for us in this life, namely, the teaching of sacred scripture. He announced this teaching through Himself and His followers so that it could illuminate the world, which was fixed in the shadows of error and ignorance. Thus it is written, "The precept of the Lord is bright, illuminating the eyes" (Ps 18:9). What, moreover, are the various colors that appear like a rainbow in the wheel if not the benefits of manifold grace, gathered for the church by the Savior and imprinted in the scriptures of truth? These, no doubt, are the riches and glory that, as it was said, are in the left hand of Wisdom, the Son of God. This one, as the apostle said, for us was made poor although He was rich so that by His poverty we could be rich (2 Cor 8:9), just as elsewhere he said that Christ would present for Himself a glorious church not having spot or wrinkle (Eph 5:27). He does that by washing her in the font of water in the word of life (Eph 5:26) and by giving her as if to His spouse earrings of obedience, a necklace of chastity, a ring of faith, bracelets of good works, anklets of discipline, and precious garments of various virtues. These things offered to the world through the dispensation of the incarnate Word, what are they if not the riches of the church in the left hand of Wisdom? And what is the glory, also in the left hand, if not the precious and innocent blood of her Savior, which was poured out for her so that He might reconcile her to God the Father and make her sit with Him in the heavens? With this blood, as if with a purple cloak, that strong, jealous lover clothes His beloved and covers over all her sins. Thus in a not unwarranted voice of exultation she shouts and says, "Far be it from me to glory except in the cross of our Lord Jesus Christ" (Gal 6:14).

It should not seem strange that I compare sacred scripture to a wheel because that quadriform wheel, which is said in Ezekiel to have appeared beside the four animals (Ez 1:15), is often compared by the fathers to evangelical teaching, doubtless for this reason. Indeed, because a wheel is round, it has nothing by which its progress is impeded. Likewise sacred teaching, trimmed all around and agreeing with itself, nowhere has the smallest part of untruth slowing it down when it should be rolling toward the minds of its hearers. Thus the Psalmist says, "The word of God runs quickly" (Ps 147:15), and just as a wheel revolves around one unmoving point, so the whole of sacred teaching turns around God, whose nature is unmoving and wholly unchanging. As a part of a wheel touches the earth, so sacred doctrine instructs the simple by stories. In that part by which it teaches morals it gradually lifts itself from the earth. And it extends itself still higher when it allegorically signifies the temporal aspects of Christ and the sacraments of the church, as in this: "A rod shall come forth from the root of Jesse and the flower shall rise from his root" (Is 11:1), and this: "The queen of Sheba came from the land of Ethiopia to hear the wisdom of Solomon" (3 Kgs 10:1–4; 2 Chr 9:1–4). It draws near the top when it reminds us about our eternal beatitude, as in this: "Blessed are the pure of heart for they will see God" (Mt 5:7). It is near the top where the glory and beatitude of the angels is spoken of, as in "Their angels always see the face of My Father who is in heaven" (Mt 18:10). At the very top is where it thunders on high about that divine substance, as in this: "In the beginning was the Word and the Word was with God, and God was the Word" (Jn 1:1). From its height it bends down again when, after the loftiness of wisdom, which is spoken among the perfect, it tempers itself for the understanding of the weak.

We can also understand that same wheel held in the left hand to be this world. This world was once wiped out by a judgment of water and is yet to be burned by a judgment of fire. These two judgments are symbolized by the image of a rainbow, which was in the wheel. Indeed a rainbow has two especially notable colors, deep blue like water and red like fire. Thus the Lord placed a rainbow in the sky after the flood in order to signify that after the judgment of water the judgment of fire would come to the world. Also, the victory by which Christ conquered the world can be symbolized by the green branch that He holds in His right hand. For the ancients returning from battle used to bear a green olive branch in their right hands as a sign of victory and peace. Thus Christ seems to offer an olive branch and wheel for the consolation of His followers in the church struggling daily on the wheel of this world while He shouts to them in the gospel and says, "In the world you will have distress, but be assured—I have overcome the world" (Jn 16:33).

Now let us continue to the other parts of your vision. Under the silver chest, as you say, appears the bronze belly, by which we can understand the gathering of people clinging to Christ, that is, the church. About this, the Lord says through the prophet: "I suffer in My belly; I suffer in My belly" (Jer 4:19). Indeed, the Lord suffers in His belly as long as they whom, as He said through Isaiah, He carries in His womb (Is 46:3), that is, the lap of the church, contend with each, torment each other, and are destroyed by each other. And not inappropriately is the church called by the name of belly. For in the belly certain frail and loose members are intermingled, like entrails and things of this kind. And there are some noble and important members, like the heart and the liver. The heart is called the vessel of the vital spirit, which spreads from there to all the members, and the liver is the font and source of the blood, which likewise is distributed to all the other members. In this way, in the lap of the church, those who are of looser life, that is, the carnal ones, are intermingled with men of virtue. These virtuous ones are the principal vessel of the multiform grace of God, which, through their leadership, teaching, example, merits, and prayers, is spread to all the members of the church of God to invigorate and strengthen them. If on any occasion any one of them should happen to be weakened from his state of fortitude, the health of the whole church is endangered. Thus the Lord, when He said through Jeremiah, "I

157

suffer in My belly," immediately, as if adding the cause, continued, "The senses of My heart are troubled" (Jer 4:19). Likewise Jeremiah, as the voice of the church, cries out: "My heart is overturned in me" (Lam 1:20), that is, it is turned from celestial to earthly things, and a little later, "My entrails are troubled; my liver is spilled out on the ground" (Lam 2:11). Truly indeed, the entrails of the church, that is, its weak members, will necessarily be troubled as long as the liver, that is, those through whom they are to receive the blood of Christ and other spiritual nourishments, is spilled out in earthly desires. Rightly, moreover, did this belly seem to have a likeness of bronze, since the church resembles the resonance of this metal. All day and all night the church rings out in praise of the Lord and expounds His glory so that this sound comes forth in every land. Also, the more vigorously this metal is rubbed, the brighter and the more like gold it is made. Likewise, the more the church is abraded by persecutions, so much brighter does it become in virtues and advance to the likeness of God. Well indeed does the luster of silver shine above the bronze belly, since the church of God must neither teach nor do anything other than what is contemplated in the wisdom of its Savior, which is above it. The bronze pillars with silver capitals in the court of the tabernacle of the Lord (Ex 27:9–10) that was in the desert also signify this.

The legs of steel and iron can be understood as the twofold foundation of the church. The apostle wrote to the Ephesians about this, saying, "Built upon the foundation of the apostles and prophets" (Eph 2:20). Indeed, the whole edifice of the church is supported by their teachings. And I compare the prophets to steel because of their unbending rigor of steadfastness. By this they strongly withstood the hammers of the devil when they so firmly endured many adversities from their own people and foreign tyrants. Thus their constancy has also been compared in scripture to the hardest rocks, as in the words of the Lord to Ezekiel: "Like adamant and flint I have made your face" (Ez 3:9). And Isaiah says about himself, "I have set my face like the hardest rock" (Is 50:7). Likewise steel, polished with long labor, resembles the luster of silver and becomes like a mirror for one looking at it. If investigated with earnest effort, prophetic teaching—which is like murky water in the clouds of the sky—is found to be most like the teaching of Christ, which is silver tested by fire, and like a mirror of the life of one who looks at it diligently. As James said, "You have the prophetic word; you do well to attend to it as to a shining lamp in a dark place" (2 Pt 1:19).

I compare the apostles to the iron of the shins not only because they too were hard and strong against persecutors, but also because Christ used them like iron hammers to overcome the hard hearts of the unfaithful throughout the whole world. And just as iron is of greater use to builders than steel, so in the construction of the church Christ used the fortitude of the apostles more than that of the prophets. This is because the prophets announced the word of God in Judea alone, but the apostles, going out to the whole world, preached to every creature. Moreover, the steel appears above the iron because just as iron is blunt for cutting anything hard unless it is plated with steel, so the preaching of the apostles would have been ineffective for cutting the hard hearts of the unfaithful had it not been strengthened and in some way sharpened by the testimonies of the prophets preceding them. Thus the Lord said to the disciples, "In this the saying is true, that there is one who sows and another who reaps. Others have labored and you have entered into their labors" (Jn 4:37–38).

And now, to what shall we compare those earthen feet? Just as by the golden head we understood the divinity of the Savior, so by the feet we could understand the human nature of the Savior existing in two substances, body and soul. That giant assumed this nature to follow our path of wretchedness when, in the height of His divinity, He could not touch the earth and dwell with humans. Nor should it seem absurd that when humanity was united with divinity (humanity, as we say, signified by the feet, divinity by the head) there was a great distance between those parts, because, although they were not separate spatially, nevertheless as much as east stands apart from west, and vastly more, does humanity stand apart from divinity and is lower through the weakness of nature. In scripture, also, the humanity of Christ is sometimes found to be called by the name of feet, as in this: "You have put all things under His feet" (Ps 8:8), and in the apostle, "He must reign until He shall put all enemies under His feet" (1 Cor 15:25). That means until His reign is to be manifested, until all His enemies know that they are subject to His humanity, which they have scorned in Him and judged unworthy of life. This will be when they see the One whom they pierced coming with great power and majesty.

The church also functions with that same humanity of Christ as its feet. Indeed, the whole machine of the human body is held up and moved about from place to place by the service of the feet. Likewise, the whole body of the church rests upon the humanity of the Savior, as upon the twofold foundation of its faith and work, because we all receive from the fullness of His grace whatever we must believe or do. Through His humanity we are redeemed and it has been fashioned like a vehicle to carry us back to our homeland. Thus also is the shoulder called the wisdom of God, for He joyfully placed the lost sheep that had been found on His shoulder and carried it back to the ninety-nine that He had left on the mountain (Mt 18:12–13; Lk 15:4–5). And iron appears next to the feet because the apostles, who are represented by iron, were planted next to His likeness, eating and drinking with Him, and touching Him with their hands, thus contemplating the incarnate Word more intimately.

But why is it that the shins and the thighs and the belly, all of which we refer to as the church, seem to be like hard, solid metals, while the feet alone, which we say pertain to the humanity of Christ, appear fragile? No doubt this shows that every strength and fortitude of the church derives its source from its root, which is the Savior's weakness, the weakness of flesh. This is because what was weak in God enables greater strength in humans. This is well represented in the first parents, when strength of bone was extracted from Adam so that Eve could be made, and from this woman was strengthened and man weakened.

Here ends the third book of Elisabeth's visions.

The Book of the Ways of God

This is *The Book of the Ways of God*, which the angel of God most high announced to Elisabeth, handmaid of Christ and of the living God, in the 1156th year of the Lord's incarnation, in the fifth year of her visitations when the Spirit of the Lord visited her frequently for the salvation of all who receive the fatherly warnings of God with grateful praise.

1. She describes when *The Book of the Ways of God* was first revealed to her. She also describes the three paths she saw extending from the base of a shining mountain up to its summit and the figure of a man she saw at its peak.

   In the beginning of the fifth year of my visitation, when the feast of Pentecost was approaching, I, Elisabeth, in a spiritual vision, saw a lofty mountain illuminated at its peak by abundant light. I also saw what appeared to be three paths extending from the mountain's base to its summit. One of them, which was in the middle directly across from me, had the appearance of serene sky or blue stone; the one to my right appeared green, and the one to my left, purple. At the summit of the mountain facing the middle path was a man clothed in a remarkable blue tunic and girded at the loins with a bright white belt. His face was shining like the sun, his eyes beaming like stars, and his hair was like the brightest wool. In his mouth he had a sword sharpened on both sides. In his right hand he had a key, and in his left hand what appeared to be a royal scepter (Rv 1:13–17).

2. She saw three paths going up the mountain.

   Again, on the solemnity of Pentecost,[224] in another vision I saw three other paths beside those of the first vision. They were on the

161

ascent of the mountain, to the left of the aforementioned man, and they varied as follows. The one appearing closer to the green path was pleasant but entirely surrounded and covered over by dense thorn bushes. Those walking on it would inevitably be pricked unless, cramped up and bent over, they proceeded[225] very carefully. There also appeared a delightful path, narrow and hardly worn. It had no thorns but on both sides was abundantly surrounded by pleasant grass and flowers of various kinds. The middle one between these two was wider than the others and smooth, as if it were paved with red tiles. While I was carefully looking at it, the angel of the Lord who was standing by me said, "You gaze upon this path and it seems lovely and easy to walk on, but it is dangerous and those advancing on it easily slip."

3. About the four paths that she saw next to the three paths of the first vision.

On the octave of Pentecost[226] at the time of the midday rest, suddenly the eyes of my heart were opened without physical pain, just as in the aforementioned visions, and again I saw everything that I already described. However, the Lord also showed me four paths in addition to those I had already seen. They were next to the three of the first vision, to the right of the man who was standing at the top of the mountain. The one next to the purple path seemed to be very difficult up to the middle of the mountain because dense thorns covered it on both sides. But its remaining part leading to the top of the mountain appeared pleasant and free from impediments, yet narrow and hardly worn. The one next to it seemed arid and rough with large clods of earth like a plowed field and very laborious for its travelers. I was thinking about the difficult courses of these two paths and the angel, who was standing by me, said, "Let those who walk by these paths take care not to stumble. If they stumble and fall and do not get up but remain on the ground, they will not see eternal light." The remaining two paths appearing with them were smooth and without obstacle and were lovely to look at, with a sheen like that of well-worn earth in a public street. While I was fixed on the sight of them, I again heard the angel, who said,

"The way of the just has been made straight and the road of the saints has been prepared" (Is 16:7; Lk 3:4).

4. She describes the interpretation of the vision about the high mountain, its diverse paths, and the figure of the man at the top of the mountain.

This is the interpretation of the first vision as I learned it from the angel. The lofty mountain is the height of celestial beatitude. The light on the top of the mountain is the brightness of eternal life. The diverse paths on the mountain are the various ascents of the elect by which they climb to the realm of brightness. The blue path is the effort of divine contemplation. Those who fix the eye of the mind in constant meditation and desire for God and celestial things walk on this path. The green path is for those who strive to be perfect and irreproachable in the active life, walking in all the commands and precepts of God without complaint. In all their works they give heed not to a transitory reward but to the unfading prize of supernal salvation. The purple path is the ascent of the blessed martyrs, who devote themselves to the justice of God by enduring the torments of suffering. They strive to cross over to the divine light in the purple of their blood. The remarkable man at the top of the mountain is Christ. His shining face signifies the brilliance of His divinity. His beaming eyes refer to His serene gaze over His chosen ones. The hair like white wool announces Him to be the Ancient of Days, even though He was born in the flesh in the most recent days. The double-edged sword in His mouth is the terrible sentence of judgment that will come forth from His mouth, striking the reprobate with a double bruising of body and soul. The key appeared in His right hand because He alone opens the gate of life that no one closes; and when He closes it, no one opens it (Is 22:22). He also unlocks the depths of God's mysteries to whomever He chooses. There is no one who can close or seal them, and there is no one who can loose His seal. The scepter in His left hand is the royal power He declared that He received according to His human nature, saying, "All power in heaven and on earth has been given to me" (Mt 28:18). The blue tunic indicates the virtue of heavenly contemplation that perfectly possessed the whole mind of the Savior. Unlike others, He did not turn to divine contemplation by degree or for a time; He received the spirit not by measure (Jn 3:34) and the whole fullness of divinity dwelt corporeally within Him (Col 2:9). The white belt designates the radiance of His inviolable innocence. He appeared on the path that signifies the contemplation of His divinity because He wills this path to endure forever while the others will not remain. He did not appear on all the paths, and yet He was on them all because they each represent the virtues through which righteous people come to the mountain, that is, to the high place, where they receive the particular rewards for their individual virtues. On all the paths of truth, God must be contemplated.

5. She reveals the meaning of the second vision.

This is the mystery of the second vision. The three ways that appeared next to the green path, to the left of the man standing on the mountain, express the nature of the three orders of the church, namely, the married, the chaste, and the leaders. The path covered with thorns is that of married people. This path appeared pleasant because from the beginning God established this life and, if legitimately observed, it is lovely and pleasing in the sight of the Lord. Those who walk in it are definitely climbing the mountain of God. But infinite brambles of worldly cares hang over it at every point. Those who travel it are inevitably pricked unless, living moderately, they constrain themselves in every way and, humbling themselves in the presence of God and others, they go forth as if bent over.

The path free of brambles and surrounded on both sides with delightful flowers is the life of the chaste. It is characteristic of them to withdraw their minds from the cares and anxieties of the present life and meditate only on those things that are of the Lord, so that they may be holy in body and spirit. This way is narrow because, for it to be legitimately and wisely observed, great discipline must be maintained to confine the course of those walking on it. Otherwise, living according to their own will, they will either slip into fornication or be counted with the foolish virgins or delicate widows who are the living dead (Rv 3:1). It is hardly worn because in comparison with the others, there are few who take this path, fewer still who persevere in it. It is delightfully surrounded with flowers of various kinds because all kinds of virtues adorn the life of the chaste.

The middle way between these two aforementioned ones, which is wider than them, is the life of the leaders. Since it was established for governing the life of either the married or the chaste or both, it is less constrained than those other paths. The people on this path have freer authority to exercise personal will. Because of this, the course of those walking on this path is more likely to become slippery, which its even surface aptly signifies. It is said to be dangerous because so many slip on it and thus very few are found to be secure on it. Moreover, that it appears to have a pavement of red tiles, which are earthen and baked by fire, signifies the anxiety of the prelates. Their minds must constantly be seething with solicitude for the people subject to them, to whom they owe the care of body and soul.

6. About the pile of books that she saw in a tent.

When I inquired about the interpretation of the third vision from the angel, my instructor, he said to me, "Behold you have begun *The Book of the Ways of God*, just as it had been declared to you." He said this because one day in the previous year, while I was in a trance, he had led me as if into a meadow. A tent was pitched there, and we entered it. He showed me a great pile of books kept there and said, "Do you see those books? All of these are still to be dictated before the judgment day." Then, raising one from the pile, he said, "This is *The Book of the Ways of God*, which will be revealed through you after you have visited sister Hildegard and listened to her."[227] And immediately after I returned from Hildegard, it did indeed begin to unfold in that way.

7. She reveals the meaning of the third vision.

This is the significance of the four paths that were shown in the third vision. The first, which was closer to the purple path and rough with thorn bushes on the lower part but unobstructed and full of flowers on the upper part, signifies the life of those who divide their days. They live legitimately in the world with the troubles of worldly affairs, and then they cross over to the flowery and

165

unobstructed life of the chaste. Constraining themselves by the rule of the chaste, they ascend the mountain of God together with them.

The arid path, rough with clods of earth, is the hardest kind of life. On this path advance holy hermits and some dwelling in contact with others. It is hardest because they torture their flesh beyond human measure and dry it out by fasts, vigils, genuflections, beatings, hair shirts, and any other severe afflictions. Indeed, all things of this kind are like the roughest clods of earth. Those walking on this path need great effort and vigilance lest by chance they stumble in its excessive roughness and fall more heavily than the others.

One of the other two ways described with these appeared more worn and less obstructed. My teacher said, "On this path advance the holy souls of young children who were sanctified in holy baptism and departed from life within seven years. Because they have not experienced the evil of the world, they come to the kingdom of God with an unobstructed and very free course." About the other he said, "This is the path of adolescents who progress a little more slowly and therefore their path appears less worn and unobstructed."

8. She affirms that these visions and their interpretations are true.

These visions and their interpretations are true. The one who opened my eyes so that I could see the visions of God, has, through His angel, proven beyond doubt that they are to be understood in this way, as was pleasing to Him.

9. How her eyes were opened and she saw a multitude of saints in a great light.

On the feast of the blessed apostle James,[228] while I was in a trance and seeing a vision of the ways of God, I was lifted up into the height and contemplated the mountain of God as if from nearby. And behold that immense light that abides on the summit of the mountain seemed to be cut through the center. I looked through it and saw a multitude of saints whose number I could not guess. My guide said to me, "Look and see and examine all those whom you see. Here you see holy martyrs, bishops and confessors of the Lord, monastic virgins of both sexes, widows and secular people, both married and chaste, those of high birth and of low, all reigning with Christ. They walked in the ways of the Lord, the holy paths that you have seen, and they arrived and received the unfading grace from Christ the Lord with His angels. Let all now contemplate their own path: If they walk on it unjustly, let them correct themselves with humility and charity and obedience and make straight their way. Because if they arrive, they will receive the eternal reward."

10. The First Sermon: The Way of the Contemplatives.

After this I was resting in my bed and had not yet fallen asleep when suddenly the spirit of the Lord visited me and filled my mouth with this sermon: "Now take heed, you who have renounced worldly desires and have chosen to follow the footsteps of the one who has called you into His marvelous light (1 Pt 2:9), who has named you as His chosen children and established you to judge the tribes of Israel at the end of time (Mt 19:28). Think about how you should live with all humility, obedience, and charity and without murmur, without slander and envy, and without pride; abstain, too, from all other vices. Love each other lest your heavenly Father be blasphemed and enraged by you and you vanish from the way of righteousness, that is, the way of His contemplation."

Then the angel of the Lord continued the sermon in this way, adding, "If indeed there are disputes among you, and dissent, slander, murmuring, anger, hatred and jealousy, haughtiness, hunger for glory, idle talk, jesting, gluttony, sleepiness, impurity of the flesh, idleness and the like, in which the children of this world walk, where will be the space for divine contemplation?" He added more, saying, "This is the word of God to you who have chosen to do battle for God among the clergy or in the monastic profession. You have chosen the best part—take care lest it be taken away from you (Lk 10:42).[229] With all diligence keep yourselves from the ways of those who outwardly bear the appearance of your piety but negate its virtue by their deeds. They honor God with their lips but blaspheme Him with their practice. Some of them seek knowledge of the Law but do not embrace its use. They turn their back on truth, and yet they glorify themselves for walking in the path of contemplation. They make the Law of God and its precepts serve their pride, avarice, and desire. They impudently seek riches and honors from those things which are of Jesus Christ, and they stir up their own impurities. The sanctuary of God and the places revered by the angels they enter with pride and pollution, and the purities of Christ's sacraments, which should be adored, they dishonor with irreverent service and unclean heart. They laugh at their accusers and afflict them with slander and persecution. Those who excel in these things are abominable in the sight of the Lord. They walk in the cloak of humility but their hearts are far from it. They multiply prayers, but what good is this when they oppose God in their hearts, when they neglect brotherly love, envy and disparage each other, and contend for preferment? They profess to disdain the world, but they venerate the things of the world and impudently seek to gain them, and are blown around by every wind of personal will. They cast off the teachings of the fathers, pour themselves into secular business, and fill the church with scandals. On account of this, behold, piety suffers contempt and faith suffers schism.

"'What more should I do for them?' says the Lord. 'Behold I shout after them and they do not listen, they repulse the voice of My admonition as if kicking it away. I visit them with unheard of grace and they do not recognize the visit—on top of that, they laugh at it. I strike them and they do not grieve; I throw them down and they do not fear. Woe to them! Alas, Mine is a horrible reckoning. Behold, it will come quickly; like an unexpected torrent it will rush upon them, tumbling into perdition those found without fear.

"'But you, My people, are not a people of false piety. You have placed it in your hearts to overcome the world and give birth to heaven in your minds. You, I say, turn aside from people of this kind and do not associate with them. Stand in the path of the vision you have chosen. Cleanse the eyes of your heart so that you may raise them in contemplation of the light in which life dwells, which is your redemption. These things purify the eyes of the heart so that they can be lifted up to the true light: rejection of worldly concern, affliction of the flesh, contrition of the heart, frequent and pure confession of sin, and the washing of tears. When all impurity has been purged, these things lift up the eyes of the heart: meditation of the marvelous essence of God, examination of pure truth, clean and strong prayer, joyful praise, and burning desire for God. Embrace these things and live in them and run to meet the life-giving light which is offered to you as God's children (Heb 12:7) and is abundantly poured forth in your minds. Withdraw your hearts from yourselves and give them to these things which you have heard and they will be filled with a divinizing splendor. You will be children of the light and like the angels of God who, in the vigor of their contemplation, do not cease to gaze at their Creator and flow back to their source.

"'Children of Adam, is it not enough for you to be made children of God? Why do you turn your face from contemplating the countenance of the one who gave such power to humans and especially to you, who have chosen to be peaceful in this world and to be conformed to angels on earth? You are burning lamps whom the Lord has established on His sacred mountain to illuminate the darkness of the world by your word and example. Take care lest the light that is in you be extinguished by the wind of pride and cupidity, which snuffed out the light of your parents in paradise. Children of peace, turn your ears away from the clamors of the world and offer silence to the spirit which is speaking within you. Observe the Sabbath of the Lord constantly in your hearts and the peace of God, which surpasses all understanding (Phil 4:7), will rest upon you and you will delight in the abundance of its sweetness. Do not be agitated and let your mind be overcome if the world spurns you and reckons you as dead and sterile. If your life is diminished by pain, suffering, and poverty, do not be sad and turn your eyes from the sight of the light that is before your face. Behold! The time is near in which this world shall pass away and its flower shall perish and you shall judge its lovers and tread upon the necks of the proud. Seeing this, they shall be amazed at your glory when your riches, which you have stored up in heaven (Mt 6:20) are revealed. Then, what is imperfect in your contemplation shall be put aside and the face of eternal light shall receive the eyes of its eagles[230] and, like an overflowing river, its brightness will flood the hearts of all who sought it in truth.'"

The angel, who was speaking to me at intervals, had not yet finished these words when a certain doubt occurred to me about distinguishing the ways of God that had been described. I asked him, "My lord, aren't we monastics on the path of contemplation as well as on the path of chastity? Can it be that we are on both?"

And he said, "The path of contemplation is shared by you and the clergy, just as the path of chastity is shared by you and them. Know, however, that there are many on the path of chastity who are not on the path of contemplation. There are also many clerics who walk the path neither of contemplation nor of chastity, and they are miserable. They think they are on the path of contemplation, but they are not."

In response, I continued by asking, "What shall we say about bishops and religious superiors and other great prelates of the church?"

He responded to me in these words: "Pride reigns in the hearts of the prelates and great ones and they reject God from their hearts. He wishes to rest only upon the humble and the quiet and those fearing His words. Indeed, once the Savior commanded His disciples, saying, "Whoever shall not receive you, leave them and shake the dust from your feet as a testimony against them" (Mk 6:11). When He comes to this place, what do you think God, the Savior and Creator of all creation, will do to those who do not receive Him but drive Him from themselves? Without doubt He shall cast them into everlasting fire, where there will be weeping of eyes and gnashing of teeth (Mt 25:41; 13:42). What good will be their pride and riches then?"

After all these words had been collected, on the day we were celebrating the memory of blessed Michael,[231] the angel again presented himself to me. I spoke to him, saying, "My lord, can we confidently confirm that all those words came from you?" I said this because he uttered some of those words in such a way that I could not see his face and some of the words were pronounced through my own mouth while I was in a trance.

At that, he looked at me with great severity and said, "Believe with your whole heart that these words that have been transcribed have come from my mouth. Blessed is the one who reads or hears the words of this book because they are true and I have never diverged from the truth."[232]

11. The Second Sermon: The Way of the Active Life.

He immediately began another sermon with these words: "I admonish those who are worn down by worldly concerns to think about the precepts of life, that is, to love God and to love your neighbor as yourself. Do not kill, do not steal, do not desire what belongs to others. Observe with zeal these and the other things that are written in the law of God and you will know that you can enter the kingdom of God.

"If they are not able to raise themselves to the height of contemplation, let them strive to fulfill the duties of legitimate action. Let them always have the fear of God in their minds and it will direct all their works. Let them visit the house of prayer with reverence and honor it with their means when necessary. Let them venerate the sacraments of the Lord in faith and humility, and freely devote their attention to the word of God; let them judge the ministers sanctified by God to be worthy of every honor, and let them meekly submit to their discipline. Whatever duty they owe to another, let them offer it peacefully, giving no one any occasion for quarrel. When they are injured, let them bear it, reserving vengeance for the Judge of the universe. Let them firmly speak the word of truth at its time and not refuse to endure distress for the sake of justice. Let them defend from oppression the orphan and widow and the one who is without an advocate, and relieve their sufferings with pious consolation. Let them refresh the hungry and thirsty, clothe the naked, take in the stranger, visit the sick and imprisoned (Mt 25:35–36). Let them lend freely and strive after works of mercy and equity. Let the more prudent teach the unlearned and recall to justice and truth those wandering and those walking amiss, and let them restrain discord among brothers.

"They must flee drunkenness and intoxication, impurity of the flesh, vain jokes and sinful speech, idleness, arrogant clothes, and the thorns of care, just as the divine word commands, casting all worry upon God (1 Pt 5:7). And they must not forget the mortification of the flesh. Moreover, I say to those who assist in charitable deeds: Do your works with a good and simple heart without murmuring and idle talk, so that you aggravate no one and you can aid the one suffering need. Guard against all avarice. Indeed, it acts in such a way that your works will be deceitful and you will defraud your neighbors and cheat and perjure the name of the Lord and gather unjust wealth, which plunges its owners into ruin. You who are in authority, do not act superior to those who are on this path, and do not oppress them unjustly, but rather, defend and protect them in every kindness and establish peace among them because you have been put in this position by the Lord. This is the way of the Lord, straight and beautiful, the way of holy actions. Those who walk in it till the end shall find life. They shall rest on the sacred mountain of God and their destiny will be with the children of light."

12. The Third Sermon: The Way of Martyrdom.

A feast day was being celebrated and we were attending the divine office when the angel appeared to me in the usual way. After I had blamed my sins for his unusually long absence, I said to him, "May it please you now, my lord, to introduce to us the discipline of the third path, that of the holy martyrs, and please do not refrain from this kindness due to any of my faults."

At that he opened his mouth and spoke, saying, "Christ the Lamb comes forth in the presence of the holy martyrs, and they follow Him with palm branches and crowns, rejoicing with Him in noble triumph. And Christ appears among them like a mirror and a model and a glorious ornament. Many are the passions by which the children of God are crowned, and no one will be crowned but the one who strives lawfully (2 Tm 2:5). Hear this and understand with your heart, you who suffer persecution for the sake of justice (Mt 5:10). Go rejoicing on this noble path, the path of warriors of the Lord, the path stained purple with the blood of the Lamb and the saints. Do not groan; let no murmur against the Lord arise in your heart as if you have been abandoned by Him and as if something new were happening to you. Read the scriptures of the Holy Spirit and think about the days of old. So many went before you on this path that you are treading; all were pleasing to God in their struggles. Through many straits they crossed into the spacious freedom of the glory of children of God.

"The first precursor of the Lamb was Abel, who, at the hand of his wicked brother, poured his blood upon the earth in the presence of the Lord as a testimony of his steadfast innocence. Abraham, father of the faithful people, was disturbed by the idolatry of an unjust nation, and he chose to be destroyed by fire rather than sin against his God, and through the hand of the Lord he was led from Ur of the Chaldeans. Because he loved innocence and accused his brothers' crime in the presence of his father, Joseph was sold to foreigners. Again, when he would not consent to immoral adultery, he endured long imprisonment with a calm mind. The prophets of the Lord, servants of truth, struggled against the transgressors of the Law to the point of death and ended their lives with many sufferings. In Babylon the young men of the Lord confidently resisted the order of the proud one whom all the earth feared. They chose to be given over to horrible fire rather than insult the Creator by kneeling before a created thing. Daniel, beloved by God because he honored the God of his fathers, was handed over to the lions' jaws. Vast is the number of saints who before the coming of the Savior offered examples of praiseworthy endurance, and in their deaths they anticipated the death of the Lord. The last of all was the innocent Baptist—among those born of women there arose none greater than he (Mt 11: 11). Because of his testimony to the truth his head was cut off and given to a girl in payment for a dance. Thus it was appropriate and pleasing to the Lord that not only blood of lambs, goats, and other animals symbolically foreshadow the blood of the Lamb who would be sacrificed for the salvation of all, but also that the blood of the children of God who would be redeemed would be poured out in offering to Him. In these last days, the immaculate Lamb, adored by the Cherubim, Seraphim, and the whole multitude of angels, and expected from the beginning of time, was sent from the mystery of the Father to atone for the sin of the world. And those whom He came to save did to Him what they pleased. There are books full of His struggles and suffering; you read about His sufferings, and yet you do not grasp it in your heart. How long will you be hard, O human children? The earth, which has no feeling, received drops of blood from the Savior's wounds and could not endure His majesty, but quaked and shook, and the hardest rocks were split. And behold, the manifold passion of the Son of God, who was killed for you, drips through the scriptures onto your heart, which does have reason, and yet you are able to suppress your groans and tears? You hear vanities that do not pertain to you, and you do not refrain from laughing."

After this, he continued, saying, "You, who go forth by the path of Jesus' tribulation, look and see if there is grief like His grief. He did not sin, He alone was born upon earth without sin, but the pains of evildoers filled His soul. The chains of the impious did not inflame the gentleness of the Lamb, nor did the false accusation, the evil mockery, the stripping and whipping, the blows, slaps, and spit, the thorns piercing His head, the cross and nails, and the lance and the outpouring of innocent blood. But in all these things His patience reigned, and in dying He destroyed the sting of death. Give heed, children of the cross, to the path of the Lamb and walk confidently in the traces of His blood. He is the guide of your journey and He shouts to you, saying, 'Be confident! I have conquered the world.'

"And why are you frightened at the face of human terror when you have an invincible leader and so many thousands of His imitators going before you with marvelous victory? Behold, not long before you, there took place countless battles of the servants of God—the apostles and martyrs and unconquered virgins. In their victories they gave glad spectacles to all the heavenly host. They loved God more than their own lives, and for His name they exposed themselves to all kinds of death and endured being trampled like mud by everyone. Lovers of the world laughed at the nakedness of the saints in the theaters and assemblies, and they were glutted with mocking the saints' shame. Like a beast devouring its prey, they delighted in the sundering of the saints' flesh, and they spattered innocent blood by cross and sword, fire and raging water, claws of iron and jaws of beasts. Whatever torture the cruelty of the impious could imagine was used in the attempt to kill them. The athletes of God rejoiced in their brokenness as if in a banquet, and they delighted in their cup of bitterness like those who take pleasure in many delights. The saints' patience was found faithful in its testing and strong beyond the strength of kings and princes of the world. On account of all this, behold, they were led into the refreshment of consolation and they rest in the embrace of the right hand of God. They have been made bright in the glory of the Lamb in the sight of God and the holy angels because they bore their ignominy in the presence of those who dwell on earth.

"Pay attention and with a vigilant mind consider again, O one who is puny in heart for enduring the sufferings of Christ. Think about the glory and joy surrounding the martyrs of the Lord, and you will not be afraid to share their pains and sufferings. But first you must disdain the substance of this world and its glory, which are here today and gone tomorrow. For if you love these things, courage will flee from you in the time of pressure and contempt. I also say this: Do not let your life be precious in your own eyes; instead, always consider it worthless and despicable. Indeed, those who love themselves and consider themselves great are not able to endure the abuse of persecution and are not fit for the contest of the saints. A happy exchange has been set before you. Refuse the life of short duration and miserable condition, and for it you will receive the life that knows no defect or uneasiness, a life full of glory and rejoicing, which no tongue knows how to describe. O person of darkened understanding, lift up your eyes and look into the future and see the blessed reformation of your body, which will come to you from your Savior when He plucks the thorn of Adam from your flesh and fashions your body according to the splendor of His own. May you thus hasten with eagerness to pour out your life in every danger in the zeal of His love, and in this way you shall reckon the loss of your life like drops shaken out onto the earth from a bucket. Why do you still worry, O person of God, at the face of the pursuer? Be comforted, be consoled, Christ is with you in persecution. His angels are with you in the struggle. They count up all your labors and support you in your weariness, for they also battle your enemies for you. Remember the word that He spoke to His servants, 'Whoever touches you, touches the pupil of My eye' (Zec 2:8). Servant of God, what do you give back to your Savior, who joined Himself to you in such a way that you cannot be wounded without injury to Him? He suffered once for you, and still daily He suffers in you and in your fellow servants and is made a mockery of (Heb 6:6). If you are sorrowful, grieve about His injuries, not your own. For yourself, however, rejoice and be glad because through tribulation you are being prepared for eternal glory and joy. You are the gold of the Lord; He tests you by fire so that He can receive you proven among His treasures."

Before the angel who was talking with me had finished this discourse, the feast of blessed Ursula and her eleven thousand companions had arrived.[233] At Matins, that divine verse, "God will render reward for the labors of His holy saints and will lead them on a marvelous path" was being sung.[234] So during the silent part of the Mass, when my instructor had appeared to me in his usual way, I took the opportunity to ask him, "Lord, show me which is the marvelous path that scripture mentions, saying, 'And He will lead them on a marvelous path.'" He immediately responded, saying, "This is the way of the holy martyrs." I questioned him again, saying, "And why is it called marvelous?" He replied, "It is aptly called marvelous. For is it not marvelous to human eyes that God inflames the mind of fragile human beings in such a way that, due to the magnitude of love for Him burning within them, they so forget their own life that they are made insensible to very harsh tortures and, without concern for themselves, they freely endure all things for His name? You can see this in those sacred virgins whose martyrdom you are celebrating today. They were fragile in sex and age and they had no protector, yet they did not fear the tyrants and their swords, but with constancy they offered their delicate members in death for the Lord. They could do this because they were strengthened spiritually by the fire of divine love so that they did not feel death physically. This indeed was extremely marvelous to human eyes, but not in the eyes of the Lord, to whom all things are possible (Mt 19:26). Have you not seen in spirit this marvelous path? Was it not more beautiful and extraordinary than all others? Thus know that the recompense of the martyrs is more outstanding than all recompense, and that nothing compares to their glory."

After this, when the feast of Saint Martin was at hand,[235] around the middle of the night, before Matins, I was suddenly awakened and sleep flew from my eyes. And behold, the angel of the Lord was standing before me and I spoke to him, saying, "I pray, my lord, that you now supply an exhortation for this sermon about the holy martyrs and bring it to a close with a suitable conclusion."

After he had made me contemplate certain sublime things in the heavens that I was not worthy to see, he fulfilled my request, saying, "Again I speak and warn you, O children of God, to pay careful attention to your predecessors described for you in this sermon. Look how they blazed in the love of Christ. Run and be strengthened and do not deliberate. Behold the Son of Peace watches over you; He receives you and rewards you beyond human reckoning. May the One who lives in perfect Trinity and reigns as true God forever and ever deign to manifest to you that spirit of Christ's love and charity which overcomes all weakness. Amen."

13. The Fourth[236] Sermon: The Way of Marriage.

I was praying and my lord appeared to me in his usual way and I asked him about the discipline of the path that was said to pertain to the order of married people. Immediately he agreed to my request and began in this way, "Behold, I speak to and warn married lay people. Restrain yourselves from the depraved acts by which you are polluted. The earth is contaminated by your worst iniquities, which are avarice, excess, fornication, adultery, murder, pride, anger, hatred, jealousy, blasphemy, and doubt. Pay attention, therefore, and examine your path and how you walk along it, since it is impossible for you to enter into it with such vices." Having said this, he withdrew.

When he appeared to me again, I asked that he continue the exhortation of the sermon he had begun. He said, "If the Lord were not kind and merciful, He would be wearied by the fact that He warns those who dwell on earth in so many ways, but they disdain His warnings and pay them no mind. They should be burning with love for His fatherly warnings, but instead they transform that love into indignation. They spurn His admonitions and are contemptuous of paying heed to those whom He sends. If it were possible for Him to worry, He would certainly be disturbed that in so many ways this world rises up against Him, this world for which He was born and suffered and worked many miracles and still does, even though no one pays attention. And behold, He gives His warnings even to those in the world who oppose Him in every way. He does this for the sake of His gracious kindness and for love of those who, although they live in the world, nevertheless love and serve Him, although, alas, their number is small. He would do this even more extensively if they would heed His warnings with better devotion."

After this, the angel opened his mouth and spoke, saying, "O irrational generation, burdensome to the Lord your God! You love with such ardor what your heavenly Father hates, and you are not afraid to provoke the Lord of heaven in whose sight the whole multitude of angels trembles. Tell me: What benefit is acquired by those who since the beginning of time have walked in the depravities that I enumerated to you and have not tried to propitiate the face of our God by the remedies of penance? What have all witnesses to the truth announced to you about such people? If you have forgotten, behold, I declare to you again in the presence of the living God: Heaven is closed to them with an eternal and indissoluble lock and the desirable face of our God will be hidden from them. They have become strangers to the eternal banquet of the joy of the saints, who abhor their evil ways. And behold, they have become consorts of the unyielding devil and his wretched angels, who ceaselessly afflict them without mercy, trample on their necks, which they had raised up against their Creator, and nourish them with their harshest afflictions. Because they have closed their eyes lest they see the light of the knowledge of God and His holy precepts, and because they have loved the works of darkness, they have been sent into the abyss of horrendous gloom, which has no exit and can never be illuminated by any light. They have disdained to have holy fear of the Lord, and they have provoked Him by the delight of their desire and have kindled in themselves the illicit burning of lust and anger and insatiable greed. Therefore, horror-filled fear, inconsolable sadness, and biting indignation hang over them. They have become coals of the eternal fire that can never be extinguished and yet are not consumed by any burning. Hear this, offenders of God, and forsake the ways of the perished while you have time for correction. Return to the pure life that God has prepared for you from the beginning and see how you can walk on it with fear of God.

"Your marriage is honorable not because of human invention but because it was instituted by the Creator of the universe in the paradise of innocence when He created your parents male and female. He spoke to them in their language, saying, 'On account of this a man leaves his father and mother and cleaves to his wife and the two become one in flesh' (Gn 2:24). Therefore, O man and woman, give honor to your order, which God has deigned to honor. Do not introduce breach or stain into your union. Let the Law of the Lord join you and sanctify you. Let there be one home, one table, a shared wealth, one bed, and one soul for you, and make room for the fear of the Lord in your midst. Fear of the Lord is the ornament of the marriage bed; the marriage bed that is devoid of it will be judged cursed and unclean by the Lord. Lust that knows no measure reigns there, and the deed unworthy of name, which nature did not ordain and which does not pertain to procreation, is practiced there. Let those who do this hear and understand that it is evil in the Lord's sight. Let them remove the stain from their beds. Let your heart be bound with fear of the Lord so that you impose restraint upon yourselves in the act allowed to you and do not follow every impulse of your desire in the manner of animals. Honor with continence feast days and days of lawful abstinence and the times of purgation, and if you add anything beyond this, the Lord will add His grace to you and your offspring. Those who do not distinguish between one day and another and one time and another by abstaining shall feel the vengeance of the Lord against themselves and their seed at an hour that they do not anticipate. Exhort each other to continence and pray for each other so you will be able to abstain and so that the spirit of uncleanness will flee from you. When, however, weakness prevails, the allowed remedy should be taken so that one does not sink to illicit things. As the doctor of the Gentiles wrote, 'A man does not have power over his own body, but the woman does; and a woman does not have power over her own body, but the man does. Therefore you cannot deny what's owed to each other' (1 Cor 7:3–4). Know, moreover, that the principal cause of your mutual knowledge must be the propagation of offspring. If it is anything else, it pertains to weakness and will be forgiven if it has the fear of God as restraint and almsgiving as remedy.

"With patience and compassion let the man support the frailties of the woman and the woman support the frailties of the man.

179

Do not disdain each other; instead, vie in showing the greater honor to each other. Bitter and contentious words should never arise between you; rather, reprove each other's excesses in the spirit of gentleness and good severity. Let the woman be obedient to the man and yield to and serve him as superior, just as the Creator ordained from the beginning. Let her tolerate the depraved ways of the man and propitiate his iniquities in the sight of the Lord with alms and prayers. She must declare her interior virtue externally by the modesty of her clothes, speech, gait, and appearance. Her eye should not linger on the face of a stranger, and she should always take care to cut off any occasion for suspicion and slander. The man who has received an intelligent and devout wife should not dishonor her with foul and bitter speech but should honor her as a vessel of the grace of God. He should show himself fit for her and give thanks to the God of heaven, who blessed him with such a marriage.

"Listen to me and groan over the evils of humankind that I am relating to you. In these days, men of great number bend their hearts to the foolishness of women and are made stupid in conforming to their insanity. Arrogance in attire, which you have seen and detested in the daughters of the world who have come to you, increases on earth beyond measure. People are crazy about their dress and thereby invite the wrath of God upon the world. They are proud to walk with steps impeded by their layers of clothes, and they uselessly try to consume what could be the bare necessities of the poor. Oh, the wretchedness! Oh, the miserable blindness! What was acquired with great effort they consign to the mud in order to attract the eyes of adulterers. Able to purchase the kingdom of God, they are buying the fire of gehenna. Men—remove this evil from the sight of the Lord! Do not glory in the vanities of your wives but be indignant that they are dressing like whores. That excess of cloth and the tight garments serve no purpose except suffocating births. The arrogant hair coverings and many things like this are the inventions of venal women and do not pertain to lawful wives.

"This is my cry from the Lord to you who have set aside virile severity and put on the softness of women. You are so stupid and vain! Why have you abandoned the serious customs of the righteous elders who have gone before you? Why have you turned toward the vanities and insanities of devilish invention that offer you nothing but the increase of your perdition? Woe to you who are proud in the pomp of splendid, superfluous, and delicately tailored garments, and who pride yourselves in despising what was eagerly sought. Woe to you who indulge in womanly hairstyles and are not embarrassed to dishonor your masculine form! Woe to you who waste your time in vain games, in revels and drunkenness! Woe to you who are eloquent in mockery and detraction, in useless storytelling, in causing sorrow, and in subverting the cause of the innocent! Woe to you who have venal words in council and rejoice to fill your belly with the distress of the oppressed! Woe to you who are contentious and haughty among your fellow citizens. Woe to you who are greedy and profoundly intent on multiplying your worldly wealth, which will vanish with you! He who set the ear in place, does He not hear? And He who fashioned the eye, does He not see this (Ps 93:9)? Children of the world, stop irritating the Lord. Behold, the time is near for Him to awaken and devour His irritators in the fire of His zeal.

"Again I say to you who are under the yoke of matrimony: Fear God, and guard your faith and unstained love for each other. Nourish your sons and daughters and family in fear of the Lord and purity. Do not delay in offering tithes for the Lord and wages for the laborer (Tb 4:15). Do not forget kindness to the poor and take care to observe the other saving works that I announced in this sermon from the Lord. This is the delightful loveliness of your path, which was shown in the mysterious vision. Blessed are those who love it. Yet those who walk in this path must have the tribulation of the flesh and the cares of the world that those who are chaste do not experience, just as is expressed in the symbol of the thorns. It is the will of God that you should turn away from them as much as possible, observing a reasonable course in everything and curbing your own will in fear of the Lord."

My brother asked me to question the angel as to why, at the beginning of this sermon, the term "fornication" was added to the other sins when fornication does not seem to apply to married people, which is what he had been discussing. Indeed, the incontinence of married people had been expressed there by the term "adultery." I began to question my lord about this uncertainty and had not yet fully explained it when he spoke to me, saying, "The earth is full of uncleanness. A man who has a spouse joined to him in a legal marriage secretly pollutes the wife of his neighbor and, in her turn, a woman takes the husband of another woman. This is the worst iniquity and vast is the number of those who offend in this way. The earth is full of the uncleanness of fornication. Everybody hurries to it as if thirsty, and scarcely anyone is found who has not rushed into this pit. When they have become inflamed with carnal desire, they can hardly wait to act it out. And when they have fulfilled their worst desires, they do not rest but again and again they return to it, thinking that they can never be satisfied. But even before they are old enough to be able to practice this depravity, they stain their innocence in many ways. Therefore, I added the term fornication in rebuking married people because they too are greatly defiled by it before they take on the law of marriage and bring down the wrath of God upon themselves. Then, coming to legitimate marriage, they are deprived of the fruit of offspring by the Lord. They wonder why it happens to them, not knowing the cause of their sterility. Those to whom offspring are conceded are struck by divine judgment in many other ways, either in the offspring themselves or in other crucial matters, and all things turn out unhappily for them."

I also asked him about the term "blasphemy." He said, "I said this on account of those who dishonor their neighbors with disgraceful insults." Then I asked about the doubts that he condemned in the sermon. He responded in this way, "There are many people in the church who appear to be Christians but nevertheless are wavering in the Christian faith. They live openly among Catholics, enter the house of prayer, receive the sacraments of the faith with the others, and yet have no faith in these practices, nor do they judge them useful for salvation. They openly confirm this in the very bad things they do. If they had true faith, they would abstain from their many evils." He continued, "There are many heresies these days, but secret ones. And there are many heretics who secretly oppose the catholic faith and turn many other people away from it."

Then I asked him, "My lord, what do you have to say about those who are called Cathars, who are said to completely condemn the life of married people?" He responded, "The life of those about whom you inquire is abominable to the Lord. They cannot criticize the life of those who lawfully contract marriage and live together in fear of God according to His law, observing holy days and fasts and showing compassion for the needs of the poor."

Again I addressed him, saying, "Lord, as I have heard, certain Cathars assert that a lawful marriage is not possible except between two people who have both guarded their virginity up until the time of lawful union. What do you say to this?"

He responded, "Where such a union is possible, it is pleasing to the Lord. But it very rarely happens in this way. Furthermore, among those who have not remained chaste, there are many who are acceptable to the Lord, have lawful unions, and walk in the commands of the Lord. Otherwise, the numbers of the people of God would be severely diminished. Those about whom you speak have nothing to condemn in the church of God because they themselves are worthy of every condemnation. Know for certain that they are the ministers of Satan, whose depraved works they do. He is their leader and goes before them with models of every evil and they follow him in all his worst works."

I said, "Lord, what is their faith or life like?" He replied, "Their faith is depraved and their works are even worse." Again I spoke, "But people see them as just, and they are praised as if they are doing good works." "That is so," he answered. "They feign the appearance of a just and innocent life and through this they seduce and draw many to themselves, even though on the inside they are full of the worst venom."

14. The Fifth Sermon: The Way of Chastity.

While we were celebrating the solemnity of blessed John the Evangelist,[237] I was engrossed in prayer after Matins and, with a strong effort of my heart, I was praying to the Lord that in His customary kindness He would deign to reveal to me the discipline of the path of the chaste, which I had seen in spirit. I was also invoking the divine evangelist and my angel guide to help me. When I was exhausted from praying, I closed my eyes a little to sleep. After a moment, I was suddenly awakened and behold, the angel stood by me and with these words began the sermon that I had been hoping for: "I say to you, O children of God, O children of light—examine your path, how it flowers and how delightful it is to run on it. Run, therefore, and hasten to meet your Spouse, who awaits you. Love chastity and preserve the integrity of your virginity for Him. The virgin runs well when adorned with chastity, love, prudence, and humility." When he had said this, he added no more.

On the following day, at the celebration of the Mass of the Blessed Innocents,[238] the Book of the Apocalypse was being read. I took the occasion of the reading to beseech my lord, who was again standing by me, "Lord, if I have found favor in your presence, I beg you to tell me what canticle the blessed martyrs sing before the throne of God and the Lamb, just as the present reading attests. Also, how it is that they follow the Lamb wherever He goes" (Rv 14:1–5)?

He responded, saying, "Why do you ask me? No tongue will ever sing this song on earth. I will tell you nothing about this. However, you also asked how it is that they follow the Lamb wherever He goes. This means that they imitate the Lamb in all His virtues. They follow Him in the virginity which is without stain in them, just as that holy Lamb is completely without stain. They were humble and simple and without guile, just like the Lamb. They had patience in martyrdom, just like the Lamb, who showed no impatience in the passion by which He destroyed the sin of the world. No virgins or martyrs follow the footsteps of the Lamb as fully as they did, except for our Queen who first guarded her virginity pure and immaculate for the Lord. That outstanding Virgin and those blessed martyrs are the mirror for all holy virgins. Many have followed them, pouring out their blood for their virginity. For this they have been crowned and glorified in the sight of the Lord. All virgins must look to them and contemplate how they have gone before them in sanctity and they must shape their lives to resemble them."

Again, on the Circumcision of the Lord,[239] when my lord had presented himself to me, I said to him, "My lord, teach me, I beg you, about the integrity of virginity. Can one who is often tempted by impure lust be pardoned if the lust has not led all the way to the deed itself?"

He said, "One is not pardoned, but rather one is polluted in many ways by the impurities of lust even if it does not proceed to effect. But, although the integrity is polluted, it remains nonetheless, as I will show you by this comparison." Then he said to me, "Extend your hand!" When I had extended it, he said, "Close it." I did so. Then I looked down and saw before my feet what looked like unclean filth.[240] And he said to me, "Put your hand in it!" When I had done this, he said, "Take it out!" When I had removed it, it was soiled. And he said, "Plunge it in again. As often as you do it, your hand will be that much more soiled and difficult to clean." I also felt a heat in my hand. He said, "It is warm and the warmer it becomes the greater will be the effort needed to cleanse it. Thus, the more one pollutes oneself in the impurities of carnal desire, it is that much harder to be cleansed of them. Nevertheless, it is possible to be cleansed by the pain of salvific penance and by tears and good works in such a way that one can become even more pleasing to God than before. Isn't your hand clean and beautiful inside? So is virginity when the uncleanness of a perverse act does not reach its inner part. It can be cleansed of pollution in such a way that its integrity suffers no harm, just as your hand, which was only externally polluted, is easily cleansed. But if the act itself is done and the uncleanness penetrates to the interior part, it would be impossible to cleanse it so that it returns completely to its original beauty. Furthermore, there are many who, although they do not draw their lust out to the act of commingling, still pollute the integrity of their virginity in many ways. They do not turn their minds and hearts to being fully purified with the remedies of penance and to making satisfaction to God, and they remain polluted until the end. Their virginity is not acceptable to God and loses its due reward."

When he had said these things, I was afraid that the order of the words might slip from my memory. Therefore, I asked him to repeat them to me, and he kindly granted my request. Moreover, when he again presented himself to me on the octave of blessed John,[241] he anticipated my words, cheerfully saying, "You want to ask me a question. Ask, and I will answer you." Just as I had been advised by a teacher, I said, "Lord, it is written that the will is to be judged as the deed.[242] Doesn't this contradict the sermon that you just delivered?"

He responded, "Not at all!" Then he added, "What you declare is written is certainly true. One may have the will to engage in a particular act. This will does not abide within the person without leading to the desired effect. Thus the will persists until the end and it is judged as deed by the Lord. If there should be any evil deed that one desired to carry out, it can be wiped away by the power of true penitence. Indeed, anything a person might have done in thought or will can be annulled in this way before the Lord as if it had never happened. Remember that I told you a second time to stick your hand in the filth and that it would then be more difficult to cleanse it. In such a way a person is first polluted by thought alone, thereafter also by will. Then one is cleansed only with greater difficulty, yet one's integrity remains."

Then he referred to a scriptural passage that I had planned to ask about, and said, "It is also written, 'One who looks at a woman lustfully has already committed adultery with her in his heart' (Mt 5:28). This is so. If a person persists in the will to act on his or her lust and does not abandon that desire, however much the desire remains, the person will lead the matter to effect. Without washing away the evil desire by the fruit of repentance, the person's integrity, although it may remain, is useless and gains no reward."

Again I spoke, adding, "Lord, some people unwillingly experience torments of the flesh in temptation and are vexed by the heat that opposes the purity of their bodies, yet are not strong enough to avoid it by any means of resistance. Will this be judged as sin?" He said, "If they are vexed by temptations of this kind and do not consent to them with their minds, they will receive the indulgence of a lighter penance for the guilt that they incur and they will attain a great reward."

Then he showed to me a person in Christ who is close to me, God knows who he or she is. This person was enduring an assault on chastity from the Adversary and crushing his or her soul with excessive afflictions because of this. And he said, "Announce consolation to this one and say that the affliction should cease. Let this one remember what is written about the chosen ones of the Lord,

'He tested them like gold in the furnace' (Wis 3:6). Let this one have joy, but not without sadness. Joy, because the Lord has deigned to impose such a thing, which prepares one for a great reward. But it is not without sadness, because guilt cannot be completely avoided in temptation like this."

I said, "Lord, how should one resist the Adversary and by which weapons will he be overcome?" He replied, "One should fight by prayer and confession and flagellation of the flesh, and with these, one will conquer. But one should not continually ask the Lord to be liberated from this torment but should pray instead for the Lord's mercy. At the time of temptation, if this one should be in a secret place, he or she should kneel three times before the Lord. If, however, there is no place to do this, three times should this one seal the heart with the sign of the cross and say, 'Savior of the world, save us whom you have redeemed by your cross and blood. Our God, we beg you to come to our aid.'"

After this, one day my tongue was set in motion with these words, "O virgins, behold! The divine voice shouts to you; the voice of your Spouse beats upon your ears. Open the palace of your heart to Him and lead Him in and embrace Him because He is more beautiful and lovable than all creatures."

To this the angel added, "The Lord of majesty, only begotten of the Most High, King of the divine hosts, filling the heavens and earth with His wondrous glory, great and awesome in omnipotent strength, sweet and lovable in incomparable kindness, and wholly desirable in the brilliance of His perfect beauty, whose marvelous face the Cherubim and Seraphim and our whole company delight to gaze upon with unceasing desire, this one, O virgins, this is the one who desires your beauty, who invites you to His pure embraces. He begs of you the glorious lilies of your virginity so that He can adorn His secret marriage chamber with them. That wedding chamber knows no defect of modesty, and nothing corrupt enters it. The precious flowers of virginity neither fade nor pass away there but remain in incorruptible beauty. The immaculate Lamb gladly sleeps among them and inhales their sweet scent. The sacred virgins gleam in the marriage chamber of their Spouse like choice and desirable pearls. He is the one who washed them in the blood of His

187

side, the Virgin who set a sign upon their faces, the Spouse who rejoices in their appearance and graciously reveals the secrets of His beauty to His dearest ones. There the organs of the elect play harmonies in the spirit of peace. There a song, lovely to hear, is sung, a song of special gladness that can be sung by virgins alone and the heavenly spirits belonging to the bridal chamber. The Spouse leads the choir in a clear and excellent voice and not one in the thousands of singers can equal Him. His voice, a voice sweet in the fullness of grace, fills all the heavens with delight—blessed are those who hear it, very blessed are those who sing with it! Among these, our leader, the Virgin Theotokos has primacy. To her alone was it given to lift up her voice above all the angels' trumpets.

"Pay attention, daughters, to the words of my minister and seal them in the hidden place in your mind. If your heart is for the noble and beautiful Spouse, the one who is worthy to be loved, why do you neglect Him? Why do you hesitate to extend your whole strength to that Spouse? Nothing in heaven or on earth is brighter, nothing more lovable than Him. If you love glory, what is more glorious than to have such a Spouse and to possess everything in Him? If you desire to have delights and pleasures, hurry to the bridal chamber of delight that has been prepared for you. Nothing that the eye has seen or the ear has heard or has arisen in human hearts can be compared to its delight and sweetness" (1 Cor 2:9).

After he had said these things, I placed in my heart the words he had said about the virgins' song, and I prepared my question, saying, "It isn't really like that, is it, my lord? Don't angels also sing this song? And do *all* the virgins?"

He said, "In fact, angels do sing this song, as do all those who make their way from this life to heaven without stain."

I continued, "How, then, should we understand the scriptural passage which says, 'And nobody was able to say the song except those one hundred and forty-four thousand' (Rv 14:3)? Are all virgins included in that number?"

"This is how it is," he said. "This is the perfect number and it signifies the perfection of those who have preserved themselves unstained just as the holy infancy of the Innocents is without stain."

The weakness of my understanding, however, could not hold onto what else he said about this number.

Again taking up the word of exhortation, he spoke, saying, "Behold your Spouse is coming. Prepare yourselves, O virgins. Go and buy wedding garments for yourselves and enter with Him to the wedding lest it be said to you, 'How have you entered here when you have no wedding garments?' (Mt 22:12) Lest perchance you be reckoned among the reprobate, think now with complete attention of your mind, how you may be pleasing to your Spouse when He comes. Be watchful, therefore, lest by chance He should find you sleeping with the foolish virgins." He continued again, saying, "Hear these words, O virgins, and open the ears of your heart, and understand how your Spouse invites you. If you knew how beautiful and lovable is He whom the whole heavenly multitude always gazes upon with every desire, you would without a doubt spurn the world with all its trappings; you would throw behind you all the glory of the age. You would direct every effort to loving fully your holy Spouse, the Lord Christ, and you would always be anxious to preserve your heart and your body clean and spotless for Him."

After this I questioned him saying, "Lord, what are those wedding garments to which you referred?"

He responded, "Virgins must go to the inner places of their hearts and there they must buy three kinds of ornaments. They must have one white and spotless vestment, which is the innocence of the flesh. Also necessary for them is a garment in which they are to be wrapped, and this is the charity with which they must love their Spouse. Their third ornament is a golden necklace, which is modesty, by which they must constrain themselves to be modest in speech, hearing, living, and doing anything that might be immodest. This is the sign about which it is said, 'He has placed a sign on my face.'" I believe that he added this because I had asked him about that on the feast of blessed Agnes[243] and he had given me no answer.

Again I said, "Lord, at what price are these ornaments purchased by the virgins?"

He said, "By chastising the body and one denarius, which is contemplation of the modesty of the Spouse. They must place this contemplation in the center of their hearts. The denarius is stamped with a royal image, since He is the King of all kings, blessed forever."

Again I inquired of him, saying, "Remember, Lord, that expression you used, 'The virgin adorned with chastity, love, prudence, and humility runs well.' There you distinguished four ornaments, and in this later distinction you have designated the first two and seem to have omitted the last two."

He said, "The one who diligently inquires about these things can be called a man of desires" (Dn 9:23).[244] Then he responded to my question, saying, "The two things that seem to you to be omitted are included under the term *necklace*. As indeed the virgin constrains her heart against everything that is shameless, it could not be done without great prudence. Moreover, humility could not be absent from her if true prudence were present."

After several days I again brought up a question about the previous sermon. "Lord, when it is well known that those virgins who are found without their wedding garments will not be able to enter the wedding with the Spouse, how then could it be said to them, 'How have you entered here, not having your wedding clothes?'" (Mt 22:12)

He responded, "This saying pertains to the Last Judgment. There will be gathered before the face of Christ all His chosen brides, adorned with their marriage clothes according to the good works they did in this world. The reprobate will also be there. They will have no garment appropriate for marriage because they neglected to do good works during their lives. Because of this, the Spouse will say to them, 'Go, cursed, into eternal fire' (Mt 25:41). From that voice they will also hear the rebuke, 'How have you entered here, when you have no wedding garments?'"

Again he exhorted, "Listen and incline your heart to me, simple virgin, beloved of the Lord. Do not emulate the daughters of the world who walk prosperously in their luxuries and who seek to please human eyes rather than God's. They strive to be well put together and adorned so that they might receive praise from those seeing them. They become a trap and the ruin of many. But just like the words of their admirers, so their beauty is also of the moment. Just as the foam on water is easily dissolved and a spark shooting up from a fire is quickly extinguished, so the beauty of the body and all of its glory is like the flower of a tree, which appears for less than an hour and is immediately shaken off by the force of the wind. But you, daughter, set your heart so that you may walk, well put together and beautiful, in the sight of your chaste, jealous one,[245] our King, who watches you from the heavens and numbers all your ways. Take hold of that beauty which neither fades with death nor perishes with old age, and which lack of perishable wealth does not darken. The more beautiful you are in appearance, the more you must take care to become attractive in mind, because the charm of appearance is false. May your glory be from within so that you please your Spouse, who looks into your heart. Examine the path of chastity and notice that it has the greenness of grass and the beauty of flowers on both sides. Make room for chastity not only in the flesh but also in the spirit, because chastity of the flesh is useless where incontinence of the spirit reigns—likewise with the other things that defile the soul. Pay attention to what I am saying, 'Just as a lamp cannot shine without the provision of oil, so continence of the flesh cannot shine before the celestial Spouse without chastity of the spirit.'"

To these words I posed the following question, "Lord, our path appeared narrow in the vision. Why is that, since scripture says, 'I shall walk in spaciousness because I have sought your commands' (Ps 118:45)? What is that spaciousness and how can I understand it in this path?" He responded in this way, "This spaciousness is the strong intention of the heart and the charity burning within with which chaste souls burn for their Spouse, Christ the Lord, who is the spaciousness and fullness of all the paths of God. Consider the freedom of this path, which has no thorns and obstacles. This is the effect of charity, which operates especially in virgins as it banishes the thorns of care and all malice so that they can be free to meditate on divine matters, on how they can please God, whom they love above all else."

When I had again asked him about the narrowness of this path, he said, "Virgins must confine themselves so that they never withdraw from themselves." I said, "Lord, are they able to depart from themselves?" "They are," he said. And I said, "How do they do this?" He said, "By idleness and gossip and all things that carry their

Spouse away from their memory." And he added, "The narrowness of the path and the narrowness of the necklace, which I have outlined to you, have the same meaning because the brides of Christ must always walk a narrow way in matters pertaining to this world."

After he had delivered these messages and it was the second Sunday of Lent, the feast day of blessed Matthias the Apostle,[246] the blessed, holy angel of the Lord appeared to me at the time of the divine sacrifice. I said to him, "I beg you, my lord, if now is the right time and if it is good in your view, to add an appropriate conclusion to the sermon to virgins of the Lord, which you have expounded up to this point."

I had hardly finished this request when he immediately opened his mouth with these words, "Behold, I will urge you again, most beloved children of the Lord. Keep yourselves from charms of vices that fight against the spirit. Utter to the Lord the thoughts of your heart and He will nourish you, as it is pleasing to Him, and He will lead you into the banquet of eternal life that has been prepared for you by Jesus Christ, Son of the living God, who lives and reigns with the Father and the Holy Spirit for ever and ever. Amen."

15. The Sixth Sermon: The Way of the Prelates.

Having concluded the preceding sermon, the angel of the Lord delayed longer than usual in visiting me. I attributed this to my failings and began to worry to myself. I struggled diligently with tears and prayers, and the members of our convent helped me by our communal prayer. When seventeen days had passed from when he had finished the previous lesson, I was standing alone in the oratory around the third hour, pouring out my heart to the Lord and saying, "In all the things you have done for me up until now, Lord, you have not regarded my merits. Rather, in your mercy you have done all these things. For this reason I beg you not to hold back because of my failings or those of anyone else, without leading to a good conclusion what you in your goodness have deigned to begin in me. About the path of the church's leaders, which you showed to me in the vision: May you deign to reveal to us the appropriate discipline, from which some fruit of correction may derive, just as you know is necessary for your people."

Just then, as I was saying this and similar things in prayer, behold, the angel of my desire suddenly appeared to me and began the sermon that I was longing for with these words, "The Lord spoke these things, 'Behold, I send My angel (Mal 3:1) so that he will announce to those of you in high power who provoke Me to anger. Moreover, I say to you that the iniquity of the earth which you hide for gold and silver rises before Me like smoke from a fire. Are not the souls that you smother in eternal fire because of your avarice worth more than gold and silver? Therefore your own religion accuses you in My presence. Behold, you have even made your sanctification stink in the view of My people and it is turned into an abomination to Me. You seized the dominion of My saints, and I did not know it; you polluted My bed, and I said nothing. Why do you exasperate My gentleness? Whence have you come up to disturb My sheepfold and burden My heart about My children to whom I gave birth in the bitterness of My spirit on the day of My struggle and sufferings?'"

He continued to speak to me, saying, "'Are not My pastors hardened as if in a heavy sleep? What should I do to awaken them for My flocks who are scattered like sheep feeding in green pastures? My people have become wanderers, following their own hearts. They run with the whole force of their soul after their own desires. My pastors have neither the voice nor the mind for gathering and rebuking those who are scattered. They have become mute,' says the Lord. 'They have become stupid, but to themselves they are wise and eloquent. Their mouth is open, their tongue is versatile and sharp for gathering the grapes of My vineyard in which they have not labored. Their foot is swift and they run about in agitation to tear out and devour the flesh of My people whose spiritual needs they do not serve, they who are slow to move a finger to rescue from iniquity the souls for whom I have tasted death. Like people who are ignorant of My name they do not fear to proceed against Me. They walk under My name and sadden the heart of My people with unfair exaction. They do not bother to remove from My eyes the iniquity of the adulterer and the fornicator, of the one who violently strikes a neighbor, of the thief and evildoer, of the liar and usurer, of the one who deceives in weights and measures, of the one who pollutes My Sabbath with shameful dalliance, of the one who transgresses a vow of purity, of the uncircumcised one who dishonors My altar, not acknowledging that it is the purest of the pure, of the one who buys and sells My sanctification and is proud about inheriting My sanctuary. By these and other practices that I have prohibited by My laws, they destroy My house as if with a flame of desolation. They make Me weary of the children of the world. My pastors are silent in their duties and they sleep in the desires of their souls. They plant their steps according to their own plans and their will find retribution worthy of their course,' says the Lord."

The angel who spoke with me at various times went on in this way, and I said to him, "Lord, what is that awakening with which the Lord threatened His pastors?"

And again, continuing to announce the threatening words of the Lord, the angel spoke as if in anger, saying, "'You who sleep at My rebukes and whose heart is blinded by sleep, I am going to make you wake up when the ancient death will come over you and that old serpent will devour you with great force because you have stored up treasures for yourself in infernal punishment. Wretched and irrational ones, open your eyes and read the scriptures and recall the religion in which your predecessors walked before you.'"

After a brief delay, he added more, saying, "Look at the great pontiff, high above all else, the Lord Jesus. Look at how in the days of His obedience He walked in the midst of His disciples, not in the stature of one who rules but in the humility of one who serves, like a pious, jealous guardian of His flock until the consummation of His death for them. Look at His seed which is blessed, the ministers of your vocation, the blessed apostles and their successors. In their seats you take pride and you feast to your heart's desire on their labors. Were their ways like your ways? Do not even think it to be so, because their ways were beautiful and righteous but your ways are polluted and there is no right order in them. They did not walk in haughty spirit, nor in the commotion of a proud escort, greed for profits, magnificence of vestments, dissolution of the heart, intoxication and drunkenness and stains of the flesh, nor the vanity of gaming and running about after their dogs and birds. Moreover, with all integrity they stuck to the footsteps of the great pastor, keeping faithful watch over the flock of the Lord day and night. In their struggles and hardships and lack of necessities, and as if in the suffering of one giving birth, they fulfilled their ministry. They endured being rejected and abused by others and persecutions which no one can number. They gave their souls to death so that they could fill the earth with the Gospel of God and bring light to the souls of the elect."

While we were celebrating the feast of Easter,[247] at the time of the divine sacrifice, after the reading of the gospel, the angel of the Lord appeared, standing before me. I asked that he might deign to make sure that no act of negligence occur during that holy communion, which we were awaiting. I also asked that he might deign to continue the sermon he had begun about the leaders of the church. He gave a brief response to this, saying, "If they were worthy, the Lord would reveal many great things about them." Having said this, he immediately went to the altar with haste, and with two other angels who had arrived at the beginning of Mass, he stood by with great attention until we had all taken communion.

On the next day, however, around the same time he came and began in this way, saying, "'The head of the Church has languished and its members are dead, for the apostolic seat is filled with pride, avarice is cultivated, and it is full of iniquity and impiety. They scandalize My sheep and make them go astray when they should have been protecting and guiding them.' These words come mightily from the Lord: 'Will My right hand forget this? Not at all! Without a doubt, unless they be converted and correct their evil ways, I the Lord will destroy them.'"

Again, on another day, he added more, saying, "The Lord says this to the great prelates of the Church: 'Think about what reason you are going to give at the frightful judgment about My sheep, whom you have received to govern and protect, since you have purchased the spiritual gifts of My people at the price of wretchedness. Therefore, I now send you fatherly warnings; lest you be condemned, see that you be converted from your evil ways and purify your consciences and I will be reconciled to you. Otherwise, I the Lord will wipe out your memory from the land of the living.'"

After this, he spoke as if announcing the word of the Lord in the spirit of mercy, and said, "'I the Lord shout and warn My pastors, yet why do they not hear the sound of My warning? I stand and knock at the door of their hearts, and they do not open to Me. Listen and understand the words of My warning and delight in My love, for I warn My pastors and My sheep with fatherly warning. Indeed, among My pastors there are some who are good and peaceful, but alas, how few they are! There are many others who are evil and perverse, who provoke Me to anger. Thus it is necessary to warn the good to become better and the evil and perverse to be converted lest they vanish from the righteous path.'"

When he visited me again, he added, "Behold the Lord continues speaking to His pastors, 'With all the attention of your mind consider your path, the straight path, and do not go astray in it. Be alert and keep the night watch over My flock, like good, jealous guardians, lest a flock of goats overcome it. The goats are the evil spirit that scatters the flocks of My sheep. You, My peaceful ones, rejoice with gladness,' says the Lord, 'and remember My words found in the present sermon. Guard yourself from the forbidden things of this world, and love My admonition. Indeed, I should be loved for such an admonition. Because if you love Me and honor My name—since indeed you have received your name from Mine— I will honor you in the presence of My holy angels.'"

While the angel was delivering this sermon about the pastors of the church, it seemed to some people a good opportunity for me to ask about something that certain doubting people take as an occasion for error. Therefore, inquiring not as one hesitating in faith but as one wishing to confirm our faith with angelic authority, I asked: "Lord, do the divine services of those bishops who enter the episcopacy in an evil way and not according to God have the same power in ecclesiastical sacraments as those bishops whose entry is good?"

He responded, saying, "Many are more corrupted than corrected in close examination of such things. The Lord would reveal such things if those to whom they pertain[248] would not sin the more freely for it." Having said these things, he was immediately removed from my sight.

But when he came to me on another day, I asked it again, repeating the same question. He said, "They have the same power, but it is more pleasing to God in the services of those who entered rightly."

I spoke again, saying, "My lord, isn't it the case that we believe that priests ordained by those whose entry is evil have the same power of consecrating the body and blood of the Lord on the altar as do priests who were ordained by those who lawfully entered the episcopacy?"

He replied, "No doubt should arise in your heart about this. Rather, be assured that all who have received priesthood in ecclesiastical ordination have the same power in consecrating the sacrament of the Lord, whether those who ordained them entered rightly or wrongly. The divine words said in the sacred canon are of such power before the Lord that the body and blood of the Lord are truly made when they are pronounced, no matter which priest pronounces them. For indeed, that consecration is not effected by the merits of good people nor is it obstructed by the sins of the evil. However, even though neither those priests nor those who ordain them are ineffective in the divine sacraments, nevertheless they are blameworthy and will be overcome by greater damnation in the future."

Because this whole sermon seemed to pertain to our fathers who exercise spiritual judgment in the church, I implored the angel of the Lord, saying, "Lord, just as up till now you have administered the words of warning to spiritual leaders, I pray that you may now deign to announce some admonitions to those who exercise secular judgments, so that they may be reformed by the Lord."

He immediately consented to my request and began the sermon pertaining to them with these words, "Behold, the Lord has appointed princes and judges above His people so that they will render judgment and justice and establish truth and peace so that all people may be pleasing before the living God. 'Now, however, My princes and judges,' says the Lord, 'are like the horse and mule who have no understanding. They walk in My presence inflated with pride and with outstretched necks. They do not give glory to God, from whom all power in heaven and on the earth comes, but they glory in their own strength. I have lifted them up above the earth and honored[249] them, and behold, they disdain to know Me and glorify Me. If indeed they knew My name, which is great and to be feared, and My strong right hand, which I have extended over them, they would perhaps be humbled under My hand and retract their necks, which they have stretched out in contempt of Me. They would bow their face to the earth from which I raised them and their fathers.

"'I say to you, rulers of the earth who reach up to the heights—the noise of your iniquity rises to heaven before Me! Listen to the voice of My rebuke and I will dispute with you in the hearing of My people. Don't you know that all the kingdoms of the world and all their glory are Mine, and that I have the power of giving them to whom I choose and I will choose the hour for taking them back again? Don't you know that all living things exist at the command of My mouth and that My word has the power to divide your spirit from your flesh in the blink of an eye? Why is your heart lifted up in these things that you have received at My command and yet you are not more concerned to serve Me in your high position and to thank Me for the extent of My kindness? Return to your heart and see what I have done for you and what you have given back to Me. I the Lord, your ruler, found you not meriting grace in My presence and yet I lifted you up, as I wished, from the whole number of many peoples. I have exalted you above the height of princes and judges of the earth. I have poured out on you the oil of My sanctification and have placed the crown of glory on your head; I have presented the rod of dominion to your right hand, and with the sword of My vengeance I have girt you. I have glorified you in the presence of all My people with riches and lofty dominion, and I have given you great strength for destroying the power of those who rebel against you, and I have spread the reputation of your name across the breadth of the earth.

"'I the Lord made you all these things so that you would magnify the praise of My name on the earth and exercise My justice among those, great and small, whom I have made subject to you. I did this so that you would unite all My people in the bonds of peace and fairness and you would give yourself as a faithful refuge to everyone who is oppressed and suffering injury. I did this so that you would be My avenger against those who violate peace and justice, and that you would calm the earth against those who disturb it and make it desolate with sword and fire and violent predation, against those who devour the labors of others and turn cultivators of the earth into wanderers and beggars, against those who dishonor My holy name by which I have marked My people and set them apart as My inheritance. This was the yoke of My servitude, which I placed upon you on the day I exalted you above the highest of My people.

"'You, however, shook it from your neck and for all the glory I gave you, you returned to Me not fear and honor, but contempt and aggravation. You have closed the eyes of your mind so that you do not look to your Judge, who is in heaven. You have overturned what is just on account of the avarice and pride of your heart, and you have strengthened iniquity on earth and established it on high. When you traverse the earth, behind you I hear the cries and groans of My people, and much complaint accuses your pride because your army is intolerable and the iniquity of those surrounding you cannot be counted. You are burdensome to My people and this is a trifle to you. But you are also grievous and abominable to the Lord your God. In the filth of your shamelessness you are not afraid to provoke Me to indignation. You dishonor My holy oil by which I have anointed you. My honorable name, which I have placed upon you, you have polluted and made to be blasphemed among a multitude of people because of the insatiable sin that reigns in you. On account of this I have sworn on the strength of My right hand,' says the Lord, 'that behold, soon I will inflict My hardest vengeance upon your heads. Just as you have sinned mightily, so I will make you mightily tormented and trampled by the unclean spirits whom you serve. Affliction shall not be withdrawn from you this time if you do not do penance and withdraw from the evil ways by which you draw My anger into your kingdoms.

"'Repent, therefore, and do not delay. With all vigilance strive to fulfill the ministry to which I have called you. I will remember My ancient compassion on you and I will be merciful on your various iniquities and will magnify you according to the magnitude of My royal servants who were before you. In My kingdom I will bestow upon you a crown of glory that will not vanish from your head for all eternity.

"'All you princes and judges who carry out the iniquity of your kings, pay attention to My words. Correct your depraved ways with the rebukes with which I chastised your kings. Retreat from avarice and deceit, you who smother My justice for the gifts and human favor and encourage the hearts of My people in iniquity so that they injure each other, trusting in your injustice. I the Lord have subjected My people to your sovereignty so that you would be their protection in the face of the violent and predatory. But behold, your heart has been lifted up in pride and you trample those who acclaim you like mud in the streets and like greedy wolves you wreck havoc on your own flock. I have compared you to My principalities, who lead the army of heaven, and you have not wished to understand this honor. Instead, you have put on a likeness to the princes of hell in the vast malice with which you have afflicted My people, in the swelling of your spirit, and in the stains of your intemperance, by which you have dishonored My face, which watches you from the heavens. Yet, I live,' says the Lord, 'and the strength of My right hand lives. If you will not hear the voice of My admonition and be converted to Me, I will drag you down from your height, which you have used wickedly, and into the depth of hell, and you will be the consorts of those to whom you have likened yourselves, in the living conflagration forever.'"

At the hour of Prime on the feast of Pentecost,[250] before the celebration of the divine office, while I was at prayer, the angel of the Lord appeared before me. He concluded the sermon announced thus far by adding these words, "Thus says the Lord, the King of kings and Lord of lords of all the earth, 'Hear and understand the words of My mouth and amend your ways in My sight. Because if you strive to please Me, the higher you are in this world, the more I will give you a named place in My kingdom that you may live and reign with Me without end. Amen.'"

16. The Seventh Sermon: The Way of Widows.

On the feast of Saint Maximus,[251] during the silent part of the Mass, I addressed the angel, saying, "May it please you now, lord, to show us the discipline appropriate to the path that appeared covered with thorn bushes on one part but on the other was narrow and pleasant with flowers, with no thorn bushes or obstacles."

I had hardly finished my request when he immediately said,[252] "Behold, I speak to you who are widowed in the world, living

200

according to the flesh in many struggles and distresses. Guard yourselves from the vices of this world and walk in the delightfully adorned path of the chaste, living according to the spirit. Withdraw from the midst of the thorns around you because, behold, the noose by which you were bound to this world has been loosened! By it you were led as if captive to serving the will of another, and you were not your own. When you acted on the will of the flesh according to all the desires of your heart, you had the excuse of conjugal obligation. If you again choose to obey the flesh, what excuse will you have? Why do you still desire to be pleasing to the human gaze in proud clothes and to embellish your appearance? Why do you still nurture your flesh—already in part dead—in delights and desires which oppose your[253] spirit and pile up unnecessary anxieties for yourself? Instead, listen to divine counsel and depart from the pleasures of this life, which are false, lest you be preoccupied with them and your latest pleasures be worse than the first. Seize peace of mind and the spiritual delights that God offers to you. Spend your remaining years in prayers and vigils, in chastising the flesh and works of piety." On the vigil of the Apostles,[254] he added more, saying, "What more can I add to warn you? Behold, I have shown you the way, I have instructed you in the teaching. Grope your way forward, consider the words, hold onto the examples, love chastity, run to the brightness of God and our Lord Jesus Christ. May He deign to manifest it to you, He who lives and reigns for ever and ever. Amen."

17. The Eighth Sermon: The Way of Hermits and Solitaries.

On the day of the Translation of our holy father Benedict,[255] I was hoping to receive the beginning of the eighth sermon, but my prayers were hindered that day by the presence of guests, and my desire was put off till the next day. Then indeed, while I was standing in prayer after the hour of Chapter, the angel of the Lord presented himself to me and I asked him to begin the sermon to those whose path had appeared in the vision to be filled with clods of earth. At once he opened his mouth and spoke these words:

"Pay attention, you who have chosen to lead a life in the wilderness, to the discretion you should have. Indeed, discretion is the mother of all virtues.[256] Rough with clods is your path because of the difficulty of your life; take care lest perchance your foot stumble. Because if you stumble, be on guard lest the light that is in you be extinguished. Discretion is necessary so that you do not quickly follow every impulse of your zeal, which drives you to the height of perfection. It is also necessary so that you do not exceed the measure of your strength in excessive struggles. Walking in audacity of spirit, many have extinguished their life by excessive affliction and have perished by their own devices. Overstepping their measure, many have overturned the human understanding in themselves and been made useless and like senseless beasts of burden. Through extreme efforts, many have been led into tedium and their strength has languished. They have turned back and been laid open to the desires of the flesh, and they have been mocked by evil spirits. Affliction of the body is good because it is opposed to the desires of uncleanness, but if it goes beyond measure it is harmful because it smothers the devotion of contemplation and extinguishes its light. On account of this, be mindful, O human, of your weakness, so that you can cautiously move forward on the hard path you have entered and so that you can act patiently lest in your speed you suffer ruin. Direct all your efforts according to the counsels of the wise, not according to your own mind, and you will not be overcome in the end. Do not test the Lord of heaven as those who heedlessly reject care of themselves and trust that the power of the Lord will be magnified in them as in ancient times. Apply to yourself the learning from the discipline of contemplation that I announced from the Lord and use it to console your despondency."

While we were sitting in the chapter hall listening to the reading from the Rule on the feast of Saint Mary Magdalene,[257] my lord the angel stood before me and concluded the sermon with an appropriate ending, saying, "O you who have chosen to lead a life in solitude and have renounced the desires of the world, pay attention to what fruit you bear. Indeed there are some who love solitude for the sake of the freedom of their own will rather than for the sake of the fruit of good works. But if you persevere in the good, the Lord will establish for you what eye has not seen, nor ear heard, nor has arisen in the human heart (1 Cor 2:9). May He deign to grant this to you, He who lives and reigns, God for ever and ever. Amen."

When it was the feast of blessed James the Apostle,[258] at First Vespers, the angel of the Lord appeared to me. I did just as the one transcribing these sermons had suggested and I asked him to deign to announce a title that could be written at the beginning of this book. He immediately assented to my petition, saying, "This is *The Book of the Ways of God*, which was announced by the angel of God most high to Elisabeth, handmaid of Christ and the living God, in the 1156th year of the Lord's incarnation, in the fifth year of her visitation in which the Spirit of the Lord visited her for the salvation of all who receive the fatherly warnings of God with grateful praise."

18. The Ninth Sermon: The Way of Adolescents.

On the fifth of August, in the morning, after Matins, while I was lying on my bed and had not yet begun to sleep, suddenly the angel of the Lord appeared to me and began the ninth sermon of this book in these words, "Behold, I have something to say to you who are in your youth. You are like the lily that is closed before the rising of the sun, and then, when the sun shines in its strength, opens itself and is delighted by the warmth of the sun. The human being is like this; one's flesh flowers in youth and, touched and opened by the pleasure of natural warmth, one's mind is delighted in many ways. Listen, therefore, children, and in the words of my minister perceive the calling of your good Father in heaven. He will give you a place of sweetest delight before the throne of His glory if you choose to walk in His counsels. Learn especially to fear the Lord of heaven and accustom yourself to bending under the yoke of His fear from the beginning of your adolescence. Behold, in cruel hell He has prepared fire and sulfur and so many torments and the harshest attacks of horrendous spirits doing evil to great and small, and He spares no age. Therefore I say to you: Learn to restrain yourselves from every evil deed and guard your innocence as if it were choice gold whose price and beauty you were still unaware of. Moreover, when your understanding matures, then you will know and taste of that fruit of gladness that no one knows except those who receive it. The counsel of the Lord, my young children, is what I am saying: Behold in your breast is a desirable treasure, more precious than all the riches of the world. This is the jewel of virginity.

Blessed are you if you guard it. Do not throw such a precious thing in the mud and do not exchange it for a cheap delight that is only momentary, because once it is thrown away it cannot be fully recovered. This is the special sign of our brotherhood in heaven and on account of it we especially delight in those on earth whom we see to be marked with our sign. So if it pleases your soul to guard it, pay attention to yourselves so that you do not defile it in your light-hearted carelessness. With a quaking heart turn away from what incites you to uncleanness, and flee the conversations and games of young girls and do not associate with their corrupters.[259] Guard your mouth from impudent speech and turn your ears from it and keep your eyes and your hands from every base thing. Hear and understand what the sage has written, 'Happy is the barren, unpolluted woman who knows no bed in sin. She shall have fruit at the judgment of holy souls. And the impotent one who has not used his hands for works of iniquity, a choice gift will be given to that faithful one and his lot will be most acceptable in the Temple of the Lord'" (Wis 3:13).

When I asked the angel about the one who wrote this, he said, "The Holy Spirit spoke this through the mouth of the sage." Immediately he was removed from my sight and did not concede to be questioned more fully about this. After this he again spoke further and said, "I will continue to speak to my brothers and fellow servants about the admonitions of their Father. Sons, make a habit of the customs of sanctity in your flowering age which you can then exercise in the time of your maturity. Adapt your habits to this so that you will be modest, gentle, and sober, humble and compassionate. Be patient when corrected; love and search into the teaching of the wise. Fly from words of deceit and malice; flee vulgarities, theft, revels, and contentions and games that avarice invented; flee as well people who offer the occasion for unclean desire. It is also useful to focus frequently on prayer, because prayer coming forth from a clean conscience is like the incense of sweetness in heaven. Beseech your Creator to keep you unstained from this world. Place no hope in longevity of the present life, because your end is uncertain. This is the beauty of your life, O unstained adolescents and youths! Walk in it and you will be children loved by the Lord and like the angels of God in heaven. To their society may you be led by Jesus Christ, our Lord, who is blessed and praiseworthy with the Father and the Holy Spirit for ever and ever. Amen."

19. The Tenth Sermon: The Way of Young Children.

The angel concluded the preceding sermon on the vigil of the Assumption of Mary, the holy mother of God. He visited me again on the day of the feast itself,[260] at the time of the divine office. He said, "Behold I do not wish to bring my sermons to an end yet. There is still time, and I have something to say briefly to young children who, because of their ignorance, do not know to protect themselves. Because of this it is necessary to warn their mothers to use the fear of God to keep them chaste and unstained, lest perchance they perish."

I responded to this by inquiring, "Why is it, lord, that you said chaste and unstained? What could young children do to stain their chastity? And if they transgress in any way, doesn't their ignorance excuse them?"

He said, "They often stain their chastity with whatever unclean words and deeds they are able to perform. And although they act in ignorance, they are not without guilt. Also, they do not entirely avoid punishment for this at death since they were not corrected by anyone else, nor did they know on their own to do penance for the sin. On account of this they must by corrected by their parents for their sins because, just as they grow accustomed to doing evil, so they can learn to do good if they are nurtured by correction. Moreover, I said 'unstained' because I was referring to those who, when they are a little beyond their seventh year, could more fully stain themselves with evil deeds. Then they know how to think more about evil since they had not been prohibited from it. Also, inasmuch as they are able, they do shameless deeds in such a way that brothers and sisters often copulate, not knowing what they are doing. If they leave this life in such a state, they will endure great punishment until they are purified, because one cannot enter the kingdom of God with any stain at all. This is why I spoke of them perishing. They are much more severely and harshly punished because they are helped less by the prayers and alms of their friends since they are not thought to need them. Therefore, I say to you parents and to whoever has custody of children: Take care that you protect them with great caution, because their sins will redound to you if you neglect them. All flesh tends toward evil. Therefore, do not bring them up in your vanities, do not incline them to drunkenness and empty and depraved stories, and do not lead them to pride through a delicate upbringing.[261] Forbid shameless and contentious words, obscene singing, evil games, quarrels, and heedless wandering. Do not laugh at their sins, but scare them off from every evil with the rod of gentleness and words of correction, for they will be stubborn if they are abandoned to their own will. So begin from their birth to bend them to the fear of the Lord and take care to instill frequently in their ears the beginnings of the sacred faith and prayers of God and everything pertaining to good habits."

He concluded this sermon on the octave of the Assumption[262] by adding these words, "Now, beloved children, how beautiful is your path! Run in it! Oh, how lovable is your Father! How precious is your reward in the kingdom of heaven! May this be granted to you by the Son, who dwells in the Father, and the Father who dwells in the Son with the Holy Spirit for ever and ever. Amen."

Here ends *The Book of the Ways of God.*

An appeal to scribes of these sermons: By the Lord and by His angel, I adjure everyone who transcribes this book to correct carefully your copy and append this appeal to the book.[263]

20.[264] The words she spoke to the Archbishops of Trier, Cologne, and Mainz: "This is *The Book of the Ways of God*, which was announced by the angel of God most high to Elisabeth, handmaid of Christ and the living God, in the 1156th year of the Lord's incarnation, in the fifth year of her visitations when the Spirit of the Lord visited her for the salvation of all who receive the fatherly warnings of God with grateful praise."

When the sermons of this book were almost finished, on the feast of the apostles Peter and Paul, before the hour of the divine office I was praying in a hidden place and the angel of the Lord appeared in my sight. While I listened he spoke these words, "To the bishop of Trier and the bishops of Cologne and Mainz. It has been announced to you by the Lord God, great and dreadful, and by the angel of the testament (Mal 3:1) of this book that these words which you find in the present book are to be announced by you to the Roman church and to all the people and all the church of God. Correct yourselves and turn from your errors. Do not receive the sacred and divine warnings unworthily, because they were not invented by human beings. Moreover, I speak to you by name because in this region you are renowned for piety. Read and hear the divine admonitions and receive them with a peaceful mind. Do not judge that they are the figments of women, because they are not. Rather, they are from God the omnipotent Father, who is the fount and source of all goodness. And what I say to you, I say to all others."

The Resurrection of the Blessed Virgin

The vision that Elisabeth saw about the resurrection of the blessed Virgin, the mother of the Lord, and what she learned from the Virgin about how long she lived after the ascension of the Lord.[265]

In the year that the angel of the Lord announced to me *The Book of the Ways of God*, on the day that the church celebrates the octave of the Assumption of Our Lady,[266] at the hour of the divine sacrifice, I was in a trance and my Comforter, the Lady of heaven, appeared to me in her usual way. Then, just as I had been advised by one of our elders, I inquired of her, saying, "My Lady, may it be pleasing to your kindness to deign to verify for us whether you were assumed into heaven in spirit alone or in the flesh as well?" I asked this because, as they say, what is written about this in the books of the fathers is found to be ambiguous. She said to me, "What you ask, you cannot yet know. Nevertheless, it may be revealed through you in the future." Therefore, for the span of that whole year I dared ask nothing further about this, either from the angel who was intimate with me or from Mary when she presented herself to me. However, the brother who was urging me to inquire about this enjoined upon me certain prayers by which I might obtain from her the revelation that she had pledged to me.

When a year had rolled by and the feast of her Assumption was again at hand,[267] I was languishing in illness for many days. Lying in bed at the time of the divine sacrifice, I came into a trance with a violent struggle. And I saw in a far-away place a tomb surrounded by great light, and what looked like the form of a woman in it, with a great multitude of angels standing around. After a little while, she was raised up from the tomb and, together with that multitude standing by, she was lifted up on high. While I was watching this, behold, a man—glorious beyond all reckoning—came from the height of the heavens to meet her. In His right hand, He carried a cross on which there was a banner. I understood that this was the Lord Savior, and there were countless thousands of angels with Him. Eagerly receiving her, they carried her with great acclamation to the heights of heaven. While I was watching this, after a short time, my Lady advanced to the door of light in which I usually saw her, and standing there she showed me her glory.

In that same hour, the angel of the Lord, who had come to announce to me the tenth discourse of the aforementioned book, was standing by me, and I said to him, "My lord, what does this great vision that I saw mean?" He said, "This vision has shown you how our Lady was taken up into heaven in flesh as well as in spirit." After this, again on the octave,[268] I asked the angel who had visited me and delivered the conclusion of the aforementioned book how many days after her death that bodily resurrection occurred. In reply he kindly informed me, saying, "She departed from this life on the day her assumption is now celebrated. But she was resurrected forty days after this, that is, on September 23."[269] He also added, "The holy fathers who established the celebration of her assumption in the church had no certainty of her bodily assumption; therefore, they solemnized the day of her death, which they called her Assumption, because they believed without doubt that she had indeed been taken up in the flesh." After this I was doubtful about publishing a text of this revelation, afraid that I might be considered an inventor of novelties.

Two years passed and on the feast of her Assumption,[270] my Lady again appeared to me. I inquired of her, saying, "Lady, shall we make manifest that message which was revealed to me about your resurrection?" And she replied, "It must not be divulged to the people, because this is an evil age, and those who hear it will get entangled and not know how to extricate themselves." I responded, "Do you wish us, then, to destroy completely what has been written about this revelation?" She said, "These things have not been revealed to you so that they may be destroyed and cast into oblivion.

Rather, they have been given to you so that my praise may be amplified among those who especially love me. You must make them known to my intimate servants. These things will be manifested to those who manifest their hearts to me. They can then offer me special praise and receive special rewards from me. There are many who will receive this message with great exaltation and veneration."

Therefore, because of these words, on the day mentioned above we celebrated the solemnity in our cloister to the extent that we could and rendered devout praise to the venerable Lady. While the mystery of the divine office was being celebrated, she appeared to me according to her custom. While she was discussing many things with me, I questioned her saying, "My Lady, how long after the ascension of the Savior did you live upon the earth? Were you assumed into heaven in the year of His ascension?" She gently responded to my words and said, "After the ascension of the Lord, I remained in mortal life upon the earth for a full year and as many days as are from the feast of the Ascension to the day on which my assumption is celebrated." Again I spoke, adding, "And were the apostles of the Lord present at your tomb?" She said, "All were present, and they commended my body to the earth with great veneration."

[The age of the blessed Virgin when she conceived the Lord Jesus in her womb at the angel's announcement was revealed to Elisabeth.]

One day while we were celebrating the feast of Our Lady's Annunciation, when my Lady was again showing me her glorious face, I dared to ask her what age she had been when, at the angel's proclamation, she conceived the Word of God in her virginal womb. To this query she deigned to offer the following response, "At that time my age was fifteen years plus as much time as there is from the celebration of my birth to the solemnity of the Annunciation."[271]

The Book of Revelations about the Sacred Company of the Virgins of Cologne

1. Preface about the sacred company of the virgins of Cologne.

To you, who cherish pious feelings for holy things, I, Elisabeth, servant of the handmaids of the Lord who are at Schönau,[272] will disclose what has been revealed to me through the grace of God about that virginal company of Saint Ursula, queen of Britain, who in days of old suffered martyrdom near the city of Cologne for the name of Christ. Although I was very resistant, certain men of good repute pressed me with their demand to investigate these things at length and they do not allow me to be silent. Indeed, I know that those people who oppose the grace of God in me will take this occasion to scourge me with their tongues. Yet I shall willingly endure it because I hope to receive a reward of some kind if so many martyrs shall receive increased honor from these things that the Lord deems worthy to reveal through my labors.

2. When it pleased the Lord to have mercy on His precious martyrs who for a long time had lain without honor under the feet of humans and beasts near the walls of the city of Cologne, certain men staying there came to the place of their martyrdom and opened many graves of the holy bodies. They lifted up those bodies and transferred them to religious places[273] around there, just as had been ordained by the Lord. These things began in the 1156th year of the Lord's incarnation, when the Emperor Frederick held the rule of the Roman Empire and Arnold II presided on the episcopal throne

213

in Cologne. Among the others was found a precious martyr in whose tomb was an inscription that read, "Saint Verena, virgin and martyr." By the hand of our venerable abbot Hildelin, she was translated[274] to our place, given to Hildelin by the lord abbot Gerlach of Deutz, who burned with much pious devotion for collecting and honoring the bodies of that sacred society.

While she was awaited by the community of our brothers who were to receive her at the entrance to the church, I was sitting in our room. Before I had heard anything about her arrival, I received from the Lord a testimony about her sanctity. I went into a trance and, on the road by which the sacred bones were being carried, I saw what looked like a very bright flame in the shape of a sphere. An extraordinarily handsome angel preceded it, carrying a smoking thurible in one hand and a burning candle in the other. They proceeded together through the air in a gentle course until they were inside the church. On the next day, when the solemnity of the Mass was being celebrated to venerate her, I was in spirit and that virgin appeared to me, standing in celestial brightness, marvelously crowned and gloriously adorned with the palm branch of victory. I spoke to her and inquired whether her name was truly such as had been related to us. Likewise, I asked about the name of another martyr whose body had been brought with hers but without a definite name. She responded, saying, "My name is as you have heard. It was almost written otherwise by mistake, but I prevented the scribe. The martyr Caesarius came with me, and when we entered this place, peace entered with us."[275]

3. On the next day, when the divine office was being celebrated for that martyr, he appeared to me in great glory. When I had asked him about his station in the world and by what circumstance he had endured martyrdom with those virgins, he said, "I was a soldier in the world, the son of the maternal aunt of the sacred virgin to whom I am now joined. She was very beloved to me and therefore when she left her country, I accompanied her. She strengthened me to undergo martyrdom and I, seeing her steadfastness in agony, suffered together with her. Our bones were for a long time separated from each other, and now the Lord has granted that they should be

brought together." These words threw me into grave doubt. Indeed, like others who read the history of the British virgins, I thought that that blessed society made their pilgrimage without the escort of any men.[276] But later I learned something else that greatly weakened this opinion.

4. When the two aforesaid martyrs were found, many bodies of holy bishops and other great men were also found among the graves of the virgins. In each of their tombs had been placed stones with titles inscribed upon them, and from these it could be discerned who they were and where they were from. Of these, two outstanding and especially notable ones were sent to me from Cologne by the aforementioned abbot. He hoped something about them could be revealed to me by the grace of God, and he wanted it to be confirmed through me whether or not they should be believed. Indeed, he was suspicious that the discoverers of the holy bodies might have craftily had those titles inscribed for profit. What those inscriptions were and what was revealed to me about them I have taken care to place before the eyes of readers throughout the present book. From this it should be understood that this holy company, which the divine paternity had deigned to honor with the escort of such elevated persons, should be very worthily attended with every honor by the faithful of Christ.

5. For a while I was thinking about these things and hoping to receive from the Lord the revelations that were demanded of me. In the meantime, the feast of the blessed apostles Simon and Jude arrived.[277] While the office of the Mass was being celebrated for them, a certain torment of heart came upon me that I used to suffer when the mysteries of God had first begun to be revealed to me. When I had been tormented for a long time, I went into ecstasy and thus came to rest. While I was in spirit, just as was customary for me, I looked to the heavens and I saw the aforementioned martyrs proceeding from the place of brightness in which I was accustomed to see visions of the saints. They came far into the lower atmosphere, and the angel of the Lord, my faithful guide, came before them. Speaking as I usually do while in trance, I addressed them,

saying, "It is from your great kindness, my lord and lady, that you have deigned to visit me now in this way, even though I was not offering you any service." At this blessed Verena responded, "We sensed that the desire of your heart strongly invited us, and therefore we came to visit you." I then inquired, "My lady, what does it mean that bodies of bishops were also found buried in the place of your martyrdom? And should we believe the titles inscribed on the stones found there? And who wrote them?"

She said to me, "Long ago God predestined you for this, that these things which up until now were unknown about us would be made manifest through you. Therefore, do not be annoyed that you are urged by the prayers of those who seek to know these things. Since the Lord has deigned to reveal to you what He has decided to make known about us, let it be your resolve to fast on bread and water on the vigil of our passion every year for the rest of your life. Or, if you are unable to fulfill this, you may redeem yourself by the celebration of one Mass. In this way, you may one day deserve to be joined to our company." After this she began to speak these words to me with great joy in her face, saying:

6. "When we first began to gather in our homeland, our sacred reputation was spread far and wide, and many people gathered from every direction to see us. At God's will, it happened that certain bishops of Britain joined us, crossed the sea in our company, and stayed with us till Rome. During the journey, blessed Pantalus, the bishop of Basel, joined us and led us to Rome, and he became a partner of our passion. His inscription said, 'Saint Pantalus, bishop of Basel, who received the sacred virgins with joy and led them to Rome. In returning, he arrived at Cologne and there received martyrdom with them.'"

After this, I juxtaposed what she had said with what is read in the history of the virgins, namely, that when blessed Ursula and the virgins accompanying her were playing in the sea, as they often did, the ships they were steering were drawn further than usual out to sea. With a sudden gust of wind, all the boats were carried away from the coast and never returned. According to this, it is likely that they set out without an escort of men. To this Verena responded,

216

"The father of blessed Ursula, the king of Scottish Britain, was named Maurus. A faithful man, he was conscious of the will of his daughter and he knew what God had ordained about her, just as she herself did. Maurus explained this to certain people close to him, and after taking counsel, he carefully arranged that when his daughter, whom he loved most tenderly, set off, she would have in her retinue men whose comfort she as well as her company would need."

7. Of the distinguished inscriptions, the most notable had this form: "Saint Cyriacus, Roman pope, who joyously received the holy virgins and, having returned with them to Cologne, received martyrdom." Another found near it said: "Saint Vincent, cardinal priest." When I asked blessed Verena about them, she said, "At the time we entered the city of Rome, a holy man named Cyriacus was presiding in the apostolic see. He came from our homeland, and because he was a prudent and noble man and accepted by all, he was raised to apostolic dignity. He had ruled the Roman church for one year and eleven weeks and was the nineteenth in the succession of Roman pontiffs. When he heard that we had come, he rejoiced with all his clergy and received us with great honor. Indeed, he had many relatives among us. Then, during the night following our arrival, it was revealed to him by the Lord that he would abandon the apostolic throne and go with us and together with us receive the palm of martyrdom. He kept that revelation to himself and gave the blessing of sacred baptism to many in our society who were not yet reborn in Christ. When he perceived the time to be right, he made his will known, and in the sight of the whole church, he resigned his high office. Everyone protested, especially the cardinals who, unaware of the divine summons impelling him, thought it was absurd for him to turn aside as if following the foolishness of little women. He, however, remained steadfast in his plan because of his love of our virginity, for he too from childhood had preserved his virginity unstained in himself. From that time on, we lost every favor that we had initially had in the sight of the Roman church, and they who had at first applauded us now considered us ignoble. Our venerable father, blessed Cyriacus, however, did not leave the city until, at his advice, Anterus had been substituted for him."[278]

8. After this, when I had examined the catalogue of Roman pontiffs and nowhere found the name of Saint Cyriacus, I again inquired of blessed Verena. One day when she presented herself to me, I asked her why he was not inscribed among the other Roman prelates. She said that this occurred because of the clergy's disdain for him since he had refused to remain in his high office until death.

9. On another day, I asked her about a certain James, whose name was found written on his tomb without anything else added. She seemed to be rather pleased by my query, and she happily responded to me, saying, "In that time there was a certain noble father, Archbishop James of venerable life, who had left our country to go to Antioch. There he rose to the honor of the bishopric and for seven years he had ruled that church. When he heard that blessed Cyriacus, one of his native people, had been elevated to apostolic dignity in Rome, he had gone to visit him and had left the city just before we arrived. When we were told this, a messenger was quickly sent to call him back, and he was found in a certain castle that was two days' march from Rome. When he heard of our arrival, he immediately returned to us and was made a companion in our journey and a sharer in our passion at Cologne. Moreover, he had some nieces in our company. With blessed Pope Cyriacus exhorting him, and because he was a prudent man, he diligently strove to learn the names of our sisters. When most of us had been killed, he inscribed the stones for our bodies. But before he was able to complete this, he was caught doing this by the impious ones and slain in our midst. This is why some of us are found with inscriptions, others without. In the hour of his passion, when he was yet to be given his deathblow, he made one request of his assailants, that his death could be delayed till he could inscribe his own name on a stone. This was granted to him." I asked about the day of his martyrdom, because it was not believable—according to this narration—that he could also have been killed on the same day on which the virgins suffered. To this she responded, "On the third day after the day of our passion he was killed by that tyrant who killed blessed Cordula."[279]

218

10. She also added something about a certain martyr whose inscription was "Saint Maurisus, bishop." She said, "Blessed Bishop Maurisus joined us while we were at Rome. He had been bishop in Lavicana for two years, although he was a native of our country. He was the son of a count from a family of great princes. He was also the uncle of the two virgins Babila and Juliana and was found buried with them. He was a man of very holy life and his preaching had great power. He was also very eager that no unbeliever, whether Jew or Gentile, who came to him should leave him without having been washed by him in the water of sacred baptism. Thus rightly did his office fit with the name Lavicana.[280] He brought with him blessed Claudius of Spoleto, whom he had ordained deacon, and the lay adolescent Focatus, his brother, who had not yet advanced to God's service. These two stayed close to our bishops and diligently assisted them and underwent martyrdom with them."

She said these things since I had inquired about them because of the inscriptions I had seen. She added further, "All the bishops journeying with us had their lodgings separate from us, but on Sundays they would come into our midst, strengthening us with the divine word and communion of the Lord's sacrament."

At another time I wanted to ask her about two bishops whose inscriptions I had received: "Saint Foilanus, bishop of Lucca, sent from the apostolic see, was killed in this place, slain by the sword and buried with these virgins," and "Saint Simplicius, bishop of Ravenna." It happened that one day we were celebrating the memory of our Lady, the blessed Virgin Mary, and she showed me her face, according to her usual kindness. After she had spoken of many things with me, I asked her about those bishops. She said, "At that time, those two had gone to Cologne, and while they were returning, they encountered that sacred company. They then joined the pope and clergy who were there and, going back again with them, they obtained the palm branch of martyrdom with them."

11. I was asked to investigate the inscription of a certain venerable monument that had been written in this way, "Here in the earth lies Etherius, who lived for twenty-five faithful years and departed in peace." Under this "Rex" was inscribed in capital letters and there

was this figure: A large R was arranged so that in it the two letters P and R could be recognized, and the two letters E and X were on the left side of the figure and on the right side of the figure was written the capital letter A.[281] On the stone found next to it was written, "Queen Demetria." Therefore I asked blessed Verena about these, and at the same time I asked about an infant who was found nearby, having the inscription: "Florentina, girl." She responded to me about everything, saying, "King Etherius, was betrothed to Saint Ursula the Queen. Demetria was the mother of Etherius, and Florentina was his sister." She continued, "I will also tell you what is signified by the letter A written on the king's inscription. Take three times that letter A and add to it the three letters X and P and R and you will have Axpara, which is the name of a duchess who was found nearby. She was the daughter of the maternal aunt of Etherius, and she was bound to him by a chain of great love. The scribe of that title wished to represent this when he intermingled her name with the king's. At that time it was not necessary for it to be expressed more openly because all these things would be revealed by you in the future."

12. I wondered about these things, thinking that it was completely unbelievable in light of the history that the fiancé of Saint Ursula was killed in this martyrdom. Then one day the angel of the Lord, who usually visited me, manifested his form to me. I asked him, saying, "Lord, we have read that that young man was betrothed to blessed Ursula. How could it be that he was united with her in martyrdom, when it is written that she fled from marriage with him?" He said, "When the company of blessed virgins was returning from Rome, on the sixth night of their journey, King Etherius, who was still in English Britain, was warned in a vision from the Lord to exhort his mother Demetria to become a Christian. His father, whose name was Agrippinus, had died in the first year after receiving the grace of baptism: It was also announced to him that he should leave his homeland and go to meet his fiancée, who was already returning from Rome, and that he would suffer martyrdom in the city of Cologne with her and receive an unfading crown from God. Immediately acquiescing to the divine warning, he made his mother consent to his exhortation and be reborn in Christ. Taking

her and his little sister, Florentina, he hastened to meet his very blessed fiancée and he became her companion in martyrdom and in celestial glory."

At this I asked, "Why is it, lord, that his inscription says that he lived twenty-five faithful years when we learn from the history that he had not yet received the Christian faith when he began to negotiate his betrothal to blessed Ursula and that he had to be imbued with the catholic faith for three years before the nuptials?" He responded, "Although this was the case, nevertheless, before receiving the Christian faith, he lived as innocently and modestly in accordance with his station of life as he later did. Therefore, it seemed to the writer of the inscription that all his years could rightly be called faithful."

13. After this, one day while our blessed Lady was speaking to me, I was instructed about a certain holy man whose inscription was "Saint Clement, bishop and martyr." I learned that the aforementioned king brought him with him when he left his homeland.

14. Again, when I had asked about a certain one whose inscription read, "Saint Marculus, bishop in Greece," I received this answer from the angel: "In the city called Constantinople, there was a certain king by the name of Dorotheus, who came from Sicily. His wife was named Firmindina, and their one daughter was called Constantia. It happened that when both parents had died, their daughter was left without the consolation of a husband, and she was unknown to any man. Therefore, her relatives betrothed her to a certain young man, the son of another king. However, he died before the time of the marriage. She rejoiced at being set free, and vowed to God the integrity of her virginity, praying and asking that He not permit her to be bound to another man. She went to a man of God, the bishop of that city, who was her uncle according to the flesh. This is the person you inquired about. She asked advice from him about guarding her virginity, and strongly beseeched him to be her helper in this matter. One night while he was worrying about this, a vision from the Lord revealed to him that Saint Ursula and her company of virgins were coming to Rome. He was also told to take his niece,

Queen Constantia, and go there quickly and be joined to that company with her. He believed the revelation of the Lord and took the girl, who, for the sake of the Lord, spurned her kingdom and all things that are of this world. He came to Rome before the virgins had arrived there. Shortly thereafter, when the virgins arrived, they joined themselves to that society. Accompanying them to Cologne, they endured martyrdom for Christ. That Constantia, moreover, is the one whom your brother recently carried to this place."

At this I responded, "Lord, they say that the one he brought here had the name Firmindina on her inscription. How is it that you say she was called Constantia?" He said, "In ancient times many people were surnamed with the names of their parents and thus were called by two or three names. She had also been called Firmindina, the name of her mother. Thus it happened by chance that when her inscription was written, this name was inscribed and her proper name, which was Constantia, was left out because the thing was done in haste. This happened to many others on the same occasion with the result that their own names were occasionally left out and others, which were not their personal names, were inscribed."

15. An inscription like this was sent to me: "Saint Gerasma, who led the sacred virgins." I was frequently asked to inquire about her because it seemed that she would have been great and remarkable as the leader of such a company must be. Although I often had the opportunity and desire to inquire, it was not granted to me to do so, because the question used to slip from my memory in such a way that I wondered why it was happening. At last the person who had asked me to inquire about her sent us three holy little bodies that were from the company of virgins. Three days after the feast of blessed Andrew the Apostle,[282] Saint Andrew appeared to me in the silent part of the Mass, and with him was a very glorious martyr and two virgins. I understood that they were those whose bodies had come to us. Therefore I asked blessed Andrew about their names, because they were completely unknown. He said to me, "Ask them, and they will tell you." When I did, one virgin responded and said, "I am called Albina, and the one who is with me is Emerentiana. We

were sisters according to the flesh, daughters of a certain count whose name was Aurelian. This martyr who came with us is called Adrian. He was the son of a king, and when he was ten years old he suffered martyrdom for Christ." I said, "Lady, how can we distinguish your bodies?" She said, "Mine is the largest, that of my sister is the smallest; the medium one is of Saint Adrian." I asked her nothing else. However, God placed this word about the name of the aforementioned martyr in the mouths of two witnesses. That this was his name and that he had been the son of a king had also been revealed by a vision in the preceding night to the brother who had brought the bodies.

After this I was thinking about that martyr and wanting to know something more specific about him. That night in a dream vision it was shown to me that I had been given a book inscribed with gold letters. I read in it a long discourse about him and his kindred and how, with his four sisters, he had left his land and how he endured martyrdom with them. I read there that his sisters were named Babila, Juliana, Aurea, and Victoria. But although it seemed to me that in the vision I carefully read everything more than once, nevertheless I was unable to remember the exact sequence of what I read.

After a few days, it was the feast of blessed Nicholas.[283] When the office of the Mass was being celebrated for him, he appeared to me according to his usual kindness, and the three aforementioned martyrs appeared again with him. Therefore I asked him to indicate something more specific to me about Saint Adrian. It also occurred to me to ask about Saint Gerasma, who was mentioned above. He responded to me with great benevolence and said, "Saint Gerasma, about whom you inquire, was queen of Sicily. She was truly from the faithful root of Aaron and had the spirit of the Lord in abundance. She converted her husband, King Quintianus, who at first had been a very cruel tyrant, and she turned him from a wolf into the gentlest lamb. He had taken her from Britain, and she was the sister of Saint Maurisus the bishop and of Daria, mother of the holy queen Ursula. She had three sons and six daughters. Saint Adrian the martyr, about whom you inquired, was the youngest of them. His older brother was Dorotheus, king of Greece, who was the father of Saint Constantia, who was brought to you. When blessed

Ursula secretly discussed her holy plan with her father, he had great concern about that plan and sent a letter to blessed Gerasma, telling her the will of his daughter and the revelations she had received from God. He explained this to her and asked to hear her advice because he knew that she was a woman of great wisdom. She, moreover, inspired by divine virtue and understanding that the word had come from the Lord, undertook the trip with four of her daughters—Babila, Juliana, Victoria, and Aurea—and her little son Adrian, who willingly undertook the pilgrimage out of love for his sisters. Leaving her kingdom in the hands of one son and two daughters, she sailed to Britain. With her advice, that whole sacred company of virgins was gathered and organized, and she was their leader all throughout the pilgrimage. She guided them and in the end she endured martyrdom with them." When he had said these things, he sensed that I was wondering greatly about this arrangement and he said to me, "With good reason do you marvel, because this whole plan was arranged by divine disposition." He also added, "The martyrs the Lord sent you are especially precious; therefore, be diligent in offering them honor and service because their arrival is the beginning of a great grace."

16. One time when blessed Verena had presented herself to me, I asked her—as I had been prompted by a certain brother—who perpetrated the martyrdom of that blessed company. For considering the preceding narration about the aforementioned pope, in no way could the instigator of that persecution be Attila, king of the Huns, as some people supposed; rather, his persecution followed after an interval of many years.[284] To this inquiry she responded: "While we were at Rome, two evil princes whose names were Maximus and Affricanus were also there. They saw that our multitude was great and that many gathered together to join us. They were violently indignant toward us and feared that through us the Christian religion would grow greatly and be strengthened. Thus, once they had discovered the route we were going to take, they sent legates with speed to one of their kinsmen, Julius by name, who was prince of the Huns. They encouraged him to lead out his army, inflict persecution on us, and destroy us. Quickly assenting to their desire, he

224

emerged with an armed multitude and rushed upon us when we had come to Cologne and there he poured out our blood."

17. What she said when I asked her about the body of that blessed Saint Ursula should not be kept silent. "Her body was never lifted up above the earth except in these days, and truly it is in the place where her inscription is preserved." I also inquired about the head of Saint Verena, asking her, "Behold, lady, your body has been brought to us, but what should we do about your venerable head, which is not here? I beg you to tell us where it is so that we may seek it and join it to your body." She responded to me, "It is in a place called Ilbenstadt, and it is poorly valued there; I would rather it be where my body is venerated."[285] To this she added, "The Lord heard our prayers and has now revealed our bodies in this way. The Lord did not wish to hear our groans any longer, groans we uttered because we were so negligently hidden and nothing of worthy praise was offered to Him for us. It will not be till the last day that our whole company will be made known."

19.[286] I received these words of the Lord's revelation on various feasts of the saints, acquired not by my own righteousness but by the merits of the holy virgins and martyrs of Christ, as was pleasing to the Lord. They were completed within the space of a little more than one year. When all these discourses were almost complete, the feast day of the passion of those eleven thousand virgin saints arrived.[287] While I was present at the divine office and the gospel reading was over, I went into a trance as usual, and I saw in the region of light, which was continually visible before my mind's eye, a great multitude of beautiful virgins. They were crowned as if with the purest gold, and in their hands was the likeness of extraordinarily flashing branches. Their vestments appeared bright and gleaming like the snow when it is illuminated by the splendor of the sun. On their foreheads was the bloody redness in testimony to the blood they had poured out in their holy confession. Many glorious men appeared with them with the same signs. Many among them were gleaming, marked with episcopal adornment. I wanted to ask something about them, but on account of the multitude of them I did not know which one to address. Immediately, two of the strikingly outstanding virgins came forward from that group and stood apart from the others, in front of them, looking at me. I understood that they had done this on my account and I spoke to them saying, "I pray, my ladies, that you might deign to indicate to me who you are and what your names are." One of them said, "I am Ursula, and the one standing with me is sister Verena, daughter of my paternal uncle, a great prince." I said to the one who was speaking to me, "I beg you, most holy lady, that since so much has been revealed about you by the grace of God to me, an unworthy sinner, may you now deign to make it complete and explain to me the means of your burial. In a time of such great persecution, who so carefully arranged your sacred bones and provided such honorable tombs for you?" She responded to me in this way:

20. "At that time, there was in Cologne a sacred bishop full of the Holy Spirit. His name was Aquilinus, and he governed the church of God there, fourth in succession after blessed Maternus. While we were about to turn back to Cologne from Rome and were already preparing for our return, the Lord made a revelation to him and he saw our whole multitude and the whole manner of the passion we would undergo. He also heard a voice telling him that he should prepare our bodies for burial and hastily procure everything necessary for our entombment. While he was attending to these things, two bishops about whom you have already heard certain things, namely, the bishops of Lucca and Ravenna, came to him and told him how a vision from God had revealed to them that they would receive martyrdom in that place. But they confessed that they were still uncertain how or under what circumstances it would happen. He, moreover, who was said in his inscription to have been sent from the apostolic see, had received advice from the prelate of the apostolic see about his journey before we had arrived. When they heard from the bishop of Cologne about the vision he had seen about us, they returned by the same route by which they had come. They met us and stayed with our group until the end."

21. When she had said these things, I followed with these words, "I would like to know, my lady, what particular cause your enemies had against you to destroy you. I especially would like for you to confirm by what kind of death you ended your life." She responded, saying, "That impious tyrant who was the perpetrator of our destruction, using both terror and flattery, demanded that we deny our Spouse who is in heaven, the Lord Jesus Christ, and unite in the embraces of him and his men. But we had not gone there on such a motive, and we steadfastly refused to consent to his evil desire. We chose to die rather than be separated from our Spouse. On account of this, they raged against us with various tortures; I was struck by the shot of an arrow in my heart. Then, while we were all lying in our own blood, that venerable bishop engaged in his work of great piety for us, just as he had been instructed. With great diligence and honor, he fulfilled the duty of burying us. The majesty of the Lord was present to him and those who worked with him on our behalf, and angels of the Lord assisted them, and the work of our burial was quickly completed. We, moreover, did not delay to beseech the Lord to render unto him a reward for his labor. Soon after this he was withdrawn from this life and God gave him special honor because of the honor he had offered us. Not many days after we had been buried, a venerable man named Clematius came and he carried some bodies that were still remaining in a certain place and he buried them with great honor, as he had been admonished beforehand by the majesty of the Lord."

Immediately I followed up with this question, saying, "Lady, was this man the same Clematius who is said to have constructed your church?"[288] She said, "Not at all, but after a long time that one did come." Finishing this conversation, she concluded, "May God reward the work of the one who has renewed our passion. To the kind and merciful Lord, who knows secret things and reveals them to whom He wishes, not respecting the great nor despising the humility of the lowly, let there now be honor and glory and thanksgiving for ever and ever. Amen."

Appendix to *The Book of Revelations About the Sacred Company of the Virgins of Cologne.* The following elements were also included in various transmissions of this text.

1. This fragment continues the narration of chapter 17. Like the next fragment as well, it is found in numerous manuscripts that transmit only this work of Elisabeth, but it is not found in any collections of Elisabeth's works.[289]

Since blessed Ursula had revealed to me that Saint James, bishop of Antioch, had inscribed the tombs of the holy virgins, a doubt had arisen within me. Some people around me discussed how this could have happened. According to what I had been told, he was killed on the third day after the virgins. But how could he have been able to inscribe the titles of so many virgins and martyrs in such a short time? I heard that a great pile of them had been preserved in that sacred place.

One day while we were celebrating the solemn office of those holy virgins, some of them—about twelve—appeared to me, preceded by one who stood out beyond all the others for her striking beauty. This indeed was Verena herself. When I asked her to free me from this doubt, she offered this response: "Our inscriptions were not written by Bishop James alone, but also by the many clerics who were with him. He had selected eleven clerics for this work, and appointed each one of them to one thousand virgins, commissioning them to the task of inscribing their names. They, together with helpers whom each of them employed, wrote the inscriptions that were found there and added them to our tombs. Certain names of the virgins were unknown to them, but they learned them from blessed James, who had diligently noted them down. Others were revealed to them by divine revelation, but many were completely omitted."

2. This fragment is found in chapter 21, either after the sentence, "May God reward the work of the one who has renewed our passion," or at the end of the chapter.

After this, within the octave of that feast, while we were celebrating the memory of that sacred company, at the time of the divine office, that glorious queen, with about twelve companions, again deigned to offer herself to my gaze. I spoke to her, just as I had been counseled by a certain brother, saying, "Most blessed queen, when I asked about the manner of your death, you said that your life was ended by an arrow shot in your heart. However, later I learned from others, who attest to having seen it, that at the discovery of your sacred body an arrow was found fixed in your arm. When your body was carried out, it still remained there. So were you killed by the wound of that arrow or a later one?" To this she responded, "The tyrant who killed me first shot an arrow in my arm. When he saw that I was not yet overcome by death, he aimed a second arrow at my heart. By the will of the Lord, that arrow withdrew from my heart and struck the heart of the one who shot it. He went crazy and, rushing wildly to the Rhine, he threw himself into the water and died."

3. This letter of Ekbert to Ulrich, the prior of the Premonstratensian cloister of Steinfeld,[290] was added to the end of the revelations about the Cologne martyrdom in the final redaction of the visionary collection. The letter is not about the Cologne virgins, but it shares the task of revealing hitherto unknown details about local patron saints.

To the elder one of good days, the man of the Lord, Ulrich, venerable father of the Steinfeld brothers, your servant Ekbert, monk of Schönau, sends these words. For a long time you have been seeking something from me. I have been anxious to address this, spurred on more by your love than your reminders. So I asked Elisabeth, handmaid of the Lord, who—as I know from undeniable experience—has the grace of holy revelations, whether she could ask the Lord to reveal to her anything about Saint Potentinus, whose body is preserved in the church at Steinfeld. Who was he? What was the mode of his sanctity and that of his companions who are preserved there? For indeed, you admit that you have not yet learned anything definite about them. I asked repeatedly and urged Elisabeth with great insistence, but for a long time she resisted because of the tongues of detractors. Then the One who knows secrets revealed to me through her what I was seeking. These are

229

the words that the faithful angel of the Lord, the one who visits that handmaid of God, spoke. He responded to what she asked him and kindly revealed these things about the aforesaid man of God and his companions.

He said that Potentinus was the son of a king of Gaul by the name of Antimius, a fierce and faithless tyrant whose royal throne was in the city of Paris. Potentinus was a boy of very gracious goodness and innocent life. Although he was not a Christian, nevertheless he always loved Christians and frequently visited their homes and delighted in hearing and examining their teachings. For this he endured bitter rebukes and punishments from his parents. Yet, he did not refrain from that holy practice. In the end he became a lover of the Christian faith and even received the sacrament of baptism when he was fifteen years old. Now clothed in the spirit of fortitude, he began to withdraw himself completely from his parents and live more openly among the Christians. He departed from the city of the royal throne to another place about a day's journey away, and there he lived. Many Christians came from every direction, and he eagerly learned the sacred scriptures from them. Progressing in every way before God, in a short time he became famous among nearby Christians for his divine wisdom and holy life. The Lord worked great miracles through him at that time. By a single prayer and a laying on of hands, he cured a woman who had struggled for more than fifty years with a paralyzing disease. Likewise he cured a man who had the same illness for thirty years. He was promoted in ecclesiastical orders, rising to the level of Levite but not to the priestly order. When he turned thirty, he was elected by a congregation of clergy for the episcopal office.

At that time, in the German kingdom, in the region of Westphalia, in the city of Münster, there were fifteen clerics gathered in the service of God. Some of them, while traveling in Gaul, saw the man of God and recognized his sanctity and wisdom. They persuaded the others to choose him as their shepherd, and this was done. They sent legates to entreat him very earnestly about this. When he had consented to their will, encouraged by the advice of his brother Castor, who was also a Christian, he set out upon the journey taking with him Castor and his sister Castrina, as God had ordained. They had been traveling for two days when their paternal uncle announced the news to their parents. Their uncle was a very cruel man who had great hatred for their confession of Christian faith. Pursuing them with savage fury, he rushed upon them and killed them. He raged more ferociously against Potentinus, the Levite of God, than the others, savagely piercing his body not only with a sword but also with many arrows. In this way, Potentinus was gloriously consummated in his holy confession. Not only were his siblings Castor and Castrina killed with him, but so were two of the legates who had been sent to lead him back. These were Simplicius and Felicius. Felicius was a priest, Simplicius a lay man. The others who were with them avoided martyrdom by fleeing. These saints of God were killed in the winter, on January 5.

When the persecutor left the place, those who had fled the martyrdom returned to the place and buried the holy bodies there. They marked the places where the bodies were and returned to their homeland to tell the brothers what had happened. After many days, the same brothers, moved by the love with which they had loved the saints of God while living, returned to the place of the martyrdom. They carried their bodies away from there, planning to transport them to their church. They made the return journey by the Moselle River. When they arrived near the place called Carden, it happened by a secret judgment of God that the bodies of the saints miraculously became heavy and could not be carried. In the end, they could in no way be moved from that spot. When those who were trying to carry them were finally exhausted by their futile efforts, they yielded to divine will, buried the martyrs there, and left. Those martyrs are of great antiquity, for they were killed before the time of Saint Maurice and his companions.

When Elisabeth, the handmaid of the Lord, relayed these words of the holy angel to me, I suggested to her that she should ask him whether or not blessed Potentinus lived at the same time as Saint Maximus, the bishop of Trier. I said this because of the song that you had shown me several days earlier, when I was with you. In this song, it is given to be understood that Potentinus did live then. It was the feast day of Saint Stephen, the first martyr, when she was to ask about this. The angel of the Lord, whom she intended to ask about this, appeared to her during the celebration of the Mass, but he stood with his face turned away from her as if in indignation. Unaware of the cause of this indignation, she was gravely saddened. She anxiously asked blessed Stephen, who appeared to her at the same time, to intervene on her behalf and propitiate the holy messenger of God who seemed angry at her. After a little while, he turned his face to her, saying, "Your brother has offended me and my brothers. He knew through the histories that the Theban league was before the time of Saint Maximus. When he enjoined this question upon you, he acted as if he were testing whether I would say something contrary to the words I had already spoken about the time of this martyrdom." He continued, saying, "You will not appease me unless you first offer in satisfaction a special honor for each of the orders of my brothers."

After this, I wanted to know whether blessed Castor had been ordained to ecclesiastical office and whether his sister Castrina was married or a virgin. Also, in what circumstances did they join their brother, blessed Potentinus, so that, without the knowledge of their mother and father, they could set out on that journey on which they would endure martyrdom with him? I also wanted to know whether there was any notable place in the area where they were killed. Therefore, I asked the servant of the Lord to inquire about these things. However, she did not remember to ask about these things until the feast of blessed Lawrence. On that day, she saw blessed Lawrence, the martyr of Christ, in a spiritual vision, as she usually did at the time of the divine office, and she asked him about these things. Kindly listening to the words of her questions, he replied, "Since blessed Castor was a Christian man, a priest, and older than blessed Potentinus, he was not afraid frequently to enter his parents' home. He instructed his sister, the virgin Castrina, in Christian law and secretly baptized her. When blessed Potentinus was thinking about leaving his homeland, with pious shrewdness, Castor asked his parents to take his sister out of the city for a little recreation. She was led, step by step, further and further from the city so that a sudden flight could not be noticed. Finally, at night, they slipped away from those who were with them and went to their brother blessed Potentinus, and in this way entered the way of the

232

Lord with him. The place where their persecutor rushed upon them had no well-known name but next to it was the church called Rufa, which was destroyed by these unfaithful ones after the time of this martyrdom. This site of their martyrdom was a pleasant place on a mountain slope next to a spring that was called Roel by the people." Among other things, he also said, "Know that the Levite of God, blessed Potentinus, is of celestial merit in God's sight and is very glorious among the martyrs of Christ."

May the divine grace always allow you, most beloved father, and all your family to be aided by the potent support of Potentinus. May you be potent in the spiritual armor to which you have devoted yourselves and destroy the enemy powers. And may you gain the exalted dignity of the desirable kingdom, which will last for ever and ever. Amen.

Letters

The letters that Elisabeth announced, not from human pre-meditation but from divine inspiration, since she was unlearned, saying not her own words but those of the Lord and His holy angel.

1. From the diocese of Metz, from an abbey in Busendorf, a monk who was very learned in sacred letters came to visit Elisabeth and investigate what God was doing with her. After he had heartily wished her joy and faithfully instructed her with good advice, when he was about to leave, he asked that he might be worthy at some point to receive a letter from her. The letter was to be of that same grace from which she had in ecstasy pronounced other things, a letter from which his mind could glean some correction and good consolation. At the same time he also asked that she send a letter advising his abbot and brothers about correcting their lives. When Elisabeth had reverently commended this to divine grace, on the night after his request, while she was at Matins, suddenly and unexpectedly she announced the letter which that brother had requested to be sent to him. Similarly, on the third night after this she announced the other letter that he had asked to be sent to his abbot and brothers. From this time, she began to have the grace of announcing letters of the kind that are transcribed below.

2. The first letter to Ludwig, monk and later abbot of Saint Eucharius in Trier.[291]

To Ludwig, servant of Christ, Elisabeth sends the grace of God.

I advise you, friend of God, to walk justly in the way of contemplation that you have entered. Do not turn aside to right or the left, but extend your hand to the one who knows how to bring every evil into good. You are rich, but be moderate in all your riches. Give glory to God from whom all wisdom comes, and do not savor what is lofty but fear it, because nothing is lacking for those who fear God. Do not exalt yourself, but always be humble; the more you are humble, the more will the height of glory follow you. Correct your life with all your power so that a crown of glory will be prepared for you which God will hand over to you on the day of solemnity and rejoicing. May He deign to offer it to you, He who lives and reigns in perfect Trinity forever. Amen.

3. The second letter, to the abbot of Busendorf.

To W., the abbot of Busendorf, Elisabeth sends the grace of God.

Servant of God, a certain divine inspiration admonishes you. Awaken and extend your pastoral staff and strike strongly, and gently take care of all your sheep, for you have undertaken to govern and guard them. Those who follow their own heart and turn aside from the path of contemplation walk unjustly. For this, God will not give you the necessities of life. Return, sons of God, sons of the light, to your heart, and examine your consciences for anything in you that is not pleasing to God before whom the whole earth trembles. Correct yourselves for the better; you have a Father who lives in the heavens and looks upon the lowly. Do not give place to your heart so that it runs here and there. For your love of the Lord, disdain the world and all its ornament, so that you may see the King in His beauty, the Creator of life, who invites you to the banquet of heavenly citizens, where dwells the Father in the Son, and the Son in the Father, with the Holy Spirit, for ever and ever. Amen.

4. To Hillin, archbishop of the city of Trier.

A certain small spark sent from the seat of great majesty, and a voice thundering in the heart of a small worm-person[292] speaks. To Hillin, archbishop of Trier.

The one who was and is and is to come warns you. Rise up in the spirit of humility and fear of the Lord your God. Extend your pastoral staff over the flocks that you have received from the Lord to govern and guard. Strike strongly and gently by imploring and rebuking, not like a hireling whose sheep are not his own (Jn 10:12), but like a faithful and prudent servant whom a master established over his household so that he might give them a measure of wheat at the proper time (Lk 12:42). Again the same Lord admonishes you, saying, "Give the reason that you have defrauded Me of My chosen pearls and precious gems, which had been sent to you from the power of great majesty. You have thrown them behind you and have not wished to obey Me. Don't you know that I have said, 'You have hidden these things from the wise and prudent and revealed them to the little ones' (Lk 10:21)? Take up and open the book and you will discover what I have said and what has been done: 'The apostolic see is filled with pride and avarice is cultivated,' et cetera.[293] If you will not tell them what has been revealed to you and they die in their sins, you will bear the judgment of God. And you should know that the one who has been chosen by Caesar is more acceptable to Me.[294] If he fears Me and executes My judgment, I will give him a new heart and place My spirit within his heart (Ez 36:26). So now, pay attention and do what is pleasing to Me and do not fear, because I am with you all the days of your life (Is 43:5), and I will not abandon you but will give you a named place in My kingdom, where the harmonies of My saints ring forth without cease, which no one knows but those who hear."

May He offer this place to you, He who is the fount and source of all goodness.

5. To the abbot of Deutz and his brothers.[295]

To the venerable abbot Gerlach and his brothers, Elisabeth wishes salvation of their souls.

A certain small spark sent from the seat of great majesty and a voice thundering in the heart of a small worm-person admonishes you, saying this. Rejoice with gladness but not without fear and trembling of heart. You have among you certain morning stars, shining in heaven before the throne of divine majesty with the brightest splendor. Be imitators of God and His saints. Like good emulators, guard yourselves from all depravity and let there not be among you pride and envy and schisms and other vices that fight against the spirit, but be like newborn infants, reasonable without guile (1 Pt 2:11, 2). Do not seek to possess anything of your own in this world and do not exercise your own will because you will be told what to do. You will be holy with the holy ones, just as the Lord said in holy scripture to His faithful ones, "Be holy, because I am holy" (Lv 19:2). With blessing has the Lord blessed you, and shown you a treasure hidden in a field for so many years, for such a long time. In joy have you bought His elect and precious treasure, choice pearls and precious gems (Mt 13:44–46). Know this without doubt: If you honor them as is proper, they will always stand before the face of God, praying for you and begging for the salvation of your body and soul.

I admonish you, venerable father, extend your pastoral staff and strike the members of the flock of the Lord with all diligence and discretion, lest they walk but haltingly in the way of His contemplation. You, father, must go before them with the example of good works and lead them with you into eternal life. There you will find prepared what eye has not seen, ear has not heard, nor human heart conceived (1 Cor 2:9). May you be offered this by Jesus Christ, Son of the living God, who lives and reigns in perfect Trinity for ever. Amen.

6. To the same abbot.

To lord Gerlach, venerable abbot of the church of God in Deutz, Elisabeth of Schönau, humble handmaid of Christ, sends greetings and prayers.

Be consoled and rejoice in the Lord. Strengthen the hearts of the brothers who are with you, because the Lord has heard your groans. He has looked upon the tribulation of your heart which afflicts you in His sight, that lamentable dropping of the divine sacrament that happened in your midst. He has acted according to His customary kindness and deigned to announce certain words to me through His angel to console you. It happened on the first Sunday of the Lenten fast, when the lord abbot was celebrating the divine office with us. While I was intent in prayer after the reading of the gospel, I suddenly languished and went into a trance. And behold, the angel of the Lord, my kind consoler, came and stood in my sight. Then, among other matters that I discussed with him, I reminded him of you, just as I had been advised by my brother. I inquired of him, saying, "My lord, what happened to that venerable sacrament which was sneezed forth from a boy's throat? Was it trampled by the feet of those standing around and destroyed?" He answered, saying, "The sanctity of that sacrament vivifies the spirit of the one receiving it. When it fell from his mouth, it was caught up by an angel of God who was present and he hid it away in a secret place." I said, "Lord, dare I ask where it was placed?" "Don't ask," he replied. In turn I said, "Lord, what service should those brothers offer to God for this negligence?" He responded, "For this offense they should offer to God a sacrifice of praise for forty days in their convent." He continued, "For Jesus Christ our Lord, I establish this penance so that whenever the body of the Lord should fall upon the earth or the blood of the Lord be spilled out in such a way that it cannot be placed among the relics, a sacrifice of praise is to be offered for this sin for forty days."[296] Lastly, he added, "The more bodies of saints that the brothers gather for themselves and keep with them, the more useful and even necessary it is for them to strive to minister to them honorably and lovingly. Likewise it is useful and necessary for them to improve their life with fear of God and diligently observe their rule. In order to warn them about this, the Lord allowed to happen what was done in their midst. If they obey His warning and do what I have said, they shall be assured that those precious martyrs will clamor for them in the presence of the Lord and assist them in every need. But if they do not obey, those martyrs will make accusations and complaints against them."

7. Letter to the abbot of Odenheim and his brothers.

To lord Burchard, venerable abbot of Odenheim, sister Elisabeth of Schönau sends greetings and faithful prayers.

On the vigil of Saint Lawrence, one of your brothers came to me as if ready for a journey he was planning to make to Jerusalem. He told me that it was your desire and plan to undertake that same journey. He told me many things and earnestly asked me to inquire about the will of God about them. That same night, while I was at

Matins, suddenly the Lord placed His words in my mouth, and I announced them in this way.

The one who was and who is and who is to come, the omnipotent one, says these things. I am the way and the truth and the life (Jn 14:6). Those who enter through Me will be saved and will come to the city of Jerusalem which is on high. There they will rest and find great reward for their labor and weariness. But there are some unrighteous people, murderers, and evildoers who need penance and go to Jerusalem, seeking the patriarch and his counsel, as is beneficial to them. But you, sons of light, are not like this! O foolish and slow hearted in believing! Don't you know that if you seek Me with all your heart, behold, I am there to help? I admonish you who are a pastor of sheep: Stretch forth your pastoral staff with all diligence and strike strongly. Gently arrange everything for all those subject to you, whom you have undertaken to govern and guard, like a faithful and prudent servant. Do not shake off My yoke from your neck, but let it be gentle and bearable to you. And I order you through My right hand: Do not do those things that are in your heart, because they do not proceed from a good conscience. They will seduce you so that you will fall into the pit. But if you do not consent to My counsels and if you despise My commands, I the Lord will destroy you and wipe out your name from the book of life. So now, attend to those who are under your rule; beseech, reprove, rebuke, admonish. Improve yourself and do not give place to the devil (Eph 4:27), who is always circling, seeking someone to devour. Receive My fatherly admonition with thanksgiving and welcome back this brother of yours with free blessing, for the Lord of all loves him and will do things in him that are pleasing in His sight. Again I warn you: Walk in the way of My contemplation, like beloved sons, with all humility and obedience, without murmuring, detraction, and envy, so that your celestial Father will not be blasphemed by you and angered, lest you perish from the just path, that is, the path of His contemplation. Walk, while there is still light in you, lest the shadows of death surround you. Walk in this way till you see the God of gods in Sion and He makes you reign with Him in glory without end. Amen.

8. Letter to the brothers in Nuwinburg.

The divine voice speaking in the heart of a small worm-person admonishes you who have built yourself a habitation in Nuwinburg.

Choose for yourselves the serene light and bring true peace into your midst and your souls will delight in fullness (Is 55:2). Walk like beloved sons in the path of contemplation of the Lord, which you have chosen. Climb the high mountain where you will find a fountain of water and flood your hearts. Joyfully drink in the waters from the fountain of the Savior and say, "We who live bless the Lord" (Ps 113:18).

There are some among you who appear to me as good and peaceful, and others who are evil and perverse, who give their foolish hearts to the world and delight in it in many ways. Seeing this, I admonish the good to become better and the evil to be converted and live because we must serve one God from whom all goodness and all sanctity come. Everything in heaven and on the earth serves God; you too must serve Him in the vesture of monastic piety, so that your interior piety may be pleasing to Him. Be like the angels of God, whose mouths are always open, praising and blessing the one who lives for ever and every. Amen.[297]

If you do these things that have been described here and other things like them, and flee pride and every impurity, you will avoid polluting your minds with great impurities and angering your heavenly Father and vanishing from the just life, that is, the way of His contemplation. Without doubt He will prepare for you starry mansions and unfading crowns. May He deign to offer them to you, He who is the fount and source of all goodness.

9. Letter to the sisters at Andernach.[298]

To the sisters at the monastery at Andernach, Elisabeth, humble handmaid of Christ, wishes salvation of body and soul and the joys of eternal life. A small spark from the seat of great majesty and a voice thundering in the heart of a small worm-person admonishes you, saying:

Rejoice always in the Lord and your souls will delight in fullness (Is 55:2). Do not delay in serving your God. Walk in the way of His contemplation, like beloved daughters, with every humility and love and obedience, without murmuring, without detraction, without envy and similar things, but like young lambs pleasing to the living God. I will break the chains of your captivity (Jer 30:8), says the Lord your God, and lead you to verdant pastures at the forecourts of My tent. Again I admonish you: Walk in the way of vision of God with all the attention of your mind and, like wise virgins, prepare your lamps (Mt 25:1–10). Love each other just as your heavenly Father has loved you (Jn 15:12), and bear each other's burdens (Gal 6:2). Be merciful, anticipating each other with honor, and take care of the sick. Give and it will be given to you (Lk 6:38) and you will receive one hundredfold, not only in this world but also in the next. Hear the fatherly admonitions of the Lord with free blessing and joyful countenance in body and soul. And be not only as hearers but as doers of the word of God (Jas 1:22). Look at the vocation to which you have been called. Indeed, God has called you into His marvelous light (1 Pt 2:9) and has chosen you as His heirs. With every effort of your mind, look to how you can please your heavenly Spouse so that you may be counted among His elect daughters. He will crown you with a crown of justice, which will be handed over to you on the day of solemnity and rejoicing. May Jesus Christ our Lord deign to offer it to you. With the Father and the Holy Spirit He lives and reigns as God for ever and ever. Amen.

10. Letter to the sisters at Bonn.

A voice thundering in the heart of Elisabeth, handmaid of the Lord, has said, "I am a small spark sent from the seat of great majesty. I speak to you sisters of the monastery in Bonn."

I advise you to walk cautiously in the way that is contemplation of the Lord, not like the foolish, but like wise and intelligent ones. This is the will of God. The days and times of this world are evil and the kingdom of God suffers violence and a great schism from you. You are like a people who do not know God and you wear your dishonor to God in your bodies. Return, daughters of Jerusalem, by a different path, one that leads to life. You still have time in your life and a place for penance. In heaven sits the one who admonishes you to conversion and, if He so determines, He will save you in an instant. The wise doctor wishes to cure the languors of your soul, first by applying pain, then later gently stroking and applying sweet ointment. In this way He will bind up your wounds, just as once the Savior came to cure the sick. Do not push away this doctor of salvation until you have received health. Do not receive unworthily the fatherly admonitions of the Lord. Indeed, those whom He loves, He corrects, like a loving father admonishes those he loves. And those who love Him, fulfill His law. Indeed He should be loved for this very admonition. Look at the whole world—how it increases then decreases. Nothing in it is secure but rather is like dust, which is blown by the wind and scattered. In this way the world and all its desires will vanish. We do not have an enduring city here, but we seek a future one where Christ sits at the right hand of God (Heb 13:14). There will be restored to us the drachma that was lost (Lk 15:8–9), and we will find the reward of eternal life. May Jesus Christ deign to offer it to us. He is the Son of the living God who lives in perfect Trinity forever. Amen.

11. Letter to the sisters of the Holy Virgins in Cologne.[299]

A small spark sent from the seat of great majesty and a voice thundering in the heart of a small worm-person shouts to the sisters of the Holy Virgins in Cologne, saying:

"My daughters are like those forsaken and they have vanished in their vanities. Like a reed blown back and forth by the wind, so are My daughters in all their ways." The Lord says, "Your foot tramples on the blood of My saints, which is poured out on the earth. From under your feet they accuse you, saying to Me, 'Why do you not avenge us, Lord Sabaoth? This people does not revere us. We who have endured great things for you are honored by but few of their great number; the earth and its kind scorn us.'"

Behold, daughters, you have stained the bed in which I should be resting with My saints. Return to your heart and recall how your predecessors went before you with all humility and chastity and how they loved their celestial Bridegroom. They imitated Him in their death and so were crowned and received the palm branch. Turn from your ways and follow them and be prepared so that when your Bridegroom comes and knocks at your door, you can open immediately and lead Him into your heart. Indeed, if it is pleasing to Him for you to be there, He will give you a named place in His kingdom. May He deign to offer you this, He who is now and forever will be, and His reign will be without end. Amen.

12. Letter to the sisters in Dirstein.

Behold I admonish you, O beloved daughters. Walk in the way of contemplation of the Lord with all the attention of your mind, with all humility and obedience and love and patience. God chose you as His heirs so that you would remain in contemplation without murmuring, detraction, and envy, so that the celestial Father would not be blasphemed and vexed by you, lest you vanish from the path on which you began to walk. And behold, He admonishes you with every gentleness; receive His fatherly admonitions with joyful blessing. While you still have the light, walk in it and you will be daughters of the light.

And behold, I admonish you, O virgin whoever you are, place Me like a seal over your heart (Sg 8:6)[300] so that no hostile deceptions can enter in there. Do not push Me away from your heart, for I have prepared inestimable treasures for you and I will lead you into the tent of My palace where the angels and archangels sing, where the harmonies of the saints ring out without cease. A crown of glory will be prepared for you, which will be handed over to you by Jesus Christ, Son of the living God, who lives and reigns in perfect Trinity for ever and ever. Amen.

13. Letter to the abbess of Dietkirchen.

Greetings from Elisabeth to the most beloved abbess of Dietkirchen. I, a lowly worm-person, broken down and exhausted by the many miseries of this world, send every debt of prayer so that God may impart to you the reward that I obtain in my own soul only with His grace.

Most beloved, I admonish you, be strong and vigorous against the ambushes of the crafty serpent who lies in ambush for your heel (Gn 3:15) and has set snares for you through the envy of many. Know for certain that those who set snares for you will themselves fall into them. And you, daughter of Jerusalem, joyfully walk in the way of contemplation of the Lord, running well in charity, chastity, prudence, and humility. Act manfully and let your heart be strengthened and endure the temptations of this world. It is through many temptations that we enter into the kingdom of God. God has planted a vineyard in the place where you live, and some beautiful little branches have sprouted there and they will bear fruit pleasing to God. Thorns and thistles have also grown there, and they are useless. What do you think that the Lord will do to His vineyard when it does not bear fruit acceptable to Him? Without doubt He will tear out the unfruitful ones and send them into the fiery furnace.[301]

With all the attention of your mind, extend your pastoral staff around those subject to you, whom you have undertaken to govern and guard. Strike strongly and gently, arrange all things with discretion, with fear of God, and with all humility. The higher you are, the lower you should be; indeed, humility is the great virtue by which one arrives at a crown. And now, rejoice and be glad in Him who has consecrated you for Himself and enabled your soul to be the bride of God, the bride of the King, the bride of the most dazzling Lamb who walks before you. Let it be sweet to run after His footsteps. Do not turn aside to the right or the left and in this way you shall come to Him. He will lead you into the upper room of His tent, you will eat with Him and He with you. There you will always rejoice with the angels. There will be cinnamon and balsam and the sweetest aroma. There will be the harmonies of the saints and the lovely song will resound before the throne of God. There no weakness will disturb, no tribulation will trouble. May God deign to offer you this joy. He lives and reigns for infinite ages and ages. Amen.

14. Letter to the abbess of Dietkirchen.[302]

I ask you, my beloved, to receive my words with thanks. I utter them as given by God without human effort.

On the Friday before Palm Sunday, two people from Bonn[303] came and greeted me from you. My brother, who was with them, reminded me that you had always desired to have some advice and consolation from me. Immediately, on the next night after Matins, while I was tormented with a very severe fever and was lying down, burning hot and covered with sweat, suddenly God placed these words in my mouth. I turned them over in my head till morning and then I could not rest until they were written down. When I had shown these to my brother, he said, "You must explain to us what this is that you have said about there being cinnamon and balsam in that celestial homeland." I promised to ask my visitor about this because I had not uttered the aforementioned words from my own understanding.

So after this, on Easter Vigil, when he appeared to me and I asked him about this, he looked cheerfully at me and said, "Cinnamon has a naturally pleasing sweetness that delights the taste. At the same time, it also has a sharp strength that inflames the palate of the one who tastes it and that becomes more piquant and aromatic the more one chews it. Such is the Lord our God to us who always wait to see His desirable face. To us He is sweet beyond all things that can be tasted; nothing among other desirable things can be compared to His sweetness. It touches us with ineffable strength and penetrates us most intimately. It ignites and continually enflames us to love Him. And the more we feast on the taste of His sweetness, the more piquant and appetizing He is for us and the course of our desire for Him will have no end.

"He is also the balsam of His chosen ones because He soothes their pains and offers them eternal health in His kingdom. They drink it constantly, quaffing it and being totally refreshed by it so that they forget all the evils they bore in this life. It also makes them incorruptible, so that they no longer hunger or thirst, nor suffer any harm from heat or cold or disease or any other injury, nor are they permanently dissolved by the wound of death. Its aroma has such abundant sweetness that if all things under heaven which have a sweet redolence were piled up, they could not exude a sweetness comparable to it. Its aroma is the sweetest delight that proceeds from Him not only to those who are now present to the face of His majesty, but also to those who still wander in this world and love His glory and pant after the homeland of seeing Him."

When he had said these things, he gently consoled me about my illness and promised me a great grace. I had been weeping much, since I would not be able to be present for the Easter joys due to the obstinacy of the fever that had been intolerably tormenting me for many days and that had changed from quartan to tertian.

But the angel was mindful of his kindness to me and he returned to me on the octave of Easter. He led me in spirit to a very pleasant place and he stood me near a most beautiful fountain. He drew from that fountain with what looked like a golden vessel and gave me to drink. When I had drunk, he made a sign of the cross above me and blessed me and said, "You are released from your illness; it will no longer touch you." When I was awakened from my ecstasy, I immediately felt relieved and began to walk with a firm step, which I had not been doing for a long time, nor has that illness ever returned. Blessed be God in all the mercies He has shown to me. I have taken care to announce all these things to you, most beloved, because of my great love for you. May you receive some consolation from them and be strengthened in the Lord.

15. Letter to Mistress G.[304]

Elisabeth, humble handmaid of Christ, sends every debt of prayer and love in Christ Jesus to her most beloved kinswoman and venerable mistress G. Most beloved! I admonish you to walk in the way of contemplation of God with all the attention of your mind, and run after the footsteps of the most dazzling Lamb who goes before you in all humility and patience. Strive to be patient against every adversity. The higher you are, the more you should lower yourself in all things. Humility is a great virtue; with it, one attains to a crown. The more humble you are, the more the height of glory will follow you. Have discretion toward those subject to you; beseech, rebuke, reprove. Indeed, discretion is the mother of all virtues.[305] It is absolutely necessary for all people who are called master or mistress to have discretion about themselves and others. Again the divine voice, the voice of your Spouse, shouts to you and to all who are under your rule, and admonishes you to walk in the way of His contemplation, just as He has done before you. Walk just as He walked. Do not turn to the right or to the left but follow His footsteps with all humility, patience, and obedience. Be without discord, without detraction, murmuring, and envy, and guard yourselves from other things of this kind so that you will be like newborn infants, reasonable without guile, living justly and piously in this world (1 Pt 2:1–2). "Be holy," says the Lord, "because I am holy" (Lv 19:2). He also says, "Be perfect just as your heavenly Father is perfect" (Mt 5:48). Walk like daughters of the light (Eph 5:8) and beloved daughters of your Father, who lives on high and looks upon the lowly. Love justice, obedience, patience, and humility. Love each other with all gentleness; lovingly bear each other's burdens (Gal 6:2). Be compassionate and merciful, just as your heavenly Father is merciful. Give offense to no one lest your ministry be slandered (2 Cor 6:3). None of you should do to another what she would not want for herself. Honor your mistress and love her with all gentleness and a sincere heart, for the Lord says, "The one who spurns you, spurns me, and the one who hears you, hears me" (Lk 10:16). So pay attention to and reflect upon the divine admonitions. Let your ears hear them, receive them with a cheerful heart and thanksgiving.

This, too, is the voice of your Spouse, "I will not rest, except upon the humble and quiet one who trembles at My word." Again He says, "My delight is to dwell among the human race" (Prv 8:31). In turn, the bride of the Lamb says, "Show me, you whom my soul loves, where you pasture, where you recline at midday" (Sg 1:6). And again, "I am my beloved's and my beloved is mine, He who pastures among the lilies" (Sg 6:2). What does this mean that He reclines and rests, pasturing among lilies? They are the chaste virgins, well ornamented with charity, chastity, prudence, and humility. The more chaste the virgin, the more humble should she be. Rejoice with gladness, daughters of Jerusalem, because God has chosen you as His heirs. Correct yourselves with all the attention of your heart. He will protect you under the shadow of His mercy and nourish you with the breasts of His consolation, until the day arrives and the shadows give way (Sg 2:17, 4:6). He will lead you to the Jerusalem on high and say, "Enter, daughters of Sion, and see the King of kings, wearing the diadem with which His Father crowned Him on the day of His betrothal, the day of His heart's joy." When was that day of His heart's joy? It was when He went out as a strong giant to contend against the king of the underworld, and He overpowered him and despoiled him, taking with Him into glory those whom He had redeemed by His blood. In the same way may it be done for us so that we may be with Him and He with us in eternal life. Amen.

Be well and pray to the Lord for me that He will create the temple of the Holy Spirit in me and accomplish in me what is pleasing to Him.

16. Letter to R.[306]

Elisabeth, humble handmaid of Christ, sends every joy in the celestial treasure to be received by you, R., her beloved.

Dearest! I admonish you to note how this world is in danger and the Lord always supports those in danger, drawing them forth, sometimes by admonition, at other times by correction, and at still other times by consolation. Like a most gentle father He corrects His children lest their earthen vessel be destroyed. So now, O friend of God, with all the attention of your mind, be mindful that this world passes away, and its flower withers and is fleeting. Who dares to say, "My foot is firm and I shall not fall?" No one can be secure in him or herself; if you are here today, you are gone tomorrow. And about your blessed house let me say, "It is a house of peace and peace rests in it. A chosen pearl has been found among you, and the Lord of all loves her. She has been preserved for Him and He calls her to be betrothed to Christ Jesus, and He will give everything that He has to buy this pearl" (Mt 13:45–46).

And behold, the divine mercy admonishes you, O venerable mother of that pearl, to love her with maternal love. See, however, that you not love her more than your soul. But if you love her as your own soul and love God more than your soul, then join these two into one, daughter to God, creature to Creator, and your soul shall receive a great reward on the day of reckoning and it will go well for you with the one who is blessed forever.

And I turn to you, father H., and admonish you above everything else to abstain from wine, since your soul suffers a great danger from this.[307] Know for certain that one who is always drunk is always oblivious to God's presence. God is patient and waits for you from day to day, and has given you days and years to improve yourself; therefore, you have no excuse. He gave you teaching and showed you a just path yet you walk along an unjust path. But this

249

patience of God is a fearful thing on the day when one will be repaid according to one's deeds. If, however, you are converted and do penance, you will find great grace from God, for He is kind and merciful and does not despise sinners but eats with them and wills not the death of sinners but that they be converted and live (Ez 33:11).

And I say to you, most beloved in Christ, R., L., and H., be comforted in the Holy Spirit and strengthen your hearts. For you are athletes of God, and you will overcome those who are enemies of chastity since you are lovers of chastity. Hence, there will be great joy in heaven for you. A crown of gladness and a great reward will be prepared for you. May He deign to offer it to you, He who lives and reigns in perfect Trinity forever. Amen.

17. Letter to Gerlach, abbot of Deutz.

To lord Gerlach, venerable abbot of the Deutz church, sister Elisabeth sends greetings and devout prayers. One of your friends asked me to announce these things to you because he understood from your letters that you desired this. While I was awaiting the return of my brother, who had set out to see you, it happened that I had a nocturnal vision. In it I saw him as if returning to us, holding in his hand three beautiful lilies. One of them was very small and looked as if it had just recently opened from the heat of the sun, but it was whiter and more lovely in appearance that the others. Placing it in my hand, he seemed to say, "Receive it, sister. She is called Euticia." After this, when he did return, he stopped first to see us, and while the brothers were preparing themselves for the procession, he told us about two sacred virgins, Fenellina and Grata, whom he brought and about that third one, the infant that he claimed was sent especially to me from you. Immediately I understood the vision of the three lilies and that the third one he brought without a name is Euticia.[308]

18. Letter to lady Hildegard. [See the *Third Book of Visions*, chap. 19.]

19. Letter to lady Hildegard. [See the *Third Book of Visions*, chaps. 20–28.]

20. Letter to the Archbishops of Mainz, Cologne, and Trier. [See *The Book of the Ways of God*, chap. 20.]

21. Letter of Elisabeth to Reinhard, abbot of Reinhausen.[309]
   When I, Elisabeth, had received your letters from the hand of your messenger and had read them, I went to the Lord and prayed to Him with all my heart that He might provide me with such a response that would offer you consolation. I had hardly finished my prayer when my mouth was filled with this sermon:
   To the venerable abbot Reinhard, Elisabeth, humble handmaid of Christ sends greetings and consolation in Christ Jesus. O venerable father, behold! The divine voice admonishes you, saying, "Be strengthened and fortified against all adversities. Be consoled in the Holy Spirit and trust in the Lord your God, because I the Lord am with you all the days of your life. I will not abandon you in the time of tribulation and suffering (2 Mc 1:15). I will rescue you and guard you like the pupil of My eye. Be strong and do not fail in the contest. Whoever contends well until the end will be saved" (Mt 10:22).
   The same divine voice admonishes you again, saying, "Reinhard, servant of God, run when you run, do what you do; let your foot not be idle; let your hand not be idle. The time is near and the days will not be long till God will have mercy on you. I Myself have chosen you and established you as a worker in My vineyard. You have guarded My vineyard and faithfully labored like a faithful and prudent servant whom a master establishes over his family to give to him a measure of wheat at the proper time (Lk 12:42). Rejoice and be glad because I the Lord will receive you as My chosen servant and I will refresh you at My banquet with My brothers and I will give you an unfading reward for your labor and exhaustion. You will rest where I Myself am and there you will rejoice with the angels and exalt with the saints without end."
   I warn you who have taken on that same appearance of piety: You must appear so not only in the presence of other human beings but in the presence of the angels and of God Himself, who dwells on high and looks upon the lowly. Let your light so shine among humans (Mt 5:16); let all your works grow bright and pay attention to what David said in the Psalter, "Those who please humans have

been confounded since God has rejected them." Don't be counted among the foolish virgins who sought external praise but be like the wise virgins who carried oil with them and whose lamps were lit (Mt 25:1–10). Be wise not among yourselves but so that you may boldly say, "All people have we won" in accordance with what Paul said, "I am a debtor to all people" (Rom 1:14). Take care lest what is written in Isaiah pertain to you: "You have destroyed My vineyard and the spoil of the poor is in your house" (Is 3:14). For this you must pay out to the poor what you have in abundance and the things you took from them. What I say to you I say even more insistently to very many other brothers. Alas, the secret business of buying and selling what belongs to God! Know beyond doubt that those who sell, sell judgment unto themselves, and those who buy, buy themselves a double-edged sword. What do you think the Lord will do when He comes to the judgment with the elders of the people and He lays down the reckoning for such servants? He will send them with hands and feet bound into the fiery furnace, where there will be weeping of eyes and gnashing of teeth (Mt 13:42).

Again, I warn everyone under the governance of the good father Reinhard: Before and above everything else, carry yourselves in all humility and obedience to the lord and father, and see the Lord our God in him. Love him with all the attention of your mind and gentleness and with a sincere heart. Honor each other; bear one another's burdens (Gal 6:2), and let there not be schisms among you, nor scandal, murmuring, or detraction. Possess nothing of your own in this world, not even your own bodies, and do not forget purity. Endure all things for the honor of God. Place nothing before the love of God for the sake of Him who loved you and handed Himself over for you as an innocent sacrifice for many sinners, and called you into His own wonderful light (1 Pt 2:9). Walk like beloved sons of your heavenly Father while there is still light in you, lest the shadows surround you. There is still time to repent. Correct yourselves and be prepared, because you do not know the hour when your Lord will come (Mt 24:42). Then, when He comes, you will immediately be revealed to Him and enter with Him into glory. There you will receive from Him the reward for all your good works, which is perfect delight, infinite exaltation, the crown and joy of all the saints. May He who is the fountain and source of all goodness deign to offer it to you.

On the day of Epiphany, my familiar angel of the Lord appeared to me. When I had asked him about what it was that had prompted you to ask those things about me, he told me, "Know without a doubt that it was I who moved him to this. Everything that he did in this affair was done according to God's plan and mine in order that the works of God would be made manifest in you." For this reason, I asked him about certain words from your letter, which I have now announced. I asked him why I said them and he explained everything to me.

22. Letter to Fulbert, abbot of Laach.[310]

To lord Fulbert, venerable abbot of Laach, sister Elisabeth of Schönau sends veneration and love in Christ. The vision I saw at Matins time as Christmas approached was like this. (From here, the text is the same as *Third Book of Visions*, chap. 5.)

To these things I would add that on the third day after this, when it happened that I had the chance to speak with the beloved of the Lord, blessed John the Evangelist, about that aforementioned doctor Origen, he said about our Lady, "The Lord has left the judgment of Origen to her decision so that whatever she might want to be done with him on the Last Day will be done." But to the words of our Lady, which she directed to me on Christmas, I immediately subjected another question, saying, "Reveal to me, I ask, Lady, about that brother who was so strangely buried at the Laach church. Should there be any hope for the liberation of his soul and should prayers be offered for him or not?" She said, "The Lord wishes absolutely nothing to be revealed to you about him since nothing from this would prove of any use for the people." I have been anxious to announce these things to you since I did not want to appear forgetful of your request. May you as well as the brothers who are with you remember to be consoled according to the discretion of your prudence.

23. Letter to Burchard, abbot of Odenheim.[311]

To lord Burchard, venerable abbot of Odenheim, sister Elisabeth sends devout prayers. On the day of Pentecost I acted on your request and asked the angel of the Lord who had appeared to me about the name of the holy virgin whose body you have and about her parentage. He responded to me, saying, "The name of the virgin about whom you ask is Viventia. Her father's name was Arian and her mother was called Leticia, and they both were upright before the Lord. When they had been married for forty years without child, they finally merited to receive this daughter from the generous Lord. Because they loved her tenderly, they wished her not to be joined to a husband. The fame of blessed Ursula and her companions had arisen, so they sent their daughter to Ursula and joined her to that society. Thus it happened that she suffered martyrdom among that number of holy virgins."

Also, I don't want you to be unaware that when I heard these things from the angel during the canon of the Mass, I did not correctly retain the name of the virgin in my memory. When my brother asked me about these things after Mass, I said that her name was Convivia. After this, at noon, that very virgin appeared to me and completely persuaded me that I had not named her correctly and showed me her garment of marvelous whiteness and around it in gold letters was written, "I am called chosen Viventia." I inquired of her, saying, "My good lady, why was I allowed to err in this way about your name and call you Convivia?" She said, "Because I was led to the banquet of heavenly mysteries."[312] When I asked her where she was born, she responded, "I was born in Bebruannia."

I also asked the angel about your holy patrons Bonosius and Abrunculus and with what kind of merit they stood before the Lord. He said, "They were saints before the Lord from their earliest age and bore much fruit among the people. Therefore, their sanctity was declared by the Lord in the many miracles that have been performed in curing the sick and raising the dead." He added to this, saying, "Know that the place where their relics are held has been sanctified greatly by their merits."

The Death of Elisabeth

A letter of Ekbert to his kinswomen about the death of lady Elisabeth.[313]

1. To Guda, Hadewig, and Regelindis, virgins dedicated to God in the congregation at Andernach, their neighbors and close ones, brother Ekbert from the monastery of Schönau sends the service of prayer and the affection of love.

Let me cry out my pain a bit to you, my dearest ones, and please receive the words of my lamentation with sweet compassion. If I cry just a bit, I will hardly mourn to the fullness of my wound. Yet this I do, lest I be thought to be wracked by carnal affection and it be attributed to my foolishness. Lo, our Elisabeth, that chosen lamp of heavenly light, that virgin outstanding and honored by the abundant grace of God, that splendid gem of our monastery, the leader of our virginal company,[314] has been withdrawn from this life before her older years. She brought me forth into the light of untried newness; she led me to the intimate ministry of Jesus my Lord;[315] with her honeyed mouth she used to offer me divine consolation and instruction from heaven and made my heart taste the first fruits of the sweetness hidden from the saints in heaven. She withdrew from this path without return, and behold, the sweetness of my soul, [the consolation of my poverty,][316] the delightful spice of all my labors no longer exists upon this earth. Thus with justice do I bind my heart with the belt of grief. I take up this worthy lament about you, my beloved, virgin so grace-filled and lovable in the holy sweetness with which the spirit of God anointed you. The innermost part of my soul mourns your premature death, O daughter of grace, and the strings of my heart sound forth the mournful song about you to my spirit.

But my grief is not like the grief brought forth by flesh and blood—which are carnal—so that I grieve [now] for the sake of sibling relationship; rather, I am saddened by the shared losses of spiritual delights that you, minister of God, used to offer many people in an unheard of way. [Through you heaven was opened to earth and secrets of God hidden from the world flowed to us through the instrument of your voice; your eloquence was more precious than gold, sweeter than honey (Ps 19:10).] Through you angels conversed intimately with us and with you mediating, the highest princes of heaven were friendly to us. [O happy woman! You saw what many kings and prophets wished to see but didn't.] The sublime palace of heaven was opened to your blessed eyes and before the time when all will see, you saw the inaccessible brightness of the immortal kingdom. You made known to us the glory of the heavenly citizens and placed it as if before our mental eyes. Your blessed accounts greatly inflamed our hearts with desire for the homeland that we await.[317] [The words of your admonition so often strengthened our minds which were wavering in the service of God, and you made us greatly amplify our praises of the Lord with holy fervor.] Oh, how many works of piety were done far and wide throughout the land because of your exhortations! How many souls of the elect obtained their desired consolations through your negotiation! [You are a blessed daughter of the Lord, for you have fruitfully negotiated between God and human beings!] O woman happily born, how have our unhappy times lost you? Lamp of God, how have you been extinguished from this world? How have you been closed, O clear window through which the eyes of the Lord looked out at us?

[It is pious, O chosen one of God, for us to weep the loss of your sweet presence and yet it is also pious for us to rejoice at the blessedness of your most excellent end. You have fought the good fight and you have happily finished the course of your martyrdom (2 Tm 4:7).] All your life from your most tender years, if correctly perceived, can truly be called martyrdom. You bore the yoke of the Lord from your adolescence, under the discipline of the Rule, always walking in poverty and manifold tribulation. [The hand of the Lord was always heavy upon you, lest at any time you be without the celestial visitation that pressed upon your soul and bruised your pitiable body with afflictions and ailments, which only He who reflects upon suffering and pain is worthy to enumerate and acknowledge.] You showed yourself cheerful and patient in every flagellation of the Lord and you always added the sacrifice of [voluntary] affliction to every pain of the wounds that His hand inflicted upon you. [Lady, may the rivers of your innumerable tears, the wearying of your knees, the rending of your tenderness that you endured from the harshness of your coarse garment, the gashes in your sides caused by your hard belt, the incredible paucity of food, and the countless holocausts of prayers remain present to the eyes of the merciful God, to whom all things are things are exposed and open (Heb 4:13). May the fount of life that you thirsted after with your whole heart now quench the burning of your holy desire for Him.] May God, the one who lifts up the lowly, look upon and honor the humility of your spirit by which you, beyond all others known to me, were always puny and worthless in your own eyes. [May the divine kindness recognize the kindness that you used to show to those who opposed you, and may it bring you to the deserved reward. Weary soul, spent soul, soul saturated with the miseries of a wretched life, go on now to the rest so long desired; may the bosom of eternal peace receive you.] May the right hand of the faithful Bridegroom embrace you, caress you, and bind up all your griefs, and give you the oil of gladness in place of distress, the crown of beauty in place of the ash of contempt, and the pallium of praise in place of the spirit of sorrow.

But how have I digressed from my intent? In my mind, my dear ones, I was planning to begin the account, to describe to you the blessed end of our beloved one, but in the overflowing of my melancholy heart I took up this plaint before my proposed narration. And now, with God's favor, may I accomplish what I intended since I trust this will be pleasing to your charity.

2. The handmaid of the Lord was comporting herself in her usual cheerful way up to the day of Pentecost. Just as it was her habit to gratify us on every solemn feast day, on that day she gladdened us with sacred revelations, telling us, among other things, how and

when the individuals assisting at the service of God would be visited by the Holy Spirit. On Tuesday after [this, around] the hour of Vespers, suddenly she fell into a very grave languor, and she began to be so seriously afflicted throughout her whole body that the whole community rushed to her, invoking the help of the Lord upon her. She remained in this affliction all night.

On the following day, that is, Wednesday, a solemn fast was observed and the congregation of brothers made a procession in albs to her cell. We carried with us in reliquaries all the relics of the society of Saint Ursula the queen, that is, the fourteen whole bodies that we had, as well as the many fragments of various bodies. While we were celebrating the first Mass of the feast of the Holy Spirit there, she went into ecstasy and for a long time, as the sisters told us, she remained still, which she usually did in her times of trance when any divine things were being revealed to her. After this, when she had returned to herself, we asked her how she was and whether she had received any divine consolation from the Lord. She responded to us, saying, "In a vision of my spirit I saw our most holy Lady. Standing next to her were blessed queen Ursula, Saint Verena, whose body is with us, and all the holy virgins whose relics were carried here. It was a numerous multitude, all marvelously crowned and robed in great brightness and having palm branches of victory in their hands. I spoke to our Lady, who stood in the midst of this holy crowd, and I said to her, '[To you, most beloved Lady, I make complaint from my whole heart about all my tribulation.] Have mercy on me, for from my youth till this day I have been worn down and afflicted by so many sufferings and such innumerable ailments, and even now I endure such intolerable martyrdom in this miserable body of mine.' She responded with great sweetness, saying to me, '[My beloved! Our Lord has appointed this life for you so that you would suffer many injuries and many afflictions and great poverty in it. But He will have mercy on you and console you well in everything.] It is the will of the Lord to purify you through these things and to work in you in such a way that when you depart from this world, you will suffer no harm [from anything else. Therefore, have patience in all the evils you endure and murmur nothing against the Lord in your heart, for He will turn all things to good for you.] Look at these women who stand around me: See how they are crowned and how great is their beauty. They suffered many agonies and extremely harsh martyrdom for the Lord. Therefore they not only have honor before God but they are even honored [greatly] by human beings and everywhere in the world are they served.' [She continued, saying, 'In truth, I say to you, that if it were possible for you to be burnt to ashes thirty times in one day and each time be returned to human wholeness, you could not sufficiently merit by that affliction the grace and glory which the God has set aside for you in heaven.'] In turn I said to her, 'Lady, I fear that people may be scandalized by my infirmities and judge that I am being tortured in this way for some very grave sins. They will use this opportunity to deride the grace of God in me and to distrust those things the Lord has done in me.' And she responded to me, saying, 'No wise person will do this.'"

From that time forward, the handmaid of the Lord was weakened by her ailments more and more each day, and a new annoyance occurred daily. She was especially contracted by pains in her vital parts, and we could offer her no relief. [In the days of this languor she took so little food that it was unbelievable that a human body could even be sustained by it for any length of time, and what she did eat was coughed up.] For the remaining days till her death, she remained so unshakable mentally that never but once was she moved to tears by the laments of the sisters and her friends who feared her death, even though she had easily burst into tears while she was healthy. [Even when she seemed to treat very gently the sisters around her who were rejoicing and speaking words of gladness, in no way did she relax her face from severity.] The violence of the pain did not allow her to lie in bed or sleep; instead, sitting up almost all through the night and day with her mental faculty undisturbed, she discussed many things that we assumed she could hardly think about.

[Before the days of this illness, she had told us that] on a certain [feast] day, while she was still healthy, she saw in spirit our blessed Lady. In most devout prayer she had commended her life and the end of her life to her, saying, "I pray, most holy Lady, by your mercy, help me to have a reasonable end of my life. Let it never happen that I depart from this world without experiencing everything pertaining to the death of a Christian." [With great kindness] Mary responded to her, saying, "You must be assured that not only will your death be like that of a Christian, but it will be like that of a saint." [Truly we saw how, through the grace of God, this promise was fulfilled in Elisabeth. For all the sacraments that pertain to the death of a Christian were fully celebrated for her and even more than that, God blessed her last days so that His special grace in her was clearly recognized and glorified by many people.]

Seeing her disease worsen and thinking that she had completely lost all bodily strength, Elisabeth requested that her spiritual father, our lord abbot, be called to her. With him present, she had the whole community of sisters gathered before her. In great pain yet as if feeling nothing bad, sitting with great fortitude of spirit, she delivered to the sisters a long and rational sermon. Even though I was present for it, only a few words of it lingered in my memory.

"Do not, my dear ones," she said, "wonder about my illness like ignorant people. Nor should you distrust the grace of God in me because of His castigation that I endure and have often endured in your midst. [My conscience is clear with the Lord and I know most certainly that through these things which I suffer the Lord prepares and adorns my crown in His kingdom.] Not on account of my merits, but on account of His mercy He has for many years worked great things in me, things unheard of in our times. I know that there are many people who have faithfully and kindly understood these things and been edified by them. But many are untrusting and have been scandalized by what they have heard about me—may God not charge it against them. [But I speak to you and, on the basis of that journey by which I hope to reach the kingdom of God, I confidently affirm that these things that you have seen in me and heard from me are true and I brought no simulation or fallacy to any of these things, as God is my witness.] May these things be always before your eyes and by them may you be more fully corrected than others, lest the Lord hold you more accountable than others who have not seen these things as truly as you have. [Give thanks to the Lord always, and praise Him in all the wonders He has worked in me in your sight, for in these things He has offered you a special honor beyond others living a cloistered life.]

"Be at peace and love each other. Preserve your order with great diligence; endure your poverty with patience. [Faithfully take care of my soul with earnest attention; neglect nothing that pertains to my debt by thinking that I do not need the suffrages of your prayers. Indeed I say this to you because those who appear pious are often neglected. People who know of their good life think that they do not especially need their help."[318]

When she had anxiously said these things, the lord abbot responded to her words, saying, "We have faith that the promise whereby our Lady promised you perpetual rest after this tribulation will be fulfilled in you. Nevertheless, we will in no way ignore what you request."

To this she responded, "I do not at all distrust the promise of our beloved Lady, but nevertheless, what is mine I must do and carefully provide for my soul." To her sisters she said, "If because of me, dear ones, you have offended God at all, may He forgive you, and I dismiss all offense from my heart. And if I did anything to you that I should not have done, please, I ask, forgive me. I have not yet received an assurance from the Lord about the end of my life, but it is appropriate for me to have this concern about the protection of my soul and to set in order those things that pertain to my death, and to this end, I request the sacrament of anointing."

When she had said this and many similar things beyond her strength, she asked the lord abbot to summon many of the senior priests and anoint her. This was done. After she had made her confession, we deliberately delayed giving her the sacrament of the Lord's body because of her stomach illness and the danger of her coughing. On the following night, her illness was so aggravated that she thought that she was going to die right away. Since she was worried about the delay in receiving the Lord's body, she lifted her hands to heaven and prayed to the Lord, saying, "Savior of the world, Lord Jesus Christ, I beg you through your holy Passion in which you stretched out yourself upon the wood of the cross to redeem the world and to embrace everything that you redeemed, do not let me depart from this world before I receive your most

261

sacred body to console and fortify my soul. Be mindful, O Lord, of how many times I received it with intimate devotion of my heart and great outpouring of tears. Do not allow me to be without this blessing in my last days."

One of the sisters keeping watch with her said, "Remember, lady, that in a particular vision the divine voice said to you, 'I have begun and I will finish.'[319] Therefore I have faith that the Lord will not allow you to die so unexpectedly that you would not first experience some obvious consolation from Him and a greater certitude about your death." Elisabeth received this point with joy. Moreover, the Lord heard her desire and her death was then delayed so that she later took communion three times before the end of her life.

Thinking that I could help her with medical skill and fearing it might be imputed to my foolishness and inhumanity if I neglected to try, I made haste to the city of Mainz to consult doctors and obtain medicine. But since it was the will of God to carry her from this world, I could not find anything I was looking for.[320]

That same night while I was in Mainz, our sick one was sitting in bed in her usual way and the sisters were keeping watch with her. Around the middle of the night, when she had most earnestly prayed to the Lord and commended the end of her life to Him, she began to be gravely uneasy, and she was so transformed from her earlier condition that it was thought that she was about to die. After much anxiety, she went into a trance. The sisters who were around her looked at her from all sides and were stunned. Thinking the end was near, they began to rush around, some to bring the shroud on which she would be laid, others to wake the rest of the convent. When they arrived, Elisabeth began to draw her breath and return to herself. One of the sisters lay down close to her, holding her in her arms, and Elisabeth spoke softly to her, saying, "I do not know what is to become of me. That light which I usually see in the heavens has been divided." She said no more.

Then each of the sisters, bending down before her, asked forgiveness from her, beseeching her to forgive them all their offenses. She did this with great benevolence and prudence. In turn, as much as she was able, she lowered herself before them, showing such discretion in everything that they clearly saw the grace of the Holy

Spirit in her. Then one of the sisters privately queried her, saying, "Dearest, has any sign from the Lord been shown to you yet or have you heard any voice from which you could learn about your death?" She replied, "I have perceived nothing like that yet." After this, she said to the sisters that the community must go to sing Matins. Indeed it was the time. When the sisters who stayed with her began to chant the psalms, she again went into a trance. When they finished the office of Matins, she caught her breath again and returned to herself. She then told some of the sisters to go and rest. Those most intimate with her stayed with her. One of them said to her, "Dearest! Tell us if you can how it was for you in this trance. If anything was revealed to you by the Lord, please make it known to us." She said, "I am not yet able. Wait a little bit."

After a little while, when she had regained some strength, she said,][321] "The Lord has now shown to me the holy visions that I used to see regularly on solemn feast days. These are the same visions that the angel told me many years ago that I would not again see until the time of my death.[322] This is a most certain indication of my death. Nevertheless, I ask you still to be silent about this and not announce it. [After this, when the community of sisters had finished singing Matins, one of the older sisters came and said to her, "Tell us, most beloved, if you have received any consolation from the Lord." She responded, "Oh, what good consolation have I received!" She did not, however, have the strength to speak, so the sisters who had heard it from her told about the vision Elisabeth had seen to that older sister as well as the others who had gathered there. And there was great weeping among them.

Then, comforted in spirit and sitting up, she addressed them all in this way, "My loved ones! In this vision, you must have certitude about my death and the true testimony of everything the Lord has done in me. I beseech and admonish you to exercise steadfast faith and never distrust the things that the Lord did in me in your presence. I believe in His works and I bear testimony to them in my death. He has worked in me up to this time and will continue until my death. You must always give special thanks to Him for all these things. Satan has always lain in wait for me and has laid many snares for me. I know that even after my death he will not stop opposing me, corrupting my reputation and obscuring those things that the Lord has done in me. From my adolescence I suffered many things among you: harsh and intolerable things in my body due to many ailments, great poverty of life's necessities, and afflictions that I willingly undertook. And after the Lord began to place His special grace in me, I suffered more severely than before, not specifically because of my iniquities but so that the things that the Lord showed to me in secret would be confirmed by my afflictions that you could see externally. Thus what I saw would be more believable to you and to others who saw my afflictions."

Then the sisters with one accord said to her, "Most beloved lady, since we can no longer have you here among us, we ask you to name one of us who, with the will of God, could have authority over us and we will joyfully receive her with all benevolence." Elisabeth replied, "It is my advice that you should accept in my place the one who was prioress after me and did all things pertaining to that office well and competently. Honor and love her and support her on account of the Lord, for as long as He allows her to live among you. The Lord knows that I say these things, not because of her kinship to me or any particular love for her, but because I trust that this is pleasing to the Lord and that it will be useful to you. May the Lord console you and teach you all things that are pleasing to Him." The sisters joyfully received her advice. Later, they requested the lord abbot to give to them as mistress the one whom Elisabeth had named and he consented to their petition.[323]]

When she finished the words she was addressing to the sisters, she said to those who were closely attending her, "Alas! What should be done about the absence of my brother? Alas for the medicine that he is trying to obtain for me. What does medicine have to do with me? I beg you, send a messenger with all haste to call him back." They did this. It was Wednesday. When morning came, the [lord] abbot was soon called. He sat in her presence and the sisters told him about the vision that assured her death. Elisabeth herself did not have the strength to tell him. When he heard the words of those speaking, he said to her, "Is it as they say?" She responded, "Yes, my lord, and from this I have the most definite testimony about my death." Soon he left, going to the service of God. He celebrated the office of the holy Trinity because the handmaid of the Lord confirmed that the mystery of the holy Trinity had been revealed to her in that aforementioned vision in the same way that it had been showed to her ten years earlier in the same vision.[324] [Having finished the divine office, the abbot fortified her with holy communion and the litany was said over her with great devotion by the brothers as well as the sisters as they wept profusely.]

After this, around Nones I returned and was received with so many tears by all that I assumed she had already died. When I questioned those who met me with such tears and they said that she was still living, I remained hopeful about her life. When I was permitted to enter, I found her sitting up and talking, and so I greatly wondered at the cause of so many tears of those around her since I saw in her no likeness of death. [After I had been sitting with her for a little while,] she addressed me, saying, "I am dying, most beloved brother, and I will definitely not recover." [My heart was pierced by these words and] I said to her, "How do you know this, my dear?" She said, "Last night the Lord showed me the great vision I had seen many years ago and about which I had been told that I would not see it again until the end of my life. Thus I am certain that the end of my life has come." When I heard this I remembered the vision and recalled the words of the angel that had predicted the end of her life—all of which I had written down [with my own hands]. At this, I set aside all hope of her life and health. [From the deep pain in my heart I began to cry in front of her, but she made no sign of grief at all. Remaining mentally unshakable,] she said to me, "Most beloved, know that my death causes me no sadness and that I am separated from you without any grief, although I love you more dearly than any other person. This is because I hunger and thirst for the kingdom of God more than for any other food or drink. [I said to her, "I do not claim to be like a prophet. Pray that your spirit may be twofold in me (4 Kgs 2:9), but if the Lord wishes to grant me your spirit singlefold, it would suffice for me." She said, "Dearest! May the will of the Lord be done in you."]

After this, when Nones was over, the lord abbot returned with the whole community of brothers. At his initiation, again the litany was said with many tears. After the blessings had been said over her,

Elisabeth asked to be heard by the whole community. Sitting up and mentally stable, she addressed us and thanked us all for every benefit extended to her and for [all] the trials we had suffered on her behalf. She very prudently exhorted us to concord, to endure our poverty, and to serve the Lord [without fail]. "Each of you," she said, "should diligently apply yourselves, lest there be any defect in your service of the Lord. [I know that it was often revealed to me by the Lord that He blessed this place with a special blessing. Praise and worship of God will not cease here until the final times.] Therefore, give special thanks to Him for this because He has honored this place beyond all other monasteries by the grace that He deigned to work in me." [When she had exhorted many things in this fashion, she added an exhortation to me. She begged and urged me to preserve the steadfastness of stability and never abandon this place, even if I happened to be called to a more honorable and wealthier place.³²⁵]

All of us joyfully received her words of advice, since we clearly saw the spirit of the Lord working in her. The lord abbot said to her, "[Now we have your pleasing admonition, most beloved.] We ask you diligently to commend us to the Lord after you have died. And always pray to Him to keep this place in His protection and peace." [She humbly agreed to his petition. After this, with hands joined together,] she extended them to the abbot and said, "To the Lord God my Creator I commend my soul, and after Him, to you, beloved father. I ask you to present it to the Lord on the last day because I am your spiritual daughter, and I have loved you and preserved the obedience owed to you, just as I was obliged."³²⁶ Receiving her hands with tears, he said, "I expect to offer you joyfully to the Lord."

[After this,] she said, "Do not marvel that I so anxiously deal with everything pertaining to my death. It is necessary for me to do this while I still have the strength lest by chance when all my strength fails I would be found unprepared in some way." [As the lord abbot was withdrawing from her, she said to him, "May that blessing by which the Lord Savior blessed His disciples when He ascended into heaven remain upon you, most beloved father." With an unwearied mind she addressed each of the brothers, advising them about progress in the virtues and commending herself to their prayers. Not only did she entreat the priests to offer the life-giving sacrifice for her, but she likewise begged the deacons to do so when they ascended to that higher office.] She also requested each of them to commit themselves to saying particular psalms in her memory. For the sake of the consolation from her tribulations that she hoped to obtain from the Lord, she asked the first to chant the psalm, "When the Lord turned again [the captivity of Sion]" (Ps 125). To another [she commended the psalm], "Praise the Lord, Jerusalem" (Ps 147). To another she said, "Praise the Lord, my soul" (Ps 145). To another, "Praise the Lord for He is good" (Ps 146). To another, "Praise is due to you, God in Sion" (Ps 64). To another, "His foundation is in the holy mountains" (Ps 86). To another, "God, in your name" (Ps 53). To another, "The Lord reigns, let the earth rejoice" (Ps 96).

We were truly amazed at the fullness and fortitude of her mind, considering the severity of her weakness and her loss of physical strength. From the beginning of her illness she had taken hardly any food that she had not coughed up from her stomach. [Moreover, from that Wednesday on which she was assured about her death up till the tenth day on which she died, she took almost no nourishment but cold water, except for one day, when we forced her and she ate a few strawberries and a little bit of an apple, but she could not keep them down.]

After this she addressed a long sermon to the sisters gathered around her, advising them earnestly about every necessary matter. Then, having affectionately kissed each of them, at the end of the sermon she added, "My dears, the angel of the Lord who was sent to guard me always had great concern for me, and showed me many good things. Through me he kindly offered consolation to you and to many others. For this I ask that you always give thanks to him and that you each offer him a special service, and every day say in his honor the psalm, "The Lord reigns, let the earth rejoice" (Ps 96).

On Thursday, at the time of the divine office, Elisabeth earnestly invoked the Lord Savior, whom she declared that she had seen in that vision which is described in *The Book of the Ways of God*.[327] She asked Him to mercifully release her from the unbearable chains of her languor. He responded to her saying, "I will come quickly and release you." [On the following Saturday, while the divine office of our Lady was being celebrated, Elisabeth saw our Lady in the heavens and likewise begged her for her release.] That one[328] said to her, "Your illness is unto death. The vision you see now will not be taken from you. You will continue to see it until the hour when I come to you with my honorable company to receive your soul and lead it to the place of refreshment where it will rest from all its labors." [Throughout that whole day, Elisabeth was seriously failing, and she constantly looked to our blessed Lady as if she were present, ceaselessly calling upon her in a weak and pitiable voice.]

On Sunday night she was comforted a bit in spirit after the longed-for arrival of our sister, a God-fearing woman whom I had called from afar for Elisabeth's funeral. Then, with the sisters gathered around her, as she was sitting in bed, with eyes raised to heaven and all the attention of her heart, she prayed to the Lord with a great outpouring of holy words, saying, "[Lord my creator, my liberator, my savior, my protector, I commend my soul to your holy majesty, to your undivided Trinity, for consolation and salvation.] I ask you, Lord, through your holy incarnation, through [your holy] birth, circumcision, presentation, baptism, passion, resurrection, and ascension, through the coming of the Holy Spirit, [and through the coming judgment], to deign to loose me from these chains of mine, and lead my soul to the place where you wish, where it may receive consolation from all its tribulations."

When she had made many prayers like this, she added the customary praises of the Lord, saying, "[To you God the unbegotten Father, to you only begotten Son, to you Holy Spirit, Paraclete, to you holy and undivided Trinity, I confess with all my heart and mouth. We praise you and bless you. To you be glory forever.][329] Blessed be the holy Trinity, the Creator and ruler of all things, now and always, forever and ever."[330] [Then she continued, saying,] "I commend my soul to [my Lady] holy Mary, the ever virgin, [to receive, console, and protect it,] and to Saint Michael and all the company of heaven, Saint John the Baptist and all the holy prophets, Saint John the Evangelist, [Saint Peter and] all the holy apostles, [Saint Stephen and] all the martyrs, [Saint Nicholas and all the holy confessors, Saint Margaret] and all the [holy] virgins, [and all the saints of God, to intercede for me with the Lord, and to receive my soul when it departs from this life and] to help it in the presence of the Lord so that it may dwell there where it may be worthy to enjoy perpetual consolation with the souls of the saints. When all the sisters had said "Amen," she greeted our Lady, saying,

"Hail queen of mercy, sweetness of life
and our hope of salvation.
We exiled children of Eve shout to you.
Weeping and groaning we sigh after you
in this valley of tears. Ah, our advocate!
Turn your merciful eyes to us and,
after this exile, show us Jesus,
the blessed fruit of your womb.
O mild, O pious, O sweet Mary.

"Nourishing mother of our Redeemer,
who remains the open gate of heaven
and star of the sea,
hasten to help your people
who fall but struggle to rise again.
With nature marveling
you gave birth to your holy Creator.
Virgin first,
later receiving that Ave from the mouth of Gabriel,
have mercy on sinners.[331]

"All the angels in heaven
praise you, holy Lord, saying,
'Praise and honor are due
to you, Lord.'[332]

"The Cherubim and Seraphim
and every heavenly order
proclaim the Sanctus and say,
'Praise and honor are due to you, Lord.'

"Savior of the world, save us all. Holy Mother of God, Mary ever virgin, pray for us. We humbly beseech the prayers of the holy apostles, martyrs and confessors, and holy virgins, so that we may

269

be rescued from all evil and may be worthy to enjoy all good things, now and forever."[333]

To these she added the Lord's prayer, the Creed, and a confession to all those standing around her. Finally, she added, "Lord my God, may you deign to hear all my words that you have given me, for I can say nothing but what you manifest to me." [Having said all these things, her strength failed so that she seemed like she was now about to die, and she remained in that weakness for a long time.]

Just as our Lady had promised her, Elisabeth was, as she told us, constantly seeing the vision that had appeared to her on the aforementioned Wednesday. This vision was clearer at some times than others, so that sometimes she could see a great light pouring down from heaven upon her and she saw our Lady, accompanied by many other saints, coming so close to her that she thought she was to be carried away. [When this happened, she directed her whole mind and all her strength there so that she could neither speak nor pay any attention to us. This led us to think that her end was now here.] After one or two days she regained her speech and began to lament piteously, saying, "Alas, what's to be done? Alas, what's to be done?" This she frequently repeated. When we asked her why she said this, she responded, "I saw them approaching and thought they were going to carry off my soul, yet they ascended again and withdrew from me, still not carrying me away." [This happened frequently during those ten days.

One day she saw the angel of the Lord who was well known to her standing by her and saying, "The Lord prolongs your death in this way so that many people will more greatly glorify Him because of you." And indeed it did happen like that.] Every day many people from near and far who acknowledged the grace of God in her, hearing that she had come to the moment of her death, flocked with great desire to see her. Although it is not our custom to admit strangers to our sick, [nevertheless, upon consideration, many who were troubling us] were admitted for the sake of edification. We did this because we feared that they might become suspicious if she were so assiduously kept from everyone's view. Yet Elisabeth, bearing this so patiently and hiding the sharpness of her pain with the fortitude of her mind, sat in their presence and was not slow in admonishing them about their salvation according to what was appropriate for each of them. She exhorted clerics in the priesthood to live irreproachably and to teach the people with their good example. She said to them, "It is your place, my beloved ones, to show yourselves to be more intimate with the Lord than other people by your good way of life and your holy ministry. Do this so that the Lord may bind you more intimately to Himself in His kingdom after this life." She urged those clerics who were not in the order of priesthood not to withdraw from intimacy with the Lord but to show themselves favorable to promotion to the sacred ministry of God and to be solicitous about divine matters. She exhorted soldiers to protect the people, succor the oppressed, give a tenth of their goods, refrain from plundering, from slashing and perforating their clothes, and from fornication, saying that fornicators will not only be struck by the punishments of hell after this life but will also be smitten in this world by childless infertility and extreme unhappiness.[334] [She urged the people to maintain fidelity to their lords and to each other, to endure their poverty patiently, to give alms as they are able, and to be devout in going to church and praying to the Lord their Creator.] She exhorted not only those present to do good, but she also sent warnings of salvation to some who were not there, and she forgave those far away for their offense of slander. She also begged everyone together to remember her with prayers and alms after her death. If I tried to present individually all the words of her reasonable sermons and the holy prayers that she uttered in those days, I would certainly be compiling a not insignificant book.

Everyone greatly marveled at her prudence and glorified the power of God in her, by whose work alone the handmaid of the Lord could endure to live in such a weak body for such a long time without any nourishment and yet sit and pour forth sermons of such discretion. [It was in accordance with her request that the Lord did this for her.] She told us that she had often requested from the Lord in her prayers that at the end of her life He would grant her an illness that would be sober and free from gluttony.[335]

Each day Elisabeth's failing advanced so that we could only await her death. Twice or more the litany was said over her, and the gospel texts [of the Lord's Passion] were also recited over her. Moreover, since she had always had a great devotion to the Passion of our Lord, the Lord destined [both] the day and hour of His Passion for her death. On Friday morning she said to those who were with her, "Today, let all [who are close to me] offer me diligent care for my hour is near. When she was removed from her bed, [sitting on a little cushion and leaning on one of the sisters,] she spoke intimately and tearfully with those who were with her. At the sixth hour, her spirit began to struggle in pain. The lord abbot came with the priests and again fortified her with blessings and the litany. When I suggested holy communion to him, he signaled to me that she did not have the strength to swallow. [I decided it would not be a danger for her to abstain then because she had taken communion yesterday when I offered it.]

After this, when we were leaving, that sister upon whose breast Elisabeth was leaning, said to her, "Most beloved one, when others of our sisters were dying, you used to indicate to us at which hour their end would come and when we should place them on the shroud. [But now we cannot know this about you unless you yourself tell us.] At this Elisabeth was silent, and then after a little while had me [hastily] called. I was with her for a little while, together with our brother, a cleric of monastic life,[336] whom I had summoned here [from afar], awaiting what would come. Then, with her eyes raised and looking [devoutly] to the heavens, she began to lose her voice, [yet still began to pray in her usual way]. Finally, as if remembering the words of the aforementioned sister about indicating the hour she should be laid out, she extended her hand and quickly signaled three times to us that she should be placed upon the shroud that had been spread out near her. When we had done this and she was lying down in moderate agony, the litany was said, once by the sisters, and a second time by the [lord] abbot and the convent of brothers. After this, around the ninth hour, as if gently sleeping, she gave up her spirit to the Lord on June 18. Then one of the priests who was standing there and who loved her in Christ, tearfully burst forth, saying, "Depart, holy soul, to your rest. Ascend like a column of smoke from the spices of myrrh and frankincense and all the powders of the perfumer (Sg 3:6). Enter into the joy of your Lord. Lord Jesus Christ, Savior of the world, receive the soul that you have created, the soul that your blood has redeemed. O Mary, mother of mercy, receive now your handmaid. O virgin of virgins, acknowledge now your virgin. Holy angel, receive the soul commissioned to you and lead it now into peace where it may rest from its labors."

The Lord looked upon the humility of His handmaid, who in everything always showed herself as if unworthy. God honored her in the end by magnificent funeral services among the people who had immediately come from all around up till the third day, that is, Sunday, on which she was buried. Indeed, while she was still living and healthy, she used to speak frequently about the approach of her death and what she, with pious intention, hoped for, saying, "May I depart from this life at such a time that those who come to my funeral [suffer no danger or intemperate weather and] can remember me with greater devotion." And this is what happened. Indeed, throughout the whole summer a time did not dawn more peacefully than those three days. As a result, despite the grief we all had because of her death, nevertheless the hearts of all were infused with a pleasant joy as we celebrated her blessed consummation. By unchangeable custom we always took care that the congregation of sisters should not go outside the threshold of their monastery. Yet, because of the veneration for the special grace of God that had clearly been at work in His handmaid, it was pleasing to our venerable father as well as to the other brothers to offer her this special honor. It was permitted for all the sisters together to follow in the funeral procession of their venerable mistress and to participate in the funeral rite at her tomb. Therefore, by the hands of the sisters she had chosen for this, as well as by the hands of Countess Beatrice,[337] who had been devotedly present for her illness and funeral, she was laid in a place near the altar dedicated to all the sacred virgins, in the church of Saint Florinus, in the thirty-sixth year of her life, in the thirteenth year of her visitation in which she was visited by the fatherly grace of the Lord our God, may He be blessed in all His mercies forever and ever. Amen.[338]

Notes

NOTES TO THE INTRODUCTION

1. That is, Elisabeth, who became mistress of nuns at Schönau; Ekbert, who became abbot of Schönau; and Ruotger, who was prior of the Premonstratensian house of Pöhlde.

2. Hans Becker, "Das Kloster Schönau (Übersicht)," in *Schönauer Elisabeth Jubiläum 1965: Festschrift anlässlich des achthundert jährigen Todestages des heiligen Elisabeth von Schönau* (Limburg: Pallottiner Druckerei, 1965), 80–81, and Wilhelm Günther, *Codex Diplomaticus Rheno-Mosellanus* (Coblenz: B. Heriot, 1822), 1:231 n.2.

3. Urban Küsters, *Der verschlossene Garten: Volkssprachliche Hohelied-Auslegung und monastische Lebensform im 12. Jahrhundert*, Studia humaniora: Düsseldorfer Studien zu Mittelalter und Renaissance, Band 2 (Düsseldorf: Droste Verlag, 1985), 142–55, 73–75.

4. See Emecho of Schönau, *Vita Eckeberti*, ed. S. Widmann, *Neues Archiv der Gesellschaft für ältere deutsche Geschichtskunde* 11 (1886): 449–50. See also *First Book of Visions*, chap. 59.

5. For comparable recourse to Hildegard of Bingen for resolving theological questions, see Anne Clark Bartlett, "Commentary, Polemic, and Prophecy in Hildegard of Bingen's *Solutiones Triginta Octo Questionum*," *Viator* 23 (1992): 153–65.

6. For the Cathars and especially their activities in this region, see Jeffrey Burton Russell, *Dissent and Reform in the Early Middle Ages* (Berkeley and Los Angeles: University of California Press, 1965), 84–86, and R. I. Moore, *The Origins of European Dissent* (New York: St. Martin's Press, 1977), 168–82.

7. For Hildegard's anti-Cathar text, see *Analecta Sanctae Hildegardis*, ed. J.-B. Pitra, Analecta Sacra, vol. 8 (Monte Cassino, 1882; reprint, Farnborough: Gregg Press Limited, 1966), 348–51.

8. Hildegard seems to have known and been influenced by Elisa-

beth's revelations about the Cologne martyrdom; Elisabeth knew Hildegard's anti-Cathar work and probably the *Scivias*.

9. There is a discrepancy about the actual date of her death. See Anne L. Clark, *Elisabeth of Schönau: A Twelfth-Century Visionary* (Philadelphia: University of Pennsylvania Press, 1992), 26.

10. See *First Book of Visions*, chap. 76, and *Second Book of Visions*, chap. 20.

11. For Ekbert's views about his role, see his "Preface to the Visions," his introduction to the *First Book of Visions* (chap. 1), and his letter to Reinhard of Reinhausen (in *Die Visionen der hl. Elisabeth und die Schriften der Aebte Ekbert und Emecho von Schönau*, ed. F. W. E. Roth [Brünn: Verlag der Studien aus dem Benedictiner-und Cistercienser-Orden, 1884], 318; hereafter this volume will be referred to as *Visionen*). See also Emecho, *Vita Eckeberti*, 448–49.

12. See, for example, the visions translated here as items 1 and 2 in the Appendix to *The Revelations About the Virgins of Cologne*.

13. Ekbert's own work that he incorporated into the visionary collection includes his introductions to the *First* and *Second Book of Visions* and to *Letters*, a prayer that he first appended to the end of the long version of the *First Book*, a long section interpreting one of Elisabeth's visions with which he concluded the *Third Book*, his letter describing Elisabeth's death, the preface to the whole collection of visions, and a letter about one of Elisabeth's visions that he added to the end of *The Revelations About the Virgins of Cologne*. Ekbert also wrote prayers, meditations, letters, and polemical works that were not associated with Elisabeth's works. For his works, see Kurt Köster, "Ekbert von Schönau," in *Die deutscher Literatur des Mittelalters: Verfasserlexikon*, 2d ed. (Berlin: Walter de Gruyter, 1980).

14. See, e.g., her appeal to scribes in *The Book of the Ways of God*, chap. 19, and her comments to Hildegard of Bingen about the circulation of letters under her name (*Third Book of Visions*, chap. 19).

15. See, e.g., *First Book of Visions*, chap. 51.

16. *Letters*, chaps. 13–14.

17. See, e.g., *The Death of Elisabeth*, where Ekbert prays for her spirit to be bequeathed to him.

18. *Third Book of Visions*, chap. 4.

19. *First Book of Visions*, chap. 12.

20. For the Latin text, see Joseph Klinkenberg, "Studien zur Geschichte der Kölner Märterinnen," *Jahrbücher des Vereins von Alterthumsfreunden in Rheinlande* 93 (1892): 150–63. For an English translation, see *The*

Passion of Saint Ursula [Regnante domino], trans. Pamela Sheingorn and Marcelle Thiébaux (Toronto: Peregrina Publishing Co., 1990).

21. Elisabeth's letter to the bishops of Trier, Cologne, and Mainz was originally appended to the end of *The Resurrection of the Blessed Virgin* and then moved to the end of *The Book of the Ways of God*; her letter to Hildegard of Bingen about the Cathars originally circulated with Hildegard's text about the Cathars and was later incorporated as *Third Book of Visions*, chaps. 20–28; three letters related to the Cologne martyrs were originally appended to the conclusion of that text but later incorporated as chapters 5, 11, and 6 of the letter collection.

22. Roth, "Die Schriften Elisabeths von Schönau," in *Visionen*, CIX-XC. Kurt Köster, "Elisabeth von Schönau: Leben, Persönlichkeit und visionäres Werk," in *Schönauer Elisabeth Jubiläum 1965*. For Köster's work on the manuscript transmission, see "Elisabeth von Schönau: Werk und Wirkung im Spiegel der mittelrheinischen handschriftlichen Überlieferung," *Archiv für Mittelrheinische Kirchengeschichte* 3 (1951): 243–315.

23. Caroline Walker Bynum, "The Female Body and Religious Practice in the Later Middle Ages," in *Fragmentation and Redemption: Essays on Gender and the Human Body in Medieval Religion* (New York: Zone Books, 1991), 195–222.

24. *Vita Sanctae Hildegardis*, ed. Monica Klaes, Corpus Christianorum, Continuatio Mediaevalis, vol. 126 (Turnholt: Brepols, 1993), 30.

25. Ibid., 28–29, 32.

26. Walter Simons, "Reading a Saint's Body: Rapture and Bodily Movement in the *Vitae* of Thirteenth-Century Beguines," in *Framing Medieval Bodies*, ed. Sarah Kay and Miri Rubin (Manchester: Manchester University Press, 1994), 12.

27. The manuscripts are catalogued in Kurt Köster, "Elisabeth von Schönau: Werk und Wirkung," 243–315, and Köster, "Das Visionäre Werk Elisabeths von Schönau," *Archiv für Mittelrheinische Kirchengeschichte* 4 (1952): 114–19. To this list should be added Cologne, Stadtarchiv MS GB 8° 60; Cologne, Stadtarchiv MS W133; and Troyes, Bibliothèque Municipale MS 946; +Trier, St. Eucharius-Matthias Abbey MS 148 (D56); and +Trier, St. Eucharius-Matthias Abbey MS 524 (I66). From this list should be deleted Trier, Stadtbibliothek 646/869 8°, a manuscript in which letters of Hildegard of Bingen are ascribed to Elisabeth. The first edition of Elisabeth's visions is Jacques Lefèvre d'Etaples, *Liber trium virorum & trium spiritualium virginum* (Paris: Henri Estienne, 1513).

28. For Roger's letter, see Ruth J. Dean, "Elizabeth, Abbess of Schönau, and Roger of Ford," *Modern Philology* 41 (1944): 209–13.

29. Dean, "Elizabeth, Abbess of Schönau," 211.

30. Alberic of Trois Fontaines, *Chronica*, Monumenta Germaniae Historica, Scriptores, vol. 23, 843, 683.

31. For the Anglo-Norman poem, see J. P. Strachey, *Poem on the Assumption* (Cambridge: Cambridge University Press, 1924). For the Icelandic and French translations, see the manuscripts listed in Köster, "Elisabeth von Schönau: Werk und Wirkung," 278, 289.

32. Jean Beleth, *Rationale divinorum officiorum, Patrologia Latina*, 202, col. 148.

33. See Dean, "Elizabeth, Abbess of Schönau," 218.

34. Peter Dinzelbacher, *Vision und Visionsliteratur im Mittelalter*, Monographien zur Geschichte des Mittelalters, 23 (Stuttgart: Anton Hiersemann, 1981), 184–99.

35. I have, however, presented *The Resurrection of the Blessed Virgin* as an independent text, which is how it usually circulated, even after Ekbert incorporated it as the conclusion of the *Second Book of Visions*.

36. *Die Visionen der hl. Elisabeth und die Schriften der Aebte Ekbert und Emecho von Schönau*, ed. F. W. E. Roth (Brünn: Verlag der Studien aus dem Benedictiner-und Cistercienser-Orden, 1884).

37. For the redactions of Elisabeth's works, see Clark, *Elisabeth of Schönau*, 45–49, 137–42. When I adopt a variant reading, the manuscript basis is given in the notes, although, to avoid unwieldiness, not every manuscript transmitting the variant is necessarily cited. Obvious typographical errors in the edition are translated as emended without citing manuscript evidence.

38. In that manuscript there are minor variations between the headings as they appear in the indices and in the body of the text.

39. See, e.g., *First Book of Visions*, chap. 47, and *Second Book of Visions*, chap. 1.

NOTE TO *THE PREFACE OF ABBOT EKBERT TO THE VISIONS*

40. This preface appears only in the final version of the visionary collection.

NOTES TO THE *FIRST BOOK OF VISIONS*

41. This is Pope Eugene III. Most manuscripts only note Eugene; some transmit the erroneous Eugene II.

42. The original version of this text reads, "in the year of our Lord 1152, she began to see visions." This is the end of the original introduction and the text continues with Elisabeth's words, "I am ready, brother, to confess to your love these most sacred things in every detail, for my soul has long desired this very thing: that I may be given the opportunity to confer with you about these things that the Lord has gloriously worked in me." See below, n. 44. The variant readings for the original version of *First Book of Visions* are from Avignon, Bibliothèque municipale MS 593, and Paris, Bibliothèque de l'Université MS 790.

43. Ekbert uses the phrase *mente excedere*, literally, "to go beyond or withdraw from the mind" to describe the ecstatic trance that Elisabeth herself refers to as being "in ecstasy" *(in extasim)*, "in a trance" *(in mentis excessu)*, or "in spirit" *(in spiritu)*. For *mentis excessus*, cf. Acts 11:5. The return from this state is described as the restoration of her spirit because Elisabeth sometimes refers to her spirit as being separated from and then returned to her body.

44. For this sentence in the original version of this text, see above, note 42.

45. The original version of this texts reads "and consider, my beloved, the afflictions of my heart...."

46. Elisabeth refers here to the circumstance described at greater length in her first letter to Hildegard of Bingen. See *Third Book of Visions*, chap. 19.

47. The original version of this sentence reads, "that you and the lord abbot are pleased for you to commit my words to writing."

48. Instead of the three preceding sentences, the original version reads, "Among all my griefs, which would be tedious to recount, and among the great lack of necessities which I endured, the consolation of the Father of orphans never failed me, so that all my grief was great joy to my heart."

49. May 18, 1152.

50. Throughout the text, Elisabeth refers to the devil in various ways that suggest his personal presence as her enemy. These terms, such as Adversary, Betrayer, and Waylayer, are capitalized in this translation to suggest her sense of his personal presence.

51. Elisabeth refers here to the mistress *(magistra)* or head of the nuns' community at Schönau. There is no abbess, since the abbot is the head of the entire community.

52. Saturday was dedicated to the Virgin Mary, a practice that was associated with the recitation of the Little Office of our Lady and the

increasing popularity of the Ave Maria. See Hilda Graef, *Mary: A History of Doctrine and Devotion* (Westminster: Christian Classics, 1963, 1965), 1:208, 230–33.

53. Elisabeth distinguishes the lower atmosphere *(inferior aer)* from the area above it in which celestial figures sometimes appear to her and from which they may even, as in this vision, descend into the lower atmosphere to approach her.

54. A gesture that recalls the activity of a bishop in the sacrament of confirmation.

55. The "salvific sacrifice" is the sacrament of the Eucharist. Elsewhere Elisabeth refers to it as the "Lord's sacrifice" or the "divine sacrifice."

56. In the context of these visions of the heavenly court, Majesty refers specifically to an image of Christ enthroned.

57. For the text of the sequence "Ave preclara," see Migne, *Patrologia Latina*, 143, col. 443. For another occurrence of this vision, see *Second Book of Visions*, chap. 13. This vision caught the attention of Caesarius of Heisterbach, a Cistercian monk writing in the first half of the thirteenth century who compiled a large collection of miracle stories. In the section on miracles of the Virgin Mary, Caesarius described this vision of Elisabeth, which he claims to have heard other monastics recount. This oral transmission of the vision, which differs somewhat from the version transmitted here, adds the following conclusion: "From that day until now, at the command of the aforementioned Elisabeth, that convent [of nuns in Schönau] continues to ask for mercy at that same versicle whenever that sequence is chanted" (Dist. 7, cap. 30). Caesarius of Heisterbach, *Dialogus Miraculorum*, ed. Joseph Strange (Cologne: H. Lempertz and Comp., 1861), 2:39.

58. June 23, 1152.

59. The prose hymn *Te deum laudamus* was usually sung at the end of Matins on Sundays and major feasts.

60. June 26, 1152.

61. The original version of this chapter concludes with the following sentence: "And while I was delighting in seeing them, they were suddenly withdrawn from my eyes."

62. June 29, 1152.

63. Antiphon from the feast of the Chair of Saint Peter and the feast of the apostles Peter and Paul. It continues: "To you have been given the keys of the kingdom of heaven."

64. In the earlier version, the quotation from 2 Timothy does not appear and instead is found this sentence: "However, Paul seemed of

greater height than Peter." There was a medieval tradition, possibly originating with Gregory the Great, about Paul's larger physical size. For a collection of medieval traditions about Peter and Paul, see Jacobus de Voragine, *Golden Legend: Readings on the Saints*, trans. William Granger Ryan (Princeton, N.J.: Princeton University Press, 1993), 1:119–20, 162–66, 340–564, and 2:34–39.

65. A prayer usually associated with the Mass of the Holy Spirit. The entire text is: "God, to whom every heart is open, and every will is spoken, and no secret lies hidden, purify the thoughts of our hearts by an infusion of the Holy Spirit, so that we may be worthy to love you perfectly and praise you worthily."

66. Feast of Saint Kilian and his Companions: July 8; feast of Seven Brothers: July 10.

67. In the early version, the sentence reads, ". . .come forward into our atmosphere, towards me, and our Lady advanced with him."

68. July 15, 1152.

69. July 21, 1152.

70. July 25, 1152.

71. The church of the monastery at Schönau was dedicated to Saint Florinus. It is interesting that this patron of the monastery does not seem to loom large in Elisabeth's piety or visions, perhaps due to the paucity of his cult. The first hagiographical description of his life was composed around 1185, two decades after Elisabeth's death.

72. Saint Peter in Chains: August 1, 1152; feast of Saint Stephen: August 3; feast of Oswald: August 9; feast of Afra and her servants: August 5; feast of Cyriacus: August 8; vigil of the feast of Lawrence: August 9. In the earlier version of this text, these visions were recounted in a slightly different sequence: Peter, Oswald, Afra, Stephen, Cyriacus, Lawrence.

73. July 27, 1152.

74. Response for Vespers.

75. August 3, 1152.

76. In the medieval exegetical tradition, the four animals referred to in Ezekiel 1:10 were associated with the four evangelists: Matthew was associated with the man, Mark with the lion, Luke with the ox, and John with the eagle.

77. It is unclear here whether Elisabeth is saying that Ekbert has seen her sink into ecstasy or has himself seen the same things she saw in her visions. For Ekbert's own visionary experience and inclinations, see Clark, *Elisabeth of Schönau*, 18–19.

78. August 13, 1152.

79. Antiphon for the first week of Advent.

80. August 14, 1152.

81. This petition is found as part of a longer prayer to Mary that was attributed to Anselm of Canterbury (See *Patrologia Latina*, 158, col. 947), but was probably composed by a follower of Anselm. See R. W. Southern, *Saint Anselm and His Biographer: A Study of Monastic Life and Thought 1059–c. 1130* (Cambridge: Cambridge University Press, 1963), 206–7.

82. Antiphon for the feast of Saint Michael: "You holy Lord, all the angels with one voice praise, saying, 'Praise belongs to you, God.'" Verse: "The angel stood next to the altar of the temple, holding a gold thurible in his hand. Alleluia."

83. September 8, 1152.

84. August 16, 1152.

85. August 29, 1152.

86. Response from feast of the Trinity.

87. Antiphon from Christmas season: "O key of David and scepter of the house of Israel, who opens and no one closes; who closes and no one opens. Come and from the prison house lead out the captive, the one who sits in darkness and in the shadow of death."

88. This petition is reminiscent of a common prayer adapted to various feasts. See *Corpus Orationum*, 9 vols., Corpus Christianorum, Series Latina, vol. 160 (Turnholt: Brepols, 1992–96), 1:106–7. In the earlier version, the following also appears, "And I added, 'By the grace of God, I am what I am,' et cetera." This is an antiphon from the feast of Saint Paul: "By the grace of God, I am what I am. And His grace has not been empty in me but will always remain in me."

89. The original version of the *First Book of Visions* ends abruptly here with the following prophecy appended: "One day in the month of July, I, Elisabeth, had withdrawn to a secret place and was preoccupied with prayer. And behold, an angel of the Lord came and stood before me and said, 'Don't you know that in a future year Easter is to be celebrated on the very day on which the Lord arose and that the feast of the Annunciation will fall on Good Friday?' And I was silent because I was truly unaware of this. He continued, saying, 'Know that in that time Satan will receive power from God for inciting people against one another so that they will destroy each other. The sun will be suffused with red and covered by shadows because there will be nothing else but an outpouring of much blood and immense sadness among the Christian people. After this, the serpent, a shedder of blood, will invisibly destroy the people and there will

be such great tribulation on the earth that anyone who escapes alive will owe the Lord everlasting praise. Moreover, if I were to tell you what is going to happen soon after these things, you could not bear it for the extent of your fear.'" This controversial prophecy appeared to cause some damage to Elisabeth's reputation and is referred to in her first letter to Hildegard of Bingen. The prophecy draws on traditional apocalyptic imagery, and the Annunciation/Good Friday coincidence, which occurred in 1155, was an apocalyptic motif since at least the ninth century. For this motif, see Bernard McGinn, *Visions of the End: Apocalyptic Traditions in the Middle Ages*, Records of Civilization, vol. 96 (New York: Columbia University Press, 1979), 88–90, and 306 nn.9–11.

90. Response and verse from the feast of the Holy Trinity.

91. Adapted from a common antiphon used on various saints' feasts.

92. Antiphon from the feast of Saint John the Baptist.

93. September 14, 1152.

94. September 29, 1152.

95. Antiphon from the feast of Saint Michael the Archangel: "The angel stood next to the altar of the temple, holding a gold thurible in his hand. Alleluia."

96. For eucharistic visions and their place in women's piety, see Caroline Walker Bynum, *Holy Feast and Holy Fast: The Religious Significance of Food to Medieval Women* (Berkeley and Los Angeles: University of California Press, 1987).

97. Antiphon from the feast of Saints John and Paul: "These are the two olive trees and two candlesticks shining before the Lord. They have the power to close the clouds of the sky and open its gates because their tongues have been made keys of heaven."

98. October 21, 1152.

99. October 31, 1152.

100. November 1, 1152.

101. November 2, 1152.

102. This reference to the custom of calling saints' feasts "their birthdays" seems to be intended to acknowledge that the feasts were in fact usually commemorations of saints' deaths, and thereby their birth into eternal life.

103. That is, the beginning of the Gospel of Matthew, the genealogy of Jesus.

104. Antiphon from Advent and Christmas: "O queen of the world,

born from royal seed, Christ comes forth from your womb like a bride-groom from the marriage bed. He who rules the stars lies here in a stable."

105. December 26, 1152.

106. December 28, 1152.

107. January 1 and 6, 1153.

108. February 2, 1153.

109. A procession with candles was a common part of the celebration of the feast of the Purification. See John Harper, *The Forms and Orders of Western Liturgy from the Tenth to the Eighteenth Century* (Oxford: Clarendon Press, 1991), 130.

110. It should be remembered that all the events described in this book are said to have taken place before Ekbert's permanent move to Schönau. Thus Elisabeth refers to his absence or to receiving letters from him (e.g., chaps. 29 and 55).

111. March 8, 1153.

112. March 15, 1153.

113. Ekbert did take up this task; see *Third Book of Visions*, chap. 30.

114. March 19, 1153.

115. April 12, 1153.

116. Response for Holy Thursday: "Pilate entered the praetorium with Jesus and said to Him: 'Are you the king of the Jews?' He responded, 'You say that I am king.' Then Jesus departed from the praetorium, wearing a crown and a purple cloak. And while He was clothed like that, everyone shouted, 'Let Him be crucified, for He has made Himself the Son of God.'"

117. April 16, 1153.

118. Antiphon for Hoy Thursday.

119. Although this chapter heading specifies that the tormentors were Jews, the text itself does not. For the increasing tendency in this period to emphasize Jews as the torturers of Christ, and especially for the role of Ekbert of Schönau in this development, see Thomas H. Bestul, *Texts of the Passion: Latin Devotional Literature and Medieval Society* (Philadelphia: University of Pennsylvania Press, 1996).

120. Verse for Holy Thursday, Good Friday, and Holy Saturday.

121. Response for Good Friday.

122. This verse is found in a praise prayer to Mary transmitted in a twelfth-century manuscript from Schönau. See *Das Gebetbuch der hl. Elisabeth von Schönau. Nach der Originalhandschrift des XII. Jahrhunderts*, ed. F. W. E. Roth (Augsburg: Verlag des Literarischen Instituts von Dr. Max Huttler, 1886), 14. The editor believes some of the prayers to be authored

by Ekbert. There are other parallels between the visionary works of Elisabeth and the contents of this manuscript, as can be seen below in *The Death of Elisabeth*, although the direction of the influence is not clear. This verse is also part of a new trend that associates Mary with martyrdom due to the torment she endured in witnessing the death of her son, despite the apocryphal traditions that portray her as dying peacefully. For another example of this development, see Honorius Augustodunesis, *Sigillum*, *Patrologia Latina*, 172, col. 498–99.

123. Response for Holy Saturday: "When the Lord was interred, the tomb was sealed with a rock rolled in front of the opening. Soldiers were stationed to guard it."

124. April 18, 1153.

125. April 19, 1153.

126. This vision juxtaposes two different resurrection accounts, that of the Gospel of Matthew, where Mary Magdalene and "the other Mary" encounter the risen Jesus and hold onto his feet, and that of the Gospel of John, where Mary Magdalene encounters Jesus and he tells her not to touch him.

127. May 28, 1153.

128. Antiphon from the feast of the Ascension: "O king of glory, Lord of hosts, who as conqueror has today ascended above all the heavens. Do not abandon your orphans but send to us the Spirit of Truth promised by the Father."

129. June 7, 1153.

130. Antiphon from the feast of Pentecost: "The Holy Spirit, coming forth from the throne, entered unseen the hearts of the apostles with a new sign of sanctification so that from their mouths all languages came forth. Alleluia."

131. August 10, 1153.

132. August 15, 1153.

133. Antiphon from the feast of the Trinity.

134. November 1, 1153.

135. Antiphon from the feast of the Trinity.

136. September 14, 1153.

137. At this point, three manuscripts include a lengthy episode about the Schönau community that never became a standard part of either the original or later version of the *First Book of Visions*. In this account, Elisabeth learned through her visions that two young monks were planning to flee the monastery and return to the world. One had been raised in the monastery since his boyhood and had led an innocent life. The other

had offered himself to the monastery after having been an armor bearer. Elisabeth sees their future temptation and is able to turn the more innocent one from his plan, urging him to repent and confess his sins. After this, the devil appears before her, complaining that she has robbed him of one. However, the other monk he still claims, and the account concludes with that monk's escape into the world of sin on the abbot's stolen horse. For this incident, see *Visionen*, IV*-V*.

138. December 24, 1153.

139. Fulda, Hessische Landesbibliothek MS Aa96 and Trier, Bistumsarchiv MS 10 record a different verse here: "Sent from the exalted dignity of the Father, He descended from the heavens, entered into the womb of the Virgin so that He could appear visible to us, clothed in human flesh without the stain of sin, and He went forth through the closed gate, God and man, light and life, maker of the world." Both versions are Christmas responses. The theme of the Virgin's conception through her ear had been celebrated in hymns since the fourth century. See Graef, *Mary*, 1:56–58.

140. Response from the Christmas Vigil.

141. See above, chap. 54.

142. Antiphon from the feast of Saints Firmus and Rusticus.

143. December 25, 1153.

144. Elisabeth later elaborates this image of walking along the good path in *The Book of the Ways of God*.

145. Ekbert himself is the unnamed deacon. A more detailed account of Elisabeth's visionary exhortations to Ekbert and his decision to seek sacerdotal ordination and then monastic profession can be found in his biography. See Emecho of Schönau, *Vita Eckeberti*, 449–50.

146. December 27, 1153.

147. December 28, 1153.

148. January 1, 1154.

149. January 6, 1154.

150. February 2, 1154.

151. March 25, 1154.

152. March 27, 1154.

153. This chapter and the following, which describe a turning point in Elisabeth's visionary career, recall the declaration with which Hildegard of Bingen began her *Scivias*. See Hildegard of Bingen, *Scivias*, ed. Adelgundis Führkötter and Angela Carlevaris, Corpus Christianorum, Continuatio Mediaevalis, vol. 43 (Turnholt: Brepols, 1978), 59–61.

154. March 28, 1154.

155. March 29, 1154.

156. March 31, 1154.

157. As in her use of the expression "man of desires," (*vir desiderio-rum*, see *The Book of the Ways of God*, chap. 14), Elisabeth uses this expression "son of man," an explicitly masculine phrase, to refer to herself. Both of these expressions are direct quotations of biblical phrases that were used in contexts of divine commission of prophets.

158. April 3, 1154.

159. April 25, 1154.

160. In Fulda, Hessische Landesbibliothek MS Aa96, there is a marginal illustration of the four wheels with the larger wheel.

161. May 23, 1154.

162. Count Rupert of Laurenburg was the son of Dudo, who founded the cloister of Schönau in 1114 as a Benedictine priory dependent on the abbey of Schaffhausen. In 1125 or 1126, Rupert converted it to an independent monastery. On May 13, 1154, Pope Anastasius IV ordered Archbishop Hillin of Trier to threaten Rupert and Count Arnold of Nassau with excommunication for seizing church property in Worms. See also *Second Book of Visions*, chap. 21, and *Third Book of Visions*, chap. 12.

163. June 28, 1155.

164. Antiphon from the feasts of the Chair of Saint Peter and of the Apostles Peter and Paul: "Peter, as God commanded, loose the chains, you who open the heavenly kingdom to the blessed."

165. Antiphon from the feast of the Conversion of Paul.

166. More detail of these events is given in Elisabeth's first letter to Hildegard of Bingen. See *Third Book of Visions*, chap. 19.

167. August 8, 1154.

168. Cf. Gregory the Great, *Dialogues: Texte critique, notes, et traduction*, ed. Adalbert de Vogue, Sources Chrétiennes, vols. 251, 260, 265 (Paris: Les Editions du Cerf, 1980), 2:35.

169. August 15, 1154.

170. Response from the feast of the Assumption.

171. Originally this book concluded with a prayer composed by Ekbert. It is a meditation on God's willingness to gracefully inspire unworthy vessels, taking no account of age, sex, status, or any external condition. It doesn't mention Elisabeth by name but has much in common with the themes he later developed in his introduction to the *Second Book of Visions*, and he later transferred this prayer to that context but omitted it altogether in the final redaction of the visionary corpus. For the text of the prayer, see *Visionen*, VI*.

NOTES TO THE *SECOND BOOK OF VISIONS*

172. In this introduction, Ekbert responds to criticism apparently elicited by the publication of the *First Book of Visions*, and he tries to explain the continuation of Elisabeth's visionary experiences after the earlier announcement that she would see no more visions until her death. The author of the chapter heading, who describes God's goodness as "unheard of," misses Ekbert's point that there has been a tradition of women inspired in this way.

173. See *First Book of Visions*, chap. 79.

174. May 14, 1155.

175. June 23, 1155.

176. Antiphon from the feast of the Beheading of John the Baptist.

177. June 24, 1155.

178. June 29, 1155.

179. Antiphon from the feast of the Apostles.

180. Antiphon from the feast of Saint Paul the Apostle.

181. July 6, 1155.

182. It is not clear whether Elisabeth's vow of reading seven Psalters refers to the Book of Psalms, the seven psalms of penance (Pss 6, 31, 37, 50, 101, 129, 142), or the Psalter of the Virgin, which was a devotional genre incorporating repeated Aves as well as hymns of praise to Mary. For this genre, see Giles G. Meersseman, *Der Hymnos Akathistos im Abendland* (Freiburg: Universitätsverlag, 1960), vol. 2, *Gruß-psalter, Gruß-orationen, Gaude-andachten und Litaneien*.

183. July 11, 1155.

184. See *First Book of Visions*, chap. 11.

185. August 10, 1155.

186. This is the end of the original version of this text. In the chapters that follow, feast days are still sometimes noted, but there is insufficient notice of the years to enable a consistent chronology of the events described.

187. Reading *soleo* from Vienna, Österreichische Nationalbibliothek Vindob. Pal. MS 488.

188. Ekbert, Elisabeth's mother's paternal uncle and the one for whom Ekbert, Elisabeth's brother, appears to have been named, had been a deacon at the cathedral at Cologne, provost of Saint Cassius in Bonn, and bishop of Münster from 1127 until his death in 1132.

189. September 28.

190. Count Rupert of Laurenburg; see *First Book of Visions*, chap. 75. Cf. also *Third Book of Visions*, chap. 12.

191. "That famous master Adam" refers to a teacher with whom Ekbert had studied before coming to Schönau, probably in Paris. Ekbert also refers to Adam in a letter to Rainald of Dassel, who had been a fellow student and later became the archbishop of Cologne and the chancellor of the Emperor Frederick Barbarossa. The mention of a friend's ordination is probably a reference to Ekbert. Ekbert's ordination in 1155 suggests a death date of 1150 for Adam, thus making unlikely his identification as the Parisian master Adam of Balsham, who is thought to have died in 1181.

192. November 1.

193. October 28.

194. The customary of Hirsau, the center of the Benedictine reform movement in Germany with which the monastery at Schönau was affiliated, states that a corporal stained with eucharistic wine was to be preserved where the relics were kept. See Wilhelm, *Consuetudines Hirsaugienses*, *Patrologia Latina*, 150, col. 1041.

195. June 29. Some manuscripts reverse the order of chapters 28 and 29 to make them follow the chronological order of the feast days.

196. For the legends about Peter's martyrdom and his tears, see Jacobus de Voragine, *Golden Legend*, 1:341, 345.

197. June 26.

198. For the legend, attributed to Isidore of Seville, about John's miraculous death, see Jacobus de Voragine, *Golden Legend*, 1:55.

199. The feast of Saint John the Evangelist was celebrated on December 27. Elisabeth's concern with the accuracy of the church calendar can also be seen in *The Resurrection of the Blessed Virgin*, where she claims that the traditional date for celebrating the assumption is incorrect.

200. July 15. For the legend about the separation of their bones, see Jacobus de Voragine, *Golden Legend*, 1:348.

NOTES TO THE *THIRD BOOK OF VISIONS*

201. Feast of John the Baptist: June 24. The dates of Pentecost and its octave cannot be determined because, as in the latter half of the *Second Book of Visions*, the visionary narratives no longer indicate the year of the events described. The visions comprising this book can only be said to have taken place probably after the spring of 1156.

202. In Vienna, Österreichische Nationalbibliothek Vindob. Pal. MS 488, the question reads, "When were those streets opened?"

203. This sentence is not found in Vienna, Österreichische Nationalbibliothek Vindob. Pal. MS 488.

204. December 27.

205. Either January 25 (the Conversion of Paul) or June 29 (the feast of the apostles Peter and Paul).

206. January 25.

207. This last sentence is not found in Vienna, Österreichische Nationalbibliothek Vindob. Pal. MS 488.

208. For Bishop Ekbert of Mainz, see *Second Book of Visions*, chap. 19.

209. This is the excommunicated army of Count Rupert of Laurenburg. See *First Book of Visions*, chap. 75 and *Second Book of Visions*, chap. 21.

210. This is the most extreme example of Elisabeth being asked to clarify confusions in authoritative tradition. For the disputed text, see *Pseudo-Dionysius: The Complete Works*, trans. Colm Luibheid, Classics of Western Spirituality (New York: Paulist Press, 1987), 164. For the influence of Pseudo-Dionysius on medieval angelology, see Paul Rorem, *Pseudo-Dionysius: A Commentary on the Texts and an Introduction to Their Influence* (New York: Oxford University Press, 1993), 73–77.

211. March 25.

212. September 29.

213. Although the Latin in this passage is grammatically clear, the overall expression is somewhat confused. The text reflects a tradition that the number of the saved will replace the number of fallen angels, a belief clearly stated in the next chapter. When this question is repeated a second time in this chapter, the focus shifts from the number of the saved to the division between the saved and the damned.

214. Some of the events described in this letter are referred to, but with less detail about the circumstances, in *First Book of Visions*, chaps. 25 and 78.

215. This passage is puzzling. Hildegard's earlier concern about Elisabeth has been seen as a reference to a letter from Hildegard addressed to the mistress of nuns at Schönau in which special care for Elisabeth is exhorted (see L. Van Acker, "Der Briefwechsel zwischen Elisabeth von Schönau und Hildegard von Bingen," in *Aevum inter utrumque: Mélanges offerts à Gabriel Sanders*, Instrumenta Patristica, 23 [The Hague: Nijhoff International, 1991], 409–17). However, Hiltrud Rissel has convincingly argued that that letter was part of a correspondence with a different Elisa-

beth ("Hildegard von Bingen an Elisabeth von St. Thomas an der Kyll: Die heilige Hildegard und die frühesten deutschen Zisterzienserinnen," *Cîteaux* 41 [1990]: 5–44). The absence of an extant letter does not preclude the very likely scenario of Hildegard's having heard reports about Elisabeth's activity and having expressed her concern, which Elisabeth learned through an intermediary such as her abbot, Ekbert, or even her angelic informant (whom Elisabeth does describe elsewhere as her consoler; see, e.g., *Letters*, chap. 6).

216. December 4, 1154.

217. January 5, 1155.

218. This letter comprises what is translated here as chapters 20–28. The editor of Hildegard's correspondence treats these chapters as two separate letters, although the manuscripts of Elisabeth's works consistently transmit this as one continuous letter, albeit sometimes divided into chapters. See Hildegard of Bingen, *Epistolarium*, ed. L. Van Acker, Corpus Christianorum, Continuatio Mediaevalis, vol. 91 (Turnholt: Brepols, 1991–), 455–58 (Epp. 202–3).

219. Elisabeth seems to be making an etymological reference to Hildegard's name, which actually means "protection in battle." (I thank Barbara Newman and Connie Schütz for their help on this question.)

220. See the prophecy that concluded the original version of the *First Book of Visions* (chap. 25).

221. The elaboration of the image from John 10:1 was part of a common rhetoric condemning simony as an abuse of pastoral care.

222. The following visions in chapters 29–30 are repeated verbatim from the *First Book of Visions*, chap. 40. At that point, Elisabeth had expressed her desire for Ekbert to interpret the visions. Now he offers his interpretation.

223. Elisabeth may have understood Ekbert's choice of example, but he does not explain it to the reader.

NOTES TO *THE BOOK OF THE WAYS OF GOD*

224. June 3, 1156.

225. Reading *incederent* from Avignon, Bibliothèque municipale MS 593, Paris, Bibliothèque de l'Université MS 790, Douai, Bibliothèque municipale MS 865, and Fulda, Hessische Landesbibliothek MS Aa96.

226. June 10, 1156.

227. Here Elisabeth indicates her personal interaction with Hildegard of Bingen and suggests the influence of Hildegard on her own visionary work.

228. July 25, 1156.

229. Contemplation is here described in the traditional terms of contrasting Mary's choice of the "best part" with Martha's association with the active life. For this tradition, see Giles Constable, "The Interpretation of Mary and Martha," in *Three Studies in Medieval Religious and Social Thought* (Cambridge: Cambridge University Press, 1995), 1–141.

230. For another example in which the contemplative is compared to an eagle looking at the sun, see Hildegard of Bingen's description of Bernard of Clairvaux. Hildegard of Bingen, *Epistolarium*, 5 (Ep. 1).

231. September 29, 1156.

232. Reading *declinavi*, from Paris, Bibliothèque de l'Université MS 790, Douai, Bibliothèque municipale MS 865, and Vienna, Österreichische Nationalbibliothek Vindob. Pal. MS 488.

233. October 21, 1156.

234. Antiphon for the feast of All Saints and for feasts commemorating more than one confessor.

235. November 11, 1156.

236. Reading *quartus* from Paris, Bibliothèque de l'Université MS 790, Douai, Bibliothèque municipale MS 865, and Vienna, Österreichische Nationalbibliothek Vindob. Pal. MS 488.

237. December 27, 1156.

238. December 28, 1156.

239. January 1, 1157.

240. Reading *cenum* from Paris, Bibliothèque de l'Université MS 790, Douai, Bibliothèque municipale MS 865, and Fulda, Hessische Landesbibliothek MS Aa96.

241. January 3, 1157.

242. The ethics of intentionality was a significant religious concern in Elisabeth's culture, a concern shaped by penitential literature that encouraged introspection and reflected in the philosophical and legal literature of scholars such as Peter Abelard and Gratian. See John F. Benton, "Consciousness of Self and Perceptions of Individuality," in *Renaissance and Renewal in the Twelfth Century*, ed. Robert L. Benson and Giles Constable (Cambridge: Harvard University Press, 1982).

243. January 21, 1157.

244. The expression "man of desires" (*vir desideriorum*) is another example of Elisabeth's use of an explicitly masculine, prophetic expression

from the Bible to refer to herself. See the note about "son of man" in *First Book of Visions*, chap. 70.

245. Several times in this text, Elisabeth uses the word *emulator* to describe God, Christ, or good pastors. It literally means "imitator," but she seems to be thinking of its implications of jealous guardianship.

246. February 24, 1157.

247. March 31, 1157.

248. Reading *pertinent* from Paris, Bibliothèque de l'Université MS 790, Douai, Bibliothèque municipale MS 865, and Vienna, Österreichische Nationalbibliothek Vindob. Pal. MS 488.

249. Reading *honorificavi* from Douai, Bibliothèque municipale MS 865.

250. May 19, 1157.

251. May 29, 1157.

252. Following all the manuscripts I have consulted, I omit repeating here the chapter title that is found in *Visionen*, 118. Similarly, the edition (*Visionen*, 119) provides a title for the last paragraph of the next chapter, which is not attested in these manuscripts and is omitted here.

253. Reading *vestro* from Paris, Bibliothèque de l'Université MS 790, Douai, Bibliothèque municipale MS 865.

254. June 28, 1157.

255. July 11, 1157.

256. Cf. *Regula Sancti Benedicti*, ed. Adalbert de Vogue and Jean Neufville in *RB 1980 The Rule of Saint Benedict*, ed. Timothy Fry (Collegeville, Minn.: The Liturgical Press, 1981), chap. 64. Throughout this section Benedict and his Rule are repeatedly evoked as Elisabeth attempts to describe a path that she sees as very different from her own cenobitic life.

257. July 22, 1157.

258. July 25, 1157.

259. This reference to avoiding young girls and their corrupters is the first point that suggests that this sermon is addressed specifically to a male audience. Thus the other references to "my brothers" and the "brotherhood" of angels can be seen as encouraging young boys to identify with the male community of virginal angels.

260. Vigil: August 14, 1157. Feast: August 15, 1157.

261. This concern about delicate upbringing could reflect Elisabeth's own experience of family life. In the *Vita* of Ekbert, she is said to have declared that she hesitated to encourage her brother to undertake the monastic life because "he had been delicately brought up since his infancy"

and thus might not be able to endure the rigor of monastic discipline. Emecho of Schönau, *Vita Eckeberti*, 450.

262. August 22, 1157.

263. This appeal to scribes, attesting to Elisabeth's concern with the correct transmission of her work, is found in all redactions of the visionary collections except the final one. For the text, see F. W. E. Roth, "Aus einer Handschrift der Schriften der heil. Elisabeth von Schönau," *Neues Archiv der Gesellschaft für ältere deusche Geschichteskunde* 36 (1911): 221.

264. This chapter was added in a redaction of the visionary works that Ekbert created after Elisabeth's death in 1164 or 1165. The letter transmitted in this final chapter was written on June 29, 1157, i.e., during the final months in which the book itself was being composed. Two years after writing this letter, Elisabeth again wrote to Archbishop Hillin of Trier, accusing him of neglecting the mandate of this first letter to preach the message of this book to the universal church. See *Letters*, chap. 4.

NOTES TO *THE RESURRECTION OF THE BLESSED VIRGIN*

265. This text circulated widely in all the redactions of the visionary collection as well as independently of Elisabeth's works. In the final redaction of the collection, Ekbert incorporated it as the final chapters of the *Second Book of Visions*, which is how it is printed in *Visionen*.

266. August 22, 1156.

267. August 15, 1157.

268. August 22, 1157.

269. Elisabeth here distinguishes between the current custom of celebrating the feast of the Assumption on August 15 and the information that she receives revealing September 23 as the true date of the assumption.

270. August 15, 1159.

271. The Nativity of the Virgin: September 8. The Annunciation: March 25.

NOTES TO *THE BOOK OF REVELATIONS ABOUT THE SACRED COMPANY OF THE VIRGINS OF COLOGNE*

272. Elisabeth's description of herself as "servant of the handmaids of the Lord" (*famula ancillarum domini*) indicates that by this point she had become mistress of the nuns at Schönau.

273. "Religious places" (*loca religiosa*) indicates that the bodies were distributed to churches and monasteries.

274. "Was translated" (*translata est*) is a technical term for the transferal of relics.

275. Here Elisabeth refers to her monastery's acquisition of the bodies of two martyrs, Verena and Caesarius. In chapter 15 below, she describes the acquisition of three more bodies. According to Ekbert, at the time of Elisabeth's death the monastery possessed fourteen whole bodies and many more fragments from the relics of the Cologne martyrdom.

276. The history of the British virgins referred to here and elsewhere in this text is the popular passion, *Regnante domino*, completed by 1100 and transmitted in over 100 manuscripts. See the description in the introduction to this volume.

277. October 28, 1156.

278. Anterus was pope from 235–36.

279. According to *Regnante domino*, Cordula was one of the eleven thousand virgins who hid in fear from the murderers, but regained her courage the next day and then gave herself up to be martyred.

280. The pun in Latin is on the imagery of baptism in which the words *lavo* ("to wash") and *lavacrum* ("bath" "waters of baptism") are evoked by the name of the city Lavicana. The name Lavicana preserves the baptismal evocation that, rather than any geographical specificity, seems primary in this text.

281. There are sketches of this figure in Fulda, Hessische Landesbibliothek MS Aa96 and St. Omer, Bibliothèque municipale MS 170. It is possible that the figure was a chi-rho monogram, standing for Christ, which was not recognized by Elisabeth or her interlocutors.

282. December 2, 1156.

283. December 6, 1156.

284. Elisabeth is referring to the discrepancy between the reign of "Pope Cyriacus" (before 235), and the invasion of Gaul by Attila (451). The reign of Cyriacus also renders anachronistic the reference to the city of Constantinople (chap. 14).

285. These last three sentences about Verena's head were deleted from the last redaction of the collection, probably reflecting Ekbert's desire to avoid this potentially self-serving critique of inadequate piety at the Premonstratensian cloister at Ilbenstadt. Text is in Roth, "Aus einer Handschrift," 221–22.

286. The inconsistent chapter enumeration from *Visionen* is retained here.

287. October 21, 1157.

288. According to *Regnante domino*, a religious man named Clematius came to Cologne from the East and built a church in honor of the martyred virgins. It's possible that Elisabeth also knew of the inscription in the church of Saint Ursula that described his building of the church.

289. Text of this and the following fragment is printed in *Acta Sanctorum*, Oct. IX, 171f.

290. Ulrich was prior of Steinfeld from 1152–70. For other connections between Schönau and Steinfeld, including Ekbert's anti-Cathar involvements and the influence of Elisabeth's revelations about the Cologne martyrdom, see Theodor Paas, "Ein Steinfelder Altarbild als Zeuge der Potentinus-Legende," *Annalen des Historischen Vereins für den Niederrhein* 102 (1918): 129–39. This letter about Potentinus, like other revelations of Elisabeth, diverged from received traditions: Potentinus was known in the liturgy of Steinfeld as a confessor, but these revelations declare him a martyr.

NOTES TO *LETTERS*

291. This superscription identifying the addressee, and therefore the investigating monk, as Ludwig, the later abbot of Saint Eucharius, is found only in Wiesbaden, Nassauische Landesbibliothek MS 4, a late fifteenth-century manuscript from Schönau. Other manuscripts identify him only as "L." Ludwig of Trier did visit Hildegard of Bingen and request letters from her, so there is external evidence for his interest in women's visionary experience to support this Schönau tradition.

292. Elisabeth's use of the image "worm-person" (*vermiculus homo*; *vermicula*) seems to have influenced Ekbert, who used it in his prayer to Mary, John the Baptist, and John the Evangelist: "Give, I beseech, the hand of your support to your supplicant, a worm-person..." (*Visionen*, 324).

293. This is a quotation from *The Book of the Ways of God*, chap. 15. Throughout this letter, there are references to Elisabeth's earlier letter addressed to the bishops of Trier, Mainz, and Cologne, in which she charged those prelates to preach the message of *The Book of the Ways of God*.

294. This letter is stating a divine preference for the "antipope" Victor IV, supported by Emperor Frederick Barbarossa. For the contested papal election in September 1159, see Peter Munz, *Frederick Barbarossa: A*

Study in Medieval Politics (Ithaca: Cornell University Press, 1969), 205–19. This letter was probably written shortly after the election.

295. The letters transmitted as chapters 5, 11, and 6 of this book were originally appended to the end of *The Book of Revelations About the Sacred Company of Virgins of Cologne*. Each of these letters, however obliquely, refers to the cult of the Cologne martyrs. The letters addressed to Gerlach of Deutz (chaps 5, 6, and 17) were written between 1156 and 1160. For Gerlach's role in the cult of the Cologne martyrs, see chapters 2 and 4 of that text.

296. For another example of concern about accidental profanation of the Eucharist, see the *Second Book of Visions*, chaps. 25–26.

297. This "Amen" suggests the original conclusion of the letter, which is how it is transmitted in Vienna, Österreichische Nationalbibliothek Vindob. Pal MS 488.

298. The Augustinian convent of St. Thomas at Andernach, where three of Elisabeth's kinswomen, the addressees of Ekbert's *The Death of Elisabeth*, lived. See also chap. 15 below.

299. This letter originally circulated appended to the *The Book of Revelations About the Sacred Company of Virgins of Cologne*, following the letter now in chap. 5 of this text, and introduced by this sentence: "Likewise, at another time God placed these words on my lips."

300. Reading "o virgo quecunque es pone me sicut signaculum super cor tuum," from Vienna, Österreichische Nationalbibliothek Vindob. Pal MS 488.

301. Although there is no direct quotation, this passage is reminiscent of the song of the vineyard in Isaiah 5:1–6.

302. Although no addressee for this letter is given in the manuscripts, it appears to be the same as the previous letter since it refers to that letter, and Bonn, the site of the Dietkirchen convent, is mentioned in this letter as the home of people who visited Elisabeth with greetings from the unnamed addressee.

303. Reading "homines de Bunna duo" from Vienna, Österreichische Nationalbibliothek Vindob. Pal MS 488.

304. The initial G. of the addressee and the description of her as Elisabeth's kinswoman suggests that this letter may have been addressed to Guda of St. Thomas of Andernach, to whom Ekbert later wrote his *Death of Elisabeth*.

305. Cf. *Regula Sancti Benedicti*, chap. 64.

306. The addressee of this letter is not known. In Vienna, Österreichische Nationalbibliothek Vindob. Pal MS 488, the initials in the letter,

R., L., H., are expanded to Rudolfus, Lu___, Hermannus. The content of the letter suggests Elisabeth's personal knowledge of this family contention about the dedication of a daughter to the monastic life.

307. Reading "admoneo vos pater H…quoniam magnum periculum patiemini de hoc in anima vestra" from Vienna, Österreichische Nationalbibliothek Vindob. Pal MS 488.

308. In *Visionen*, this letter is concluded with a sentence added by an eighteenth-century hand in Wiesbaden, Nassauische Landesbibliothek MS 3: "Farewell always in God your Savior."

309. This letter was not transmitted as part of the letter collection. It is found in a manuscript, probably from Reinhausen, which is a collection of works by Elisabeth. Ekbert also wrote a letter to Reinhard to accompany this one, and his letter indicates Reinhard's interest in Elisabeth's works. Both letters were probably composed in the last year of Elisabeth's life.

310. Written after 1155, when Fulbert became abbot at Laach.

311. This letter was not transmitted as part of the collection created by Ekbert but is found in a manuscript transmitting a collection of hagiographical materials, including Elisabeth's *Book of Revelations About the Sacred Company of Virgins of Cologne*. For the text of the letter, see Ph. Schmitz, "'Visions' inédites de Sainte Élisabeth de Schoenau," *Revue Bénédictine* 47 (1935): 181–83.

312. This explanation relies on a pun on the Latin word for banquet, *convivium*. The other name of the virgin, Viventia, would also have evoked an etymological resonance for a Latin audience, suggesting "one who lives."

NOTES TO *THE DEATH OF ELISABETH*

313. The title in Vienna Österreichische Nationalbibliothek Vindob. Pal MS 488, is "To the consecrated virgins in the monastery of Andernach about the death of Saint Elisabeth."

314. This praise echoes descriptions of Saint Ursula in *The Book of Revelations About the Sacred Company of Virgins of Cologne*.

315. Ekbert is probably referring here to Elisabeth's role in persuading him to be ordained to the priesthood. See *First Book of Visions*, chap. 59.

316. This text exists in short and long versions, the former being transmitted only by Vienna, Österreichische Nationalbibliothek Vindob.

Pal MS 488. Throughout this translation, the material not found in the short version is placed in brackets.

317. Cf. Gregory the Great, *Dialogues*, IV.60.

318. This seems to have been an abiding concern of Elisabeth. See *Second Book of Visions*, chaps. 7–8.

319. See *Second Book of Visions*, chap. 18.

320. Trier, Bistumarchiv MS 10 includes the following incident at this point: "While there I heard an announcement of her future death that struck sharply at my heart. A certain venerable old person asked me how my sister was doing. 'She is sick,' I responded. He immediately said to me, 'My lord, after fourteen nights she will be with her friends.' Then it occurred to me that within that term she would have migrated from this life, just as has indeed happened. Disturbed by his response, I was silent and did not dare to question him further about this statement."

321. This long section within brackets is not found in the shorter version of the Vienna manuscript due to a missing page within that manuscript. It cannot now be determined how much of this section was part of the short version of the text.

322. See *First Book of Visions*, chap. 79 and *Second Book of Visions*, chap. 2.

323. Not only did this female relative become the next mistress of Schönau, but another relative, Simon, a nephew of Elisabeth and Ekbert, later became abbot after Ekbert's tenure.

324. See *First Book of Visions*, chap. 20 and *Second Book of Visions*, chap. 4.

325. According to his biographer, Ekbert was offered the care of "a great church" in the diocese of Utrecht, which he declined. Emecho, *Vita Eckeberti*, 452.

326. Cf. *Regula Sancti Benedicti*, chap. 2.

327. See *The Book of the Ways of God*, chap. 4.

328. Either Christ or Mary, depending on which version of the text is read. Later Ekbert refers to Mary as the one who said this, which suggests the priority of the long version of the text.

329. Responsory from the Office of the Holy Trinity, found in a twelfth-century manuscript from Schönau. See *Das Gebetbuch*, 16, 19.

330. Antiphon from the Office of the Holy Trinity, in *Das Gebetbuch*, 20.

331. These are the well-known Marian hymns *Salve Regina* and *Alma redemptoris*, here freely translated. For their composition, liturgical use, and widespread popularity, see Graef, *Mary*, 229–30.

332. A short prose hymn from Matins.

333. Antiphon from the feast of All Saints.

334. Halle (Saale), Universitats- und Landesbibliothek Sachsen-Anhalt MS Yc 4°6 transmits this sentence as referring to incest rather than fornication.

335. Halle (Saale), Universitats- und Landesbibliothek Sachsen-Anhalt MS Yc 4°6 transmits this sentence somewhat differently, saying that Elisabeth prayed for the Lord to grant her an illness that would be sober "and would force her not to eat much."

336. This is probably their brother Ruotger, who had been provost of the Premonstratensian house at Pöhlde.

337. Countess Beatrice was the widow of Rupert of Laurenburg. For Rupert's relationship to the monastery at Schönau, see *First Book of Visions*, chap. 75. For evidence of Elisabeth's relationship with Beatrice, see *Second Book of Visions*, chap. 21.

338. Some manuscripts include the following sentence: "So that you may know the vision by which, as I said above, the handmaid of the Lord was assured of her death, I have noted it in the very words in which it is described in the book of her visions."

Bibliography

TEXTS:

Emecho of Schönau. *Vita Eckeberti*. Edited by S. Widmann. *Neues Archiv der Gesellschaft für ältere deutsche Geschichtskunde* 11 (1886): 447–54.

Roth, F. W. E. "Aus einer Handschrift der Schriften der heil. Elisabeth von Schönau." *Neues Archiv der Gesellschaft für ältere deutsche Geschichtskunde* 36 (1911): 219–25.

———, ed. *Die Visionen der hl. Elisabeth und die Schriften der Aebte Ekbert und Emecho von Schönau*. Brünn: Verlag der Studien aus dem Benedictiner-und Cistercienser Orden, 1884.

STUDIES:

Bynum, Caroline Walker. *Holy Feast and Holy Fast: The Religious Significance of Food to Medieval Women*. Berkeley and Los Angeles: University of California Press, 1987.

———. *Fragmentation and Redemption: Essays on Gender and the Human Body in Medieval Religion*. New York: Zone Books, 1991.

Clark, Anne L. *Elisabeth of Schönau: A Twelfth-Century Visionary*. Philadelphia: University of Pennsylvania Press, 1992.

Coakley, John. "Gender and the Authority of Friars: The Significance of Holy Women for Thirteenth-Century Franciscans and Dominicans." *Church History* 60 (1991): 445–60.

Dinzelbacher, Peter. "Die 'Vita et Revelationes' der Wiener Begine Agnes Blannbekin (1315) im Rahmen der Viten-und Offenbarungsliteratur ihrer Zeit." In *Frauenmystik im Mittelalter*, ed. Dinzelbacher and Dieter R. Bauer. Ostfildern: Schwabenverlag AG, 1985.

Ferrante, John M. *To the Glory of Her Sex: Women's Roles in the Composition of Medieval Texts*. Bloomington, Ind.: Indiana University Press, 1997.

Graef, Hilda. *Mary: A History of Doctrine and Devotion*. Westminster: Christian Classics, 1963, 1965.

Greenspan, Kate. "Autohagiography and Medieval Women's Spiritual Autobiography." In *Gender and Text in the Later Middle Ages*, ed. Jane Chance. Gainesville: University Press of Florida, 1996.

Grundmann, Herbert. *Religious Movements in the Middle Ages*. Translated by Steven Rowan. Notre Dame, Ind.: University of Notre Dame Press, 1995.

Johnson, Lynn Staley. "The Trope of the Scribe and the Question of Literary Authority in the Works of Julian of Norwich and Margery Kempe." *Speculum* 66 (1991): 820–38.

Köster, Kurt. "Elisabeth von Schönau: Werk und Wirkung im Spiegel der mittelalterlichen handschriftlichen Überlieferung." *Archiv für Mittelrheinische Kirchengeschichte* 3 (1951): 243–315.

———. "Das Visionäre Werk Elisabeths von Schönau." *Archiv für Mittelrheinische Kirchengeschichte* 4 (1952): 79–119.

Küsters, Urban. *Der verschlossene Garten: Volkssprachliche Hohelied-Auslegung und monastische Lebensform im 12. Jahrhundert*. Studia humaniora: Düsseldorfer Studien zu Mittelalter und Renaissance, Band 2. Düsseldorf: Droste Verlag, 1985.

Newman, Barbara. *Sister of Wisdom: St. Hildegard's Theology of the Feminine*. Berkeley and Los Angeles: University of California Press, 1987.

Stock, Brian. *The Implications of Literacy: Written Language and Models of Interpretation in the Eleventh and Twelfth Centuries*. Princeton, N.J.: Princeton University Press, 1983.

Vauchez, Andrè. *La Sainteté en Occident aux derniers siècles du Moyen Age*. Bibliothèque des Écoles Françaises d'Athènes et de Rome, 241. Rome: École Française de Rome, 1981.

Index

Abelard, **xiv**
Abrunculus, 254
acedia, **xii**
Adrian, Saint, 223–24
Affricanus, 224
Albina, 222–23
Andrew, Saint, 222–23
Anterus, 217
Antimius, 230
Aquilinus, 226
Arnold, **xv**
Arnold II, **xv**, 213–14
Attila, 224
Aurea, 223, 224

Babila, 219, 223, 224
Beatrice, Countess, **2**, 273, 300n.
    337
Beleth, John, **34**
Bernard of Clairvaux, **33**
Bonosius, 254
*Book of Revelations about the Sacred
    Company of the Virgins of
    Cologne* (Elisabeth of
    Schönau), **xvi, 18–19**; and the
    apostles, 214–15; appendix,
    228–33; burial of the virgins,
    226–27; and the martyrs,
    215–16, 295n. 275; text of,
    213–33; and the virgins'

journey to Rome, 216–17,
    221–22; vision of the glorified
    virgins, 225–26. *See also*
    Andrew, Saint; Cyriacus,
    Pope; Dorotheus, King;
    Ursula, Saint; Verena, Saint
Book of the Ways of God (Elisabeth of
    Schönau), **xiv–xv, 6–7, 13,
    16–17, 19, 20, 24, 27, 29, 33,
    37**, 161, 165, 209, 267; advice
    to various archbishops, 206–7,
    277n. 21, 294n. 264; eighth
    sermon, 201–3; fifth sermon,
    183–92; first sermon, 167–70;
    fourth sermon, 177–83; ninth
    sermon, 203–5; and the saints,
    166–67; second sermon,
    171–72; seventh sermon,
    200–201; sixth sermon,
    192–200; tenth sermon,
    205–6; text of, 161–207; third
    sermon, 172–77; translations,
    33–34, 35–37; and visions of
    the paths, 161–65, 165–66
Bynum, Caroline, **31–32**

Caesarius, 214, 280n. 57
Castor, 230–31, 232
Castrina, 230–31, 232
Cathars, **6–7**, 142–43, 144–45, 147

303

Other Volumes in This Series

Other Volumes in This Series

Other Volumes in This Series